D1068269

My Home, My Prison

My Home,

RAYMONDA HAWA TAWIL

My Prison

HOLT, RINEHART AND WINSTON

NEW YORK

First published in 1980 by Holt, Rinehart and Winston,
383 Madison Avenue, New York, New York 10017.
Published simultaneously in Canada by Holt, Rinehart
and Winston of Canada, Limited.

Library of Congress Cataloging in Publication Data
Tawil, Raymonda Hawa.
My home, my prison.
1. Tawil, Raymonda Hawa.   2. Palestinian Arabs—
Israel—Biography.   3. Jordan (Territory under
Israeli occupation, 1967-   )   4. Jewish-Arab
relations—1949-   I. Title.
DS113.7.T38   1979   956.94'004'927 [B]   79-10496
ISBN: 0-03-049301-3

Originally published in Hebrew by Adam Publishers,
P.O. Box 3329, Jerusalem, Israel.
First American Edition

Designer: Ellen LoGiudice
Printed in the United States of America
1   3   5   7   9   10   8   6   4   2

THIS BOOK IS DEDICATED TO THE YOUNG GENERATION OF PALESTIN-
IANS AND ISRAELIS IN THE FERVENT HOPE THAT THEY WILL LIVE SIDE
BY SIDE IN DIGNITY AND PEACE.

I would like to express my appreciation to all those who rallied to my side during my period of house arrest, and who—by their visits and letters, by their public protests and media coverage—reassured me that I was not alone in my struggle.

My special gratitude is extended to the many Israelis—leftists for the most part—who came to encourage me during my detention. Many of them are mentioned in the pages of this book; the others are too numerous to name. By their active help and sympathy to me, they gave further convincing proof of their opposition to their government's oppressive policies toward the Palestinian people.

For particular mention, I would like to single out Peretz Kidron, who visited me regularly and frequently throughout my period of arrest, giving unstintingly of his time, energy, and talent in helping me to assemble this account. Naomi Gal revised and edited the manuscript, greatly enriching it with her feminist insight; she provided warm and consistent encouragement at all times.

Contents

My Home, My Prison

1

Custody

AUGUST 12, 1976. My phone rings early. A sleepy voice on the other end—Captain Duddy of the military-government bureau—orders me to report to the office of the Ramallah military governor.

I look at the time: six A.M. The early hour is not a good omen. What can they want of me? I think, anxious and uneasy. The Israeli military authorities are all-powerful, and they are swift to unleash that power against those who anger them. What have I done?

My thoughts go back two weeks to the interview with the Shin Bet (security services) officer, a tall, powerful man speaking fluent Arabic. He addressed me courteously enough, but his manner grew noticeably gruffer when he rebuked me for some of the press reports I had sent. "Your news reports," he said sternly, "are false, and harmful to the security of the state of Israel."

"False?" I said. "What did I write that was false?"

He brushed the question aside. "This is a warning, Raymonda. You'd better heed it!"

Does this morning's summons have anything to do with his "warning"?

I have been summoned for eight o'clock. But the minutes tick by, and I am left to wait outside: The military governor has not arrived. As time passes, my suspense and anxiety grow. My private worries interweave with the black shadow hanging over us all: Tel al-Za'ater. For weeks now, the Palestinian refugee camp on the outskirts of Beirut has been under siege by the Falangists. Thousands are trapped there; hundreds—men, women, and children—have been killed or injured by the incessant bombardment from Falangist artillery; the survivors are locked in a desperate battle, their ammunition running low, while the noncombatants suffer from hunger and thirst. It seems that the camp can't hold out much longer. The twin anxieties run through my mind: What will happen to the people of Tel al-Za'ater? What will happen to me? Time passes slowly: past nine, and still no sign of the military governor. An Israeli woman soldier enters. Without so much as a glance at me, she brings a broom and starts sweeping. Taking my mind off my own concerns for a moment, I gaze at her with interest. She is young, little more than a child. But in her khaki uniform, she represents all Israeli women: proud, emancipated, and free. Arab men show little regard for women, but even they respect the Israeli woman soldier, the symbol of victorious Israeli might.

Why, then, I ask myself, is this girl doing the traditional woman's chore of sweeping?

I address her: "Why are *you* sweeping the office? Doesn't the Israeli army have equality for women?"

She seems startled—as much by the question as at my fluent Hebrew. Flinging me a look of surprise, she answers offhandedly, "That's my job. I sweep the office, I answer the phone, make coffee for the officers."

"Why do *you* make coffee for them?" I persist. "Why don't they make it themselves?"

She shrugs. "They have *their* job, I have *mine.*" With that, she leaves her sweeping and takes a trayful of coffee cups to the various offices.

Left alone, I return to my own concerns. Why are they leaving me here to wait like this? I glance at my watch: ten. How long will they keep me? What do they intend to do with me? Do they want to interrogate me? Or place me under arrest? What do they have against me? It's so hard to know what angers them, and even harder to guess how they will react. They can be so ruthless and arbitrary at times. Maybe they intend to send me to prison? Or perhaps even worse—to deport me?

After a few minutes, the woman soldier comes back. She has been in the offices—perhaps she knows what they plan to do with me? I gaze at her, trying to read her eyes, to guess what is in her mind. But I can find nothing, no hint of anything in her clear features.

I notice that she is returning my stare. Clearly, our earlier exchange has left her intrigued. Coming closer, she gazes curiously at the badge on my coat lapel: SELF-DETERMINATION FOR PALESTINE. (I put it on especially for my interview with the governor, a token of defiance.) Glancing at the badge for a moment, she shakes her head contemptuously: "You Palestinians! You ought to give up. Accept the situation. You're finished."

Finished? What does she mean? Somewhere in one of the offices I can hear a radio. Has she heard news? Tel al-Za'ater?

"What do you mean, 'finished'?" My tone is sharp, reflecting my anxiety and uncertainty.

"Everybody hates you. The whole world is against you!" Her voice is triumphant, vindictive. "Even your own Arab brethren. Nobody is on your side. You're finished!"

Her hostility is painful to me. In my present tense and distraught mood, I am tempted to answer her in the same spirit. But I look at her again; she reminds me of my own daughter, Dianna; she is almost the same age, with the same ingenuous eyes. I make a great effort to be patient.

"You say we should give in? Accept the situation?" I smile sadly. "When the Jews were in the ghettoes, did *they* give in? Did they 'accept the situation'? No, they didn't. Well, neither will we. You say no one likes us, no one is on our side. But who liked *your* people? Who was on the side of the Jews? No one! But the Jews fought. Even when everyone around was trying to annihilate you!" Her face had lost its vindictive expression; she gazed at me in wonder.

"Well," I add, "we Palestinians are just like you Jews!"

She is astounded. "How can you talk like that? You? You're a terrorist! I know that. I know that you support the PLO terrorists!"

She *has* heard something! One of the officers must have talked about me in her presence. "Support the PLO." That could be a grave charge on the part of the Israelis. People accused of support for the PLO often find themselves being led to the Jordan bridges at dawn. Deportation! Could they do that to me? But what about my children . . . ?

I fight down my rising panic, trying to concentrate on talking with this angel-faced representative of Israeli power. Keeping my tone gentle, I answer her onslaught. "What the PLO does isn't terrorism. It's self-defense! When the whole world turned against us, we picked up the gun!" She stares at me skeptically. I feel a sudden violent urge to convince this girl, to explain, to overcome the hostile reserve in her eyes. I tell her of an interview given by Golda Meir where she recalled a pogrom she lived through as a child in Kiev, how her father barricaded the entrance with furniture and nailed the door shut so as to protect his family from the Cossacks. Golda concluded her tale with, "Thank God, now we have an army to protect us. We are no longer helpless victims."

Gazing at the woman soldier, I add, "We Palestinians are just the same. We don't want to be victims. We want to be able to defend ourselves. The whole world denied the existence of the Jewish people—but it *does* exist! I respect *your* fight for survival and dignity. You should respect *ours!*"

An officer enters. Seeing the two of us immersed in conversation, he grins at the woman soldier. "Careful!" he says, half playful, half in earnest. Jerking his head toward me, he tells the girl, "Be careful, she'll brainwash you!" Still grinning to himself, he walks out.

I stare after him resentfully. It's easy for *him* to make jokes. But how would he feel if he were in my position?

I turn my head and catch the eyes of the woman soldier watching me. Her gaze is respectful, perplexed; clearly, I have given her something to think about.

She leaves me to go back to her work. I am left alone once more, a prey to my uncertainties.

The minutes tick by slowly.

What is going to happen?

It is after eleven. I have been waiting for three hours. These people are crazy! I am thirsty and tired. Is this waiting a prelude to my interrogation? If only I could find a radio and hear the news. What's happening at home? They must be terribly worried.

An officer enters. "The military governor has arrived."

At long last. Whatever is in store for me, at least I won't have to wait any longer to find out.

I follow him into the office. The military governor is seated at his desk, but he is not alone. There are other officers in the room. Army, police. Various badges and insignia. Different shades of khaki and blue uniforms. They are all seated around the military governor's desk. They are talking as I enter; but when the military governor motions me to a vacant seat, they fall silent. All eyes are fixed on me. I glance around, trying to read their expressions; some are vacant, others hostile. All look stern and formal.

As I look at them, I sense a wave of anger. These men—what are they doing here in Ramallah? Foreigners, outsiders, representatives of an alien army—and yet they have the power to summon me here, to issue orders to me, to rebuke me, to subject me to suffering. How painful! How humiliating! How helpless I am in the face of the might they represent!

But—precisely because they are so strong—I must not show weakness. I stare back at them, boldly, defiantly. Whatever happens, they won't have the satisfaction of seeing me bow my head!

The military governor addresses me, his voice stiff and impersonal. "We met before," he reminds me, referring to our first encounter a few weeks earlier; on taking up his post, he had invited me to his office, together with other Ramallah citizens whose acquaintance he wanted to make. "That was an informal meeting," he says, "but this one is very formal." His voice becomes more official, emphatic. "I'm sorry. You were warned, but you chose to ignore the warning. We are left with no choice. We must now follow our instructions."

He motions to the police officer sitting nearby. The man clears his throat and picks up a sheet of paper. I watch him, fascinated. It all seems so dreamlike, so unreal.

The police officer begins to read from the paper. The text is in Arabic. He reads it out in a harsh, toneless voice.

By my authority under paragraph 86 of the Security Instructions order, I hereby order that Mrs. Raymonda Habib Jerais Tawil, ID card number 99770512 of Ramallah, Number 26 Mario Hanna Street, shall be subjected to special supervision from 8.12.76 at 10:00, until another order be issued.

During the period in which she is under special supervision, the aforementioned Raymonda Habib Jerais Tawil shall remain behind the doors of the house in which she resides in Ramallah, throughout all hours of the day and night.

Signed—Colonel Ya'akov Katz, Military Governor, Ramallah District. Dated—seventeenth of Menachem-Ab, 5736—August 12, 1976.

Today.

Now.

As of this moment, I am under house arrest.

Within me, a voice shrieks, "By what right?!"

How can they do this to me, turn my home into a prison? How dare they tell me what I may do and what I may not do? Who are they to place me under "special supervision"? Why? Because they have guns and I am unarmed? Because they are Israelis and I am a Palestinian? Because they are men and I am a woman?

The police officer lays down the sheet of paper. They are all looking at me. I clench my fists to control my anger. There is a brief silence.

Finally, making a supreme effort to keep my voice level, I say, 'May I ask a question?"

"Yes," says the military governor indifferently, "but I am unable to answer." Helpfully, he adds: "If you want, get yourself a lawyer."

"This isn't democratic!" I protest. "I'm supposed to know what I did to deserve punishment!"

"I have no answer for you," he mutters, averting his eyes. They are intense green, I notice.

I look about the room, studying the officers' expressions. They are expectant, curious to see how I take it.

To my surprise, I am very calm now. I try to grasp the significance of this punishment. Clearly, my activities have angered the occupation authorities. In spite of my predicament, I feel absurdly pleased at the thought that I have annoyed them.

The military governor is addressing me. He is polite but firm.

"Do you have your car?"

"No. I'll call a taxi."

"We'll take you," says one of the officers. (How gallant, I think.)

"To ensure that you don't escape," he adds.

"I don't escape my responsibilities!" I retort, fighting to keep my pride.

Silently, I walk out to the courtyard. They usher me into a car. The driver is an Arab. Turning his head, he scans me somberly.

"Tel al-Za'ater has fallen," he mutters.

A pang of pain stabs my heart. What a calamity! "God is great," I whisper.

He nods his head. "A black day," he says.

Two policemen get into the car with me. We set off, with a military jeep leading the way, and another army car following behind me. I am being escorted in style, I think bitterly.

The drive passes in silence. The car halts outside my home. The children are at the gate, terrified.

Wordlessly, I get out.

"Mama, what's happening?"

"What do they want?"

"Mama, what have you done?"

Briefly, I tell them of the detention order. They are thunderstruck. "But why?"

What can I answer?

Several officers escort me to my door. Captain Duddy comes into the house with me, walks over to the phone, and lifts the receiver.

"What are you doing?" I demand.

"I'm making sure that the phone is disconnected," he says calmly. Suddenly, I grasp what he has said. Not only am I under detention, they are doing everything to cut me off from the world. I am a prisoner within my own home, and they want to gag me as well!

The children are dazed by what is happening. They are clinging to me, clamoring for explanations, for reassurance. Suddenly, Captain Duddy turns to them. "Don't worry, children," he says in what is probably meant as a comforting tone. "Don't worry, your mother is going to stay at home with you."

For a moment, the children fall silent. They stare at him, their expressions a mixture of bewilderment and hatred.

All this time, my husband, Da'ud, has scarcely spoken a word. Now he gazes at me reproachfully. "I always expected something like this," he murmurs sadly. "This is how the Israelis pay you back. You welcomed them into your home—and this is your reward." He is depressed and sad. "But despite it all, you're still lucky. You are at home, you're unharmed. At Tel al-Za'ater there are hundreds dead."

In Lebanon—at Tel al-Za'ater and elsewhere—Palestinians are

being massacred. Here in the occupied territories, young demonstrators are clubbed, gassed, or shot.

And here am I—locked up, confined, and gagged.

A policeman is posted outside my house, day and night. He has a double task: to provide "special supervision" by ensuring that I don't leave the house and to check visitors' identity papers, making a note of their names. Some people refrain from coming to see me, afraid of having their names on the authorities' list of "undesirables." Those braver souls who do come tell me what Israeli officers are saying about me: "We are going to isolate her. She is going to be punished. We'll break her!"

Day by day, I have to contend with this terrible sense of confinement, of being trapped and caged. No visits to friends, no shopping! No walks in the marketplace, no visits to my children's schools. Only this house, the four walls, the door with the policeman sitting outside . . .

To tell the truth, my lot isn't unbearable. I'm not in jail. Unlike thousands of Palestinian patriots languishing for years in the prisons of Israel, Jordan, and other lands of the Middle East, I am not confined to a narrow cell. I can enjoy the comforts of my own pleasant and roomy home, with its wonderful vistas of the Samarian hills and the coastal plain, and occasional glimpses of Tel Aviv. I have my family around me; the constant stream of visitors proves that I have not been forgotten by my friends. I am detained in luxury. A cage.

I am imprisoned nevertheless.

Worse—my prison has many walls: No sooner do I scale one than I'm faced by another. The policeman outside my door is only one of the countless captors. In the course of my life, I have been denied my freedom in many ways:

as a Palestinian, belonging to a people deprived of rights and dignity;

as a woman in a semifeudal, patriarchal society;

as a citizen of a territory under foreign military occupation;

as an individual in a traditionalist, oppressive environment that restricts individual liberties.

Even when the authorities see fit to release me from house arrest, my regained "freedom" will have a bitter flavor. Like all Palestinians, I will bear my prison with me in my heart wherever I go. As a woman, I will suffer a double alienation.

But in the meantime, in my own home whose walls have become my prison, I shall record the story of all my prisons, all my walls. . . .

The last time I was arrested, I was touring Nablus with Terence Smith of *The New York Times*. PLO chief Yassir Arafat had been invited to address the United Nations General Assembly. After years of hostility and indifference, the world acknowledged the existence of the Palestinian people, and recognized the PLO! A wave of euphoria swept the West Bank, and in Nablus, too, the streets were filled with exultant young demonstrators. All stores and businesses were closed, Israeli troops were out in force, hauling the shopkeepers from their homes—some were brought in their pajamas!—to reopen their shops and thereby "restore normalcy." "Normalcy" always has high priority with the occupation authorities.

Terence went off to interview the military governor, and I was left standing alone in the center of town. Suddenly, an Israeli military vehicle drew up, and the soldiers brusquely ordered me to get in. They would not even give me a moment to inform Terence I was being taken into custody.

He found out anyway; some of the demonstrators hastened to him, shouting, "They're taking the girl!" ("The girl"—what a compliment!) Terence came running up just as the military car pulled away from the curb.

"What's happening?" he called to me.

"Terry, this is democracy!" I shouted back, and the car drove off.

(Terence's intervention with the military authorities ultimately helped to secure my release, even though an Israeli officer told me he didn't give a damn for "that American journalist of yours.")

At police headquarters, I was still buoyed up by my sense of euphoria. I felt no fear at finding myself under arrest. Relaxed and confident, I watched the young demonstrators being hauled in. Most of them were smiling, and we made the V sign in greeting. Behind me, I heard the policeman mutter in angry Hebrew, "They're happy because that murderer's gone to the United Nations." They regarded the invitation to Arafat as a personal affront.

I was called in to the military governor. His manner was markedly hostile. He interrogated me about the press reports I had sent off. "You have been issuing false news!" he said accusingly. "This morning you reported that the town was on strike—before it even happened!" He was furious. "I was in town this morning, and all the shops were open!"

I gave him a superior smile. "Every journalist tries to report events as they occur—earlier, if possible!"

The governor ranted on about "a bunch of irresponsible youngsters" who had intimidated the shopkeepers into closing their businesses. "The shopkeepers don't want the PLO!" he proclaimed flatly. "I know that. They want King Hussein, and not Arafat!"

Unrepentant, I reminded him that he had only been in the town a few months, while I had lived there for sixteen years. "I know the merchants, too—after all, my husband is a bank manager!" I tried to explain how people felt about Jordan, and the Jordanian regime. "We are a part of the Arab world, and we have close links with Jordan," I told him. "There are economic interests and family ties. But that doesn't mean we are prepared to forfeit our own identity, as Palestinians. We want our independence, our right to a state of our own!"

"Under that terrorist?" he asked sarcastically, referring to Arafat.

I refused to be provoked. "Those ministers and members of the Knesset who now rule Israel—men like Begin or Dayan or Rabin— what were *they* called when Palestine was under British rule? Do you remember? 'Members of the illegal military organizations' . . . 'marauders' . . ." I smiled and added softly, "Terrorists."

On another occasion, I was arrested when the Nablus military authorities were about to demolish some houses. Whenever the Israelis accused a person of belonging to the resistance, it was their regular practice to demolish his or her home. A whole family could be made homeless because one of its members was "guilty" of illegal acts. On this occasion, too, several families faced the danger of being turned out into the street if the houses were blown up.

At the Arab Women's Union we were highly concerned. We sent off a telegram to Israeli Defense Minister Moshe Dayan, demanding that he halt the demolitions. There was no response.

The time was drawing near for the order to be carried out, and still no answer from Dayan. Tension built up; our anxiety grew. Would the houses be demolished before we could do anything to prevent it? Something had to be done! At the very least, we wanted an answer.

Together with the parents and the families of the imprisoned fedayeen (guerrillas), a group of us from the Arab Women's Union marched to the military governor's office. The soldier at the gate would not let us pass. I asked him to contact the governor; he refused. "This is urgent!" I insisted, but in vain.

"Very well!" I shouted. "We shall hold a sit-in right here, at the main gate!" We promptly made preparations to carry out our threat.

Some officers came outside to see what the fuss was all about. On learning what we planned to do, the Israelis found themselves in a quandary. It would obviously have been highly embarrassing for the governor to be besieged by a crowd of old men and women and young children. The Israeli officers adopted a conciliatory approach: One of them—a captain by the name of Amnon—offered to see us in his office.

Hoping to find someone to talk to, we trooped inside. In response to our demand, Amnon phoned the military governor, Segev, and asked him to receive us. Captain Amnon listened for a moment, then laid down the receiver; Segev would not see us, he told me. "He says he knows already what Dayan's answer will be," Amnon added.

The fact that Segev refused point-blank to speak to us made us even more angry and frustrated. We felt powerless and humiliated.

We left the military-government building, our anxiety growing. I led a group of women to a meeting with Nablus mayor Haj Ma'azuz al-Masri. The situation was grave, we told him. We suggested pitching tents near the condemned houses to provide shelter for the evicted families until a better solution could be found. Haj Ma'azuz agreed, and promised to send municipal employees with tents.

Returning home, I found a journalist from *Time*—Marmon—who had come to see what was happening. I took him to where one of the houses was being sealed off (thereby making it unfit for occupation—this is the procedure whenever the proximity of another building makes it impractical to blow up the "guilty" dwelling). The municipal employees had just arrived, and they were putting up the tent for the evicted family. Marmon promptly began to take pictures of the scene: the house with its entrance being blocked, the family outside with its possessions, the tent.

All this was happening opposite the military governor's office, and our activities must have been clearly visible from there. The moment Marmon put away his camera and departed, military-government officials stormed the scene.

"Whose damned idea was this?" they shouted. "We've got enough of your tents and your refugees! Do we need new tents?" They ordered the municipal employees to take the tent away.

The next morning I was arrested, and my fingerprints were taken. I was furious at being treated like a criminal. How shocking to find myself being penalized for showing humane concern for my fellowmen! I felt tears of anger fill my eyes. Formally, I was charged with making offensive remarks to the soldier on guard outside the military governor's office. It was alleged that I had called him "an ass." Strictly speaking, the accusation was untrue. I didn't call the soldier anything—at least, not to his face. However, I must admit that, when talking to one of the officers, I asked him in exasperation, "What kind of an ass did you put on guard here?" Offensive language indeed!

The story reached the Israeli progressive weekly *Ha'Olam Hazeh,* which printed the whole account, accompanied by some heavily sarcastic remarks about the military-government officials. After that, the case against me was dropped.

It is not only the Israeli authorities who have detained me on various occasions. As a Palestinian, it has also been my "privilege" to enjoy the attention of the Jordanian security services. On one occasion, I set off on a trip abroad with my husband, Da'ud. We decided to go by way of Jordan. To cross over from Israeli-occupied territory, we had to use one of the bridges over the Jordan River.

Crossing the river is always an ordeal, since both Israelis and Jordanians subject travelers to the most rigorous searches and checks, which last an eternity. In addition, the Jordan Valley is hot and airless, making it agony to wait at the unshaded transit points. As though all that were not enough, at this time, the Jordanians were making things even worse than usual. After the events of September 1970—the notorious Black September, when they killed thousands of fedayeen as well as unarmed Palestinians, civilian refugees—the

Jordanians were trying to reestablish their influence in the Israeli-occupied territories. As a result, Palestinians crossing the bridges underwent the most detailed and rigorous checks, while the Jordanian security agents hunted for "hostile elements." During our hours-long wait, we heard names called out, and Palestinians were taken away for questioning. Some persons were brutally interrogated for expressing sympathy with the PLO or for criticizing the Jordanian Hashemite regime. Others were accused of "contacts with the enemy," often for the most innocuous matters. I met a small shopkeeper from Nablus whose interrogators accused him of selling Israeli chocolate and cigarettes! He was trembling with fear that the Jordanians would fling him into one of their fearful jails.

Da'ud and I stood there in the sun, along with the others, slowly filing past the Jordanian officials, who subjected us to their laborious vetting. It was a nerve-wracking process; I thought it would never end.

At long last, we reached the end of the long line of officials. But precisely when we breathed a sigh of relief at having finished, our names were called out for questioning. We were on the blacklist!

The security men took us into custody beside the bridge, but we were not interrogated there. They drove us to El Salt, a deserted city in the mountains. On arrival, we were shown into a small room in a military barracks and left there, alone. For a long time, we sat there waiting, and absolutely nothing happened. Our ordeal was all the worse, even though—or, perhaps, precisely because—we were not subjected to interrogation. Instead, our captors gave plenty of time for our imaginations to play up our fears and forebodings. On top of that, as though our anxieties were not sufficient torment, the unventilated room soon grew intolerably hot.

The guards brought us food, but we refused to touch it. We demanded to know what was happening, why we were being detained, what they intended to do with us. But no one seemed to know anything about it. The Jordanians just shrugged and took away our valises, presumably so as to search through our belongings.

At long last, our interrogation began. We found ourselves confronted by two men in civilian clothes—who were, nevertheless, military officers. One—apparently the superior—sat to one side listening intently to the exchanges. The interrogation was conducted by the other officer—a haughty, arrogant man.

It was a strange, unnerving kind of interrogation. There were almost no direct questions; instead, the officer would fling out remarks or stories or terse comments, challenging me to defend myself against the implied accusations they carried.

"We heard that you receive Israeli officers at your home," he hurled at me angrily.

I did not deny the "charge." "Yes, at Christmas, the Israeli military governor paid us a courtesy call, though we did not invite him." I reminded him that the identical custom was followed before 1967, when Nablus was under Jordanian rule: Every Christmas the Jordanian governor paid official visits to the town's leading Christian families. The Israelis were merely following the Jordanian precedent.

My interrogator looked furious; he probably found it highly offensive that I was placing the Jordanian and the Israeli military governors on the same plane. For good measure, I added, "I receive other Israelis too, not just officers." My defiant attitude angered the interrogator, and he sought other "crimes" to accuse me of.

"We heard that you attended a reception for Israeli officers!" he shouted, staring at me accusingly. He mentioned the name of David Parhi, a senior official in the Israeli administration. "What were you doing there?"

"It wasn't a reception," I hastened to correct him. "Nablus mayor Hamdi Kna'an invited a few people—Arabs and Jews—to his office to take leave of Hanoch, an Israeli officer who had been very helpful to the refugees in the Nablus area."

My interrogator was clearly perplexed and indignant that any Arab should take a favorable view of an Israeli officer. As patriotic Arabs, we were expected to regard every Israeli as a monster!

Unrelentingly, he continued his line of questioning, trying to uncover my "treasonous" leanings. Suddenly, he asked, "Do you own Ben-Gurion's book?"

Surprised, I shot back, "Is there anything wrong in possessing Ben-Gurion's book?"

"Answer the question!" he shouted.

"No, as it happens, I don't . . ."

And so it went on, this stupid, unimaginative interrogation. I felt disgusted. Was it not enough that I found myself in daily confrontations with Israelis? What else did I have to do to convince this man that I was a patriot? As I patiently answered his attacks and insinuations, I suddenly had a feeling of *déjà vu*. Surely this had all happened before somewhere. . . . Of course! During the 1948 war, my mother's philanthropic relief work brought her into contact with the Israeli authorities; as she devoted herself to alleviating sufferings of our people, rumors went about that she was a "collaborator" with the Israelis. The Iraqis accused her of "treason" and sentenced her to death in absentia. And now it was *my* turn to bear accusations of "collaboration with the Israeli enemy."

That night we were taken to Amman.

On arrival, there was a shock in store for us: Da'ud was to be released, but I was ordered to remain in custody. This separation was the last straw. Hitherto, I had succeeded in keeping calm, but now, after a whole day in detention without food or drink, I lost all restraint. While Da'ud tried in vain to calm me down, I poured out my fury at the security officers. "What do you want of us? The Jordanian army surrendered! You Jordanians delivered the West Bank to Israel! *Now stop this farce and release me!!!*" Totally out of control, I abused them all: Da'ud, the officers, the regime, the king.

My shouts reverberated throughout the building. The startled Bedouin sentries stared at me in stupefaction: They had never seen a woman behave in this fashion. *Their* womenfolk were quiet, obedient, submissive.

My onslaught took the officers by surprise. They went off to report to their superiors and returned with unexpected news: I was to be handed over to the civilian security service. I was not quite certain what this presaged, but it was a relief to get away from the military "intelligence" officers.

Henceforth, my interrogation was conducted personally by a senior security officer, an awe-inspiring figure and a man of great personal power. At a word from him, suspected opponents of the regime were arrested, tortured, imprisoned. Some spent years in prison camps; some never returned. He was no man to trifle with, but I was too furious to be prudent. My "interrogation" turned into a political confrontation where I answered his charges by flinging accusations of my own against the regime he represented.

"Why do you keep attacking Jordan?" he asked me aggressively. "We read your declarations. You should focus your criticism on Israel alone!" He went into a long harangue defending the actions of the Jordanian government in September 1970. "We had to protect ourselves," he said plaintively.

"Protect yourselves?" I shouted. "By killing thousands of Palestinians in the refugee camps? Those killings left a black stain on the Jordanian government; they left a great hatred for Jordan in the hearts of Palestinians!"

"But you're Jordanian," he reminded me.

"I am a Palestinian," I said haughtily.

"You bear a Jordanian passport."

"I don't care!" I retorted angrily. "I didn't choose it!"

"If I take your passport away from you, what will you do?" he asked, trying to trap me.

"I'll keep an Israeli identity card!" I shouted.

My interrogator was clearly taken aback that I didn't consider a Jordanian document infinitely more desirable than an Israeli one. I told him why, complaining of the way the Jordanians treat us West Bankers. I told him of the way people were bullied and harassed at the bridge; I complained of the interrogations, of the disappearance of Palestinians taken into custody by Jordanian security men.

He listened to it all and then gave me a reassuring smile. "Why do you believe all this propaganda?" he asked. "After all, I'm a Palestinian myself!"

Indeed, the man is of Palestinian origin—but then, he is not the only Palestinian to serve the Jordanian regime. In my eyes, this officer personifies the dilemma of those Palestinians who serve the Jordanian regime. Such men are continually torn between their loyalties to the Hashemites and their concern for our people.

This conflict came out in my interrogation. After questioning on various issues, the security officer suddenly came to the real reason for my detention. His tone aggressive and hostile, he asked: "Why did you accuse the Jordanian government of complicity in the killing of the three Palestinian leaders?" (He was referring to the Israeli raid on Beirut, in which three PLO leaders were gunned down in their own homes, in front of their wives and children.) Even though the actual killing was done by Israeli soldiers, I was able to confront him with the proof we possessed concerning Jordanian collusion in the raid. He was clearly furious about charges that he was personally involved. "Those three men were my friends!" he said indignantly.

It is not easy for a Palestinian to serve the Hashemites. . . .

Leaving the issue, my interrogator's questions now took on a political hue. "Why do you want a Palestinian state of your own?" he asked me. "A Palestinian state will be of no use to you. Israel will find it easy to swallow you up! The big fish eat the small fish. The Palestinians are much better off with Jordan!"

I rejected his view with considerable passion, reminding him how the Jordanian government mistreated the Palestinians. It was a fiery confrontation. Showing little respect for the man's rank, I argued with him on every point, contradicting him repeatedly. Both of us raised our voices, and the commotion attracted considerable attention. At one point, a group of Jordanian officers crowded into the room, forming a circle around me. They had come, they told me, to catch a glimpse of *al-jassissa al-hassna* (the beautiful spy). An outsider might find the term flattering, but it carried a sinister ring. Their hostile, contemptuous expressions showed the real motive for their inspection of me. They resented my "intrusion" into male preserves; in revenge, they wished to dehumanize me, to reduce me to the status of an object.

My exchange with this man was long and violent. It was very foolhardy and reckless on my part to subject him to such an onslaught. Senior Jordanian officials are accustomed to being addressed respectfully.

Finally, having completed my interrogation, he decided to release me. When he handed me my passport, he gazed at me with a strangely bemused expression. Then he said thoughtfully, "If the West Bank is restored to Jordanian rule, we'll find it very difficult to deal with you Palestinians."

I am not easily overawed by police interrogations—perhaps because I made my acquaintance with them at any early age, following the Israeli conquest of Acre in 1948. A policeman knocked at the door of our home one day and asked to speak to Mother. I was just a little girl at the time, and I remember gazing in fright at this strange-looking being in his unfamiliar uniform. I became panic-stricken. I did not know what he wanted of Mother, but I feared that something was going to happen to her. In the end, I told him that she was at work, and he went away.

In the evening, Mother came home, and I told her of the policeman's visit and of his inquiries about her. Her response left me totally mystified: Indifferently, with no sign of fear or concern, she just sat down and lit a cigarette—without saying a word. Her calm reaction taught me that a police interrogation is not, after all, the end of the world.

On other occasions, policemen found her at home and questioned her there in my presence. But no matter who it was they asked her about, she invariably denied having heard of the name.

On one occasion, she was asked about a certain Acre man. As usual, she denied knowing anything about him, and the policemen were forced to accept her denial. But the fact was that she *did* know him—she knew him very well indeed! In fact it was she who smuggled him out of the Acre prison, after dressing him in a male-nurse's uniform. Then she drove him to a point near the Lebanese border; from there he slipped away and escaped into Lebanon. The Israeli authorities must have suspected Mother, but they could never prove that it was she who helped him get away.

The policemen used to have a difficult time getting Mother to answer their questions. She possessed a very strong personality, and they found it hard to pin her down. She had a wonderful knack of drawing her interrogators off into side issues. When she faced some particularly awkward question, she would employ a "feminine" ruse: She excused herself and went into the kitchen to make coffee. Mother must have made a very deep impression on some of these Israeli officials and policemen. Much later, after the 1967 war, I met the Israeli who had been the first military governor of Acre after 1948. He remembered Mother well; he told me at length of his many clashes and confrontations with her, speaking of her with great respect.

"Do you know," he said wonderingly, "many Arabs accused your late mother of being a 'collaborator with the Jews'? What fools! She was a great woman and an Arab patriot. There'll never be one like her again!"

These sincere and heartfelt words of praise, coming as they did from an adversary of my people, only confirmed my own deep admiration for her. Mother was, indeed, a woman of great courage. I loved her deeply, and I know that she has been a powerful influence upon me. In many of my thoughts and deeds I have followed in her footsteps, consciously or unconsciously taking her as my model.

As a child, I would become terrified whenever Mother underwent interrogations. Although I was still very young, I was old enough to grasp that these men had it in their power to take her away from me—and if there was one thing I feared, it was a renewed separation. Hadn't I lost her long enough, when my father sent me off to convent school, telling me that Mother was dead?

After being reunited with Mother, I remained fearful of a renewed separation. Whenever police came to question her, I sensed an awful danger: Was I about to lose her once more? Anxious and distressed, I would wait impatiently for the end of the interrogation, when I could run to her and fling myself into the safety of her arms.

At seventeen, I was separated from my mother once more. I moved to Jordan, while she remained behind in Israel. The border was sealed, and although we were no more than a few miles apart, we might as well have been on different planets, so rare were the opportunities to meet.

Looking back, my life has been a long series of restrictions and prohibitions, which have hampered my freedom, my elementary human right to go to the people and the places that I love. When I was in the convent, I was deprived of my mother; living in Israel, I was cut off from my brothers; later, when I moved to Jordan, I was parted from my parents; and throughout all these years, wherever I lived, Arab society, with its conventions of masculine domination, has locked me into the prison where Arab women are condemned to spend their lives. Perhaps that is why I found house arrest halfway tolerable: After all, it is only a further variation on the deprivation of liberty that has been a persistent oppressive theme of my life. I do not remember what it was like to live in harmony, with access to all of my family and without the fear that some impending war or other calamity would again divide us. Now, confined to my home, I know that, like hundreds of Palestinians before me, I might at any moment be deported by the Israeli occupation authorities; one stroke of the pen, and I could be separated from my family, from my children. . . .

During the fifties, when my family was divided, with my parents in Israel and my brothers and I in Jordan, our only opportunity to meet was at Christmas, when for one day the authorities of the two countries permitted Israeli Christians to cross over into the Jordanian section of Jerusalem. The transit point was at the Mandelbaum

Gate, on the demarcation line. For me, as for many other Palestinians, that "gate" became the hateful symbol of the double separation: separation from our dear ones and separation from our beloved homeland. That was, indeed, a gateway of tears—tears of joy at reunification, tears of sorrow at renewed separation.

One Christmas when I went to the Mandelbaum Gate to receive Mother, she did not come at the appointed time. Deeply disappointed, I inquired about her and was informed that she was in the hospital. I begged permission to go visit her, but my entreaties were in vain. The Jordanian officer on duty, Major Kaldi, was very kind to me; he treated me like a daughter, bringing me coffee to calm me down. I noticed that he had tears in his eyes; I did not understand why.

A mood of desperation took hold of me; for a moment, I toyed with the insane idea of making a dash for it—after all, the Gate was no more than a bar, with a few soldiers on guard. Perhaps I could get through? I would hurry to Mother's sickbed, to fling myself into her arms and tell her of my remorse over my abandonment of her.

But I quickly banished the thought of running past the sentries; such a foolhardy act was tantamount to suicide. I would be shot down without mercy.

I did not know then that Mother was already dead.

Major Kaldi knew. Later on, he broke the news to me. Nobody had the heart to tell me, he said. He told me how touched he had been by the tears on my cheeks and the heartbroken look in my eyes.

"You looked like the sad Madonna," he said, "the tragedy of the Palestinians was imprinted upon your face."

2

"Say Good-bye to Your Mother!"

"SAY GOOD-BYE TO YOUR MOTHER!" Father commanded.

We children were silent, sensing that something unusual was about to happen.

Mother was wordless and tearful; Father looked somber; the maid was hurrying to and fro, busy with mysterious preparations. Something was wrong; with a deep feeling of anxiety, I stood dumb and expectant. My fingers lingered almost unconsciously on Mother's face. Putting my two small arms around her neck, I held her tenderly, sobbing, "I won't go! I won't go!" Mother put her arms about me in a last strong tender embrace. I felt her softness, inhaling the familiar scent of her perfume and gazing into her beautiful face.

The car came to the door. My father addressed us. His voice was gentle but authoritative. "Say good-bye to your mother!" he repeated firmly. I could remain silent no longer; collapsing on the floor, I burst into bitter, angry tears. I sat on the floor, refusing to budge. "No, no! I won't leave Mummy! You go alone!" George turned away his face to hide his tears; it was not manly for a boy to weep openly.

In the end, my father picked me up by force and carried me out kicking and screaming. In my despair, I flung my favorite doll on the floor, and it smashed. Father tried to comfort me, promising to buy me another doll. "I don't want a doll!" I sobbed. "I don't want you! I want Mummy!"

Father thrust me in the car and drove us to Tiberias. We stayed there with Grandma, Father's mother; we were to remain there until the end of the school vacation. It was strange and lonely there without Mother. Father used to sit morosely in the café of Abu Elias, on the promenade at Tiberias. Abu Elias knew Father's special requests; without waiting for an order, he would bring arrack and *mazza* (pickles).

Father was silent and withdrawn; he drank a lot. Friends surrounded him; he was a well-known figure among the Palestinian elite of Nazareth and Tiberias, and his acquaintances came to keep him company and cheer him up.

When the school year began, my brothers—twelve-year-old George and Yussuf, who was five at the time—were taken to a boarding school in Jerusalem. I was seven; I was sent to a Nazareth convent school.

The convent's mother superior received Father and Grandma. Their conversation was conducted in French. Father made it quite clear that I was forbidden to see my mother. Hearing him proclaim the prohibition, I felt a renewed sense of loss and deprivation. In my pain, I cried bitterly, full of anger at Father. Then Father and Grandma took their leave, and I remained, forlorn and sad.

The convent school opened up a new world for me. I felt eager to learn; everything had meaning for me; each name gave birth to an idea. Secretly I treasured Mother's tender command: "Go to school and study so that I will be proud of you." I learned many interesting things, things that made the world come alive for me. That was by day; but at night I would lie in bed crying softly to myself. The English nun who watched over us came in, hurriedly covering up her hair as she hastened to my bedside. "Mummy will come to see you on Sunday," she assured me, trying to staunch my tears. But I clung to her and wept in anguish: "No, no! Mummy won't come, only Father!" I saw the tears in her eyes: "God is merciful," she sighed. "He won't leave you alone, He will bring your Mummy." She looked shocked; only the mother superior knew of my father's ban on Mother's visits.

Father came on Sundays. I welcomed his visits, but I never mentioned Mother to him; somehow I sensed that he would not want to talk about her. The nuns told me that Mother was dead.

Mother belonged to a Palestinian family hailing from Kfar Yassif. She herself was born in America and spent her early years there. Growing up in that relatively emancipated society, she imbibed ideas of personal freedom quite foreign to Arab traditions. As a girl, she took ballet lessons; she dreamed of studying medicine, but her family decided to return to Palestine and she could not realize her dream. Back in her father's village, she continued to behave as she had been accustomed to behaving in America; her behavior incurred considerable criticism from the villagers, who found it far too emancipated for their tastes.

Later, when she married Father, she could never accept the passive role of the obedient wife. Society at that time left her with few alternatives; for a long time, she was obliged to bow to Father's authority, but she did it unwillingly and with deep resentment. She did not believe that a woman need be blindly obedient.

Father did. He adhered closely to Arab traditions of male supremacy. He was always courteous toward Mother, but he would tolerate no questioning of his authority or privileges. Father treated me with affection, but he made it clear to me that as a girl I had to accept male authority. Mother was affectionate with all three of us, but as her only daughter, I claimed special attention. She told me stories of great women, like Florence Nightingale, teaching me to take them as my models and to respect myself as a woman. Thanks to her, I was never made to feel inferior as a woman. On the contrary, I was petted and made to feel special and unique.

Mother's driving force was her desire for freedom. She dreamed of a life without ties or restrictions. She believed that she had a special role to play in furthering the welfare of her people. Her stable, sheltered life in Father's mansion of Montfort was very unsatisfactory for Mother's ambitious nature; she sought the glamor of adventure, stimulation, struggle.

Driven by the urge to assert herself, Mother finally decided on the courageous step of divorcing Father. Even today, such an act on the part of a woman is still very rare in Arab society; at that time, it was almost unheard of, although it was perfectly acceptable for a man to divorce his wife. In the Arab world, there is no one so despised as a divorced woman. But Mother cared little for the opinions of others or for the conventional morals of Arab society. She knew she would be treated as an outcast, but that did not deter her; she went her own way.

Mother's quest for freedom took her on a path of suffering. She was made to pay the heavy price Arab society exacts from "rebellious" women: She was deprived of her children. She was not allowed even to see us. Coming on top of the divorce, the 1948 war and the partition of Palestine divided her irrevocably from her sons, my brothers. Barring a few brief and heartrending meetings, she did not see them again for the rest of her life.

Her tragedy was also ours. Torn away from her at a tender age, we grew up motherless. It was a bleak, unhappy existence, and the memories of that suffering will always remain with me. Indeed, it is more than mere memory; in Arab society, children are answerable for the "misdeeds" of their parents. Mother's "scandalous" behavior is a blot on every member of our family, and we, her children, are considered to blame; in certain quarters, her "misdeed" harms our standing to this very day.

I will never forget the dreary misery of those first months at the convent: the painful longing for Mother, the agony I suffered when the nuns told me she was dead.

Alone in the convent school, I felt lost and abandoned. I was closed and withdrawn; receiving love from no one, I withheld my affections. A bewildered little girl, I nursed my lonely misery.

Then, one day, one of the sisters secretly brought me a picture of Mother. "Your mother is well, I have seen her, she sends you her kisses. She is tormented because she is not allowed to come to see you. She wants you to study hard; when you grow up and are free to do what you wish, you will see her again."

Enraptured, I gazed at Mother's picture, the token of her love for me. It was a small thing to seize on, but the snapshot helped me out of my depression. Previously I had refused to play with my schoolmates; but now, reassured of Mother's tender love, I felt free to reach out to the other girls.

That Christmas, at the end of 1947, the nuns were very cheerful. We attended midnight mass, and then, holding candles, we marched all over the convent in a long procession, singing Christmas carols: *"Mon bon Sapin," "Il est né le divin enfant,"* and "Silent Night." In the chapel, a French nun played Renaissance music on the organ. After the ceremony, we all trooped into the dining room, splendidly decorated, the tables loaded with sweets and chocolate. After midnight, the Terra Sancta orchestra came in to play for us, while outside, the bells of Nazareth pealed out and fireworks exploded in the air.

While the festivities lasted, I was gay and happy. Then we went to bed, to await Father Christmas with his gifts. But lying in bed in the dark, I felt a sudden longing for my mother and brothers. I remembered Christmas at home, with the wine and champagne and the stuffed turkey; I remembered my father telling Christmas legends and humorous stories, while I lay in Mother's lap, sensing her warm caressing touch until I fell asleep.

After Christmas vacation, when the girls came back with their stories of family festivities, I felt jealous and resentful.

The Orthodox Christmas falls on January 7. That year, Father came to the convent and took me to the home of my aunt in Haifa. My brothers came too, from the boarding school in Jerusalem. At that first reunion, we children were silent. Then, gradually, as we broke through the wall of silence, we began to talk about the previous Christmas, with Mother. Together, we dredged up half-forgotten episodes, our follies and escapades and pranks of that cherished past. We laughed and laughed until the tears ran.

But in Father's presence, we never dared to mention Mother's name; she was silent music in our hearts.

Christmas in Haifa was as enjoyable as in Nazareth, but the atmosphere was different. In the Greek Orthodox church, the service was conducted in both Greek and Arabic. The *suq* (marketplace) was closed, with the Moslems joining in our celebrations. The Greek Orthodox scouts paraded, headed by their band.

We spent the evening at my aunt's house. She played classical music for us on the piano, while Father sat very straight and proud. He was very affectionate toward me, embracing me warmly and praising my aunt's playing. He wanted me to follow her conservative, traditional ways.

Father talked to my aunt about his financial difficulties. "But I would die rather than sell my land to the Jews," he said firmly. "That's a matter of principle!" Refusing the high price offered by the Jews, he sold his lands around the Palais de Montfort to an Arab. The Palais, the Jeddin fortress built by the Crusaders, had long belonged to our family, who brought it from the sons of Daher al-Omer, the warrior chief who controlled the area in the nineteenth century. The land was resold later and was ultimately bought by the Jews, who made the castle into a museum.

Father's difficulties stemmed from a great calamity he suffered in his business affairs. He was a grain contractor for the British navy; that year, the British ordered him to hold up his shipment, and as a result the wheat was ruined by rain. Hoping to make good his losses, Father ordered the captain of his ship to scuttle the vessel. Father hoped that the insurance payment would see him through. The gamble did not come off; he forgot that the insurance company was only obliged to pay thirteen months later.

Matters got worse. Father had an open credit with Barclay's Bank of £100,000 Palestine. But things went wrong there. I never quite understood what happened, but Father was arrested and placed on trial, together with the bank manager. Father had studied law, but he never practiced it. Nevertheless, even though his father—my grandfather—was prepared to get him the best lawyers in Palestine, Father decided to conduct his own defense. In court, Father managed to save the bank manager, but he himself lost heavily. Needing money to cover Father's losses, Grandfather sold off thousands of dunams of his land; it was a heavy price to pay for Father's spirit of adventure. Several years later, Mother took me to Haifa's Hadar Hacarmel quarter, where she showed me the roads laid on land that Grandfather sold, at seven Palestine piasters a square meter, to pay the debt. But despite his predicament, Father never sold any land to the Jews: That was a matter of principle with him.

Equally, it was a principle with him to help others. When I went out walking with him, he was often accosted by people who appealed to him for help with their difficulties. Whether it was a matter of intervening with the British authorities on behalf of some unfortunate, or endeavoring to obtain pardons for the condemned prisoners, if there was a dispute and he was needed as arbitrator or peacemaker, he was always ready to help. He was generous and charitable too, and beggars were sure of his assistance. One day, I asked him why he gave money to poor people. I shall never forget his answer: "Give and God will give unto you." He quoted the Koran: "Never scorn an orphan, and the beggar never insult or refuse." Looking at me earnestly, he added, "One day your father will lose his money, and then God will send his angels with gifts."

Now Father's somber prophecy was coming true: He had lost most of his former wealth. Nevertheless, that Christmas at the beginning of 1948 there were gifts for all, and the atmosphere at my aunt's house in Haifa was festive. I do remember feeling a profound unease, however. It was only a short time before that we had all been separated from Mother; and now there were all these mysterious conversations among the grown-ups, talking of Jewish acts of terror and retaliation by Palestinian groups. It was very vague. I comprehended little of what was happening. But in some ways I sensed that all these strange acts they spoke of constituted some kind of personal threat to me and to my brothers, to the remnants of warmth and tenderness that I still found in my home after Mother's departure. I sensed a foreboding: Would we meet again at Easter? But I did not dare to express my fears and anxieties.

On the eve of our departure, my aunt played the piano for us. She played *"Ce n'est qu'un au revoir,"* and we all sang the words with her. Then we separated; my brothers returned to boarding school in Jerusalem, and I went back to the convent.

I did not meet my brothers again for six years.

A few months later, at Easter 1948, I was at my aunt's home again on King George Street, Haifa. The British were about to leave the country. By now the war for Palestine was raging everywhere. Haifa was the scene of heavy fighting. The Palestinians fired from our balcony at the Jewish Hagana positions on the other side of the street. At night we saw the soldiers—Jews as well as Arabs—clearly visible by the flickering light of the fires. From all sides came the sound of shellfire, explosions, flames. The next-door house was completely destroyed. My aunt took her five children and me and moved to another house in the German colony. We left in such haste she had no time to pack even a suitcase.

The Hagana were rapidly gaining control of the town, and the

Arab inhabitants fled in the thousands toward the port, to find a boat that would take them to safety. The question has often been asked: Why did the Palestinians flee—in Haifa and elsewhere? The answer is simple: Some were driven out by Israeli forces; others simply fled from the fighting, as unarmed civilians do in every war. Israeli propaganda has made great play of the story that Haifa's Jewish leaders tried to persuade some of the town's Arab inhabitants to remain. I do not know whether that story is true or not. All I know is that my aunt was driven by the basic instinct of self-preservation—and the same is true of hundreds of thousands of Palestinians who abandoned their homes during the 1948 war.

In the eighth year of my life, I witnessed terrifying things: men with guns and helmets—a man killed outside our home—houses blown up. My aunt was too weak, physically and psychologically, to deal with the situation. She had her own five boys to take care of, as well as me, and she sank into a terrified passivity, unable to do more than wonder out loud: "Who will bury the dead?" My aunt's attitude only served to increase my terror and bewilderment. I could not understand what was happening, and she made no attempt to explain or to help us cope with our fears. Listlessly, she talked of appealing to our Arab friends in the National Defense, or to our Jewish friends in the Hagana, to guarantee our safety, so that we could get away. But the idea of leaving brought new fears: "Suppose we are killed on the way, who will bury us?"

In the end, by some miracle, my aunt roused herself to take her family to Lebanon. Father was also making preparations to leave for Lebanon, and he was concerned for my safety. Shortly before the British left Palestine, he persuaded two British officer friends of his to take me to Nazareth. Nazareth was not a battle zone, and he was sure that I would be safe in the convent. All this was considered temporary—my aunt only intended to go to Lebanon for a few days or weeks; when things quieted down, she promised to return.

In the convent, I was troubled and anxious. The peace and quiet of Nazareth was a welcome relief after the terrors of Haifa, but I was concerned about Father. My young mind fell prey to fears and fantasies. Suppose Father was killed? What would happen to me? Would I be left all alone? Where was Mother? What was happening to my brothers in Jerusalem?

The fighting dragged on. Nazareth was still outside the battle zone, but we heard terrifying stories of masses of Arab refugees fleeing for their lives from the fighting. Thousands of men, women, and children, carrying a few personal possessions, were trudging across the Galilee hills, heading toward the sanctuary of the Lebanese border. Battles were raging all over Palestine, fire, death, and destruction were engulfing the whole country.

The weeks passed, and there was no news of Father. Gently, the nuns hinted that he might have died in the fighting. Desperately worried, I listened to the nuns talking among themselves, trying to comprehend what they were talking about. What would become of me?

The war came to Nazareth. It was brief, but terrifying nonetheless. Israeli forces approached from the west. We spent hours in the convent shelter, huddling around the nuns for security and reassurance. Many of the Nazareth townspeople came to seek sanctuary in the convent, where the flags of France and the Vatican seemed to promise some measure of safety.

There was almost no fighting in Nazareth itself. After what seemed like endless hours of terror, we heard the booming of a loudspeaker. The town had capitulated; the mayor asked the townspeople to hoist white flags and to remain calm; the Israeli occupation forces had guaranteed the safety of the population. Civilians were ordered to remain in their houses. Anyone who went outside did so at the risk of his life.

The conquest of Nazareth made little or no difference to my daily life at the convent. When the fighting ended and the Israelis took over the town, the nuns quickly restored our normal daily routine: lessons, meals, prayers.

There was still no news of Father or of the other members of my family. One day a nun told me that there was no one to pay my fees. "We have to consider you as an orphan," she said bluntly. From her point of view, it was a simple administrative matter; with no one paying for me, I was considered a charity case, and therefore they had to transfer me to the orphans' wing.

It was a terrible blow to me. I had lost everything now: Mother, Father, brothers, family, home. What would become of me? Solitary and inconsolable, I cried into my pillow. There was no hope, no source of light anywhere.

At that time, I had a recurrent nightmare: I was on a ship that had been abandoned. Everyone else, crew and passengers, had launched the lifeboat and set sail, leaving me all alone. In that fearsome solitude I heard a heart-piercing cry, sad and lonesome. And then I would awake to find the moonlight streaming in through the windows and my face wet with tears.

One day, some time after the Israeli occupation of Nazareth, Mother came to the convent. She arrived in an ambulance; she had been working as a voluntary nurse with the Red Cross in Acre, during and after the fighting, helping to evacuate the wounded, risking her life under fire. Now she commandeered the ambulance to come and see me.

The convent sisters, mindful of my father's orders, refused to let her in. She was forbidden to see me, they explained firmly. But Mother was equally firm and unyielding. Sister superior relented a little, offering to let her in if she brought written permission from my father. But there was no news from Father at that time—he might be in Lebanon; he might be dead. How could she bring his permission?

The argument went on and on. Finally Mother lost her patience. Unless she was allowed to see me immediately, she would go and fetch the Israeli police and force her way in!

Seeing that she was in earnest in her threat, the nuns gave in. She was permitted to come inside.

When I saw her, I ran toward her, flinging myself into her arms with sobs of happiness and relief.

I shall never forget my feeling at that moment: I had been rescued, brought back to life! Clutched in my mother's arms, I felt myself submerged in a torrent of tenderness. The Red Cross personnel accompanying Mother, as well as the nuns standing nearby, were deeply touched by the joy and passion of our reunion. Finally, reassured that this was indeed my mother, I flung a challenging, triumphant glance at the nuns, as though to say: You see, I'm *not* an orphan! Happily, I fingered the dresses she brought me, but her greatest gift was the hope she restored to my young heart. Once again, I was transferred, from the orphans' section back to the section where I had been housed previously. Glad as I was to regain my old place, I felt uncomfortable at this distinction between the or-

phans and those girls with parents to pay for them. Didn't the orphan girls deserve warmth and affection, not just charity? When I
myself was in the status of an orphan, I hated the nuns who sighed
their pity for me: I did not want their commiseration!

Not long after Mother's first visit, Father also appeared. I burst
into tears of joy on seeing him again, after all these months of uncertainty whether he was alive or dead. I told him of my transfer to the
orphans' section; later, when he went to pay my tuition fees, he
asked pointedly who had spread the news of his death? The nuns
were too embarrassed to reply, but later they scolded me for telling
him!

Father's arrival was as unexpected as Mother's. Even if he had
survived the war, I knew he had to be in Lebanon; I also knew that
any war refugee trying to return home was regarded by the Israelis
as an "infiltrator," and the border guards were authorized to shoot
him. Those refugees who managed to get through into Israel faced
imprisonment or deportation if they were caught without the correct
documents. How, then, had he come? I asked anxiously. Was he an
"infiltrator"? I had visions of the police coming to take him away
from me.

Father hastened to reassure me. True, he had crossed the Lebanese border illegally. Making his way on foot, he slipped across the
hills, hiding in olive groves along the way. But then he was spotted
by an Israeli patrol; the soldiers opened fire, and Father was
wounded in the leg and taken prisoner. The soldiers took him to
their headquarters in a nearby village. On the way there, he felt very
apprehensive about the fate in store for him. But when he was
brought in for questioning, he had a pleasant surprise: The officer in
command of the unit was an old friend, Bechor Shitrit! The two men
embraced warmly, to the consternation of the soldiers, who were
unused to seeing their officer giving such a warm welcome to an
"infiltrator"! Shitrit had Father sent to the Italian hospital in Haifa
to have his leg treated. He also provided him with the necessary documents to remain in Israel legally.

Later, Father took me to Shitrit's home in Tel Aviv. Shitrit belonged to an old Sephardi Jewish family that had long maintained
close relations with their Arab neighbors and shared many Arab

customs and traditions. That may be why I found such a striking resemblance between Shitrit and my father—the same wisdom, the same way of thinking. Before 1948, they had been on an equal footing, but now there was a great difference between them: Father was a member of a powerless minority, while Shitrit belonged to Israel's ruling circles. (Later, he was made minister of police in the Israeli cabinet.) I was deeply struck by this strange relationship between two men who were simultaneously friends and foes. It was not the last time in my life that I would encounter such an ambiguous relationship.

I was genuinely overjoyed at having Father back, alive and well. But my pleasure was overshadowed by the fear that he would once again prohibit Mother's visits. I did not tell him that she had come to see me, but he brought up her name. "Your mother came to see me in the hospital," he told me. "I'm glad she visited you. You must have been terribly lonely." I could not believe my ears: Father knew of Mother's visits, and he wasn't angry at all!

I was a young child, and I could not comprehend the depths and complexity of the relationship between Father and Mother. Father's treatment of Mother was dictated by the tradition in which he had been brought up. Prior to their divorce, he was the incarnation of tenderness and consideration. But when Mother struck out for freedom, Father deprived her of her children—for such is the retribution that Arab society exacts from a mutinous woman. But now, after the war, everything changed. Father was not the same man he had been two or three years previously. The calamities he endured before the war had cost him most of his wealth; what little he had left was destroyed during the fighting and by the Israeli government's expropriation measures after the war. He was left penniless. Suddenly, he found himself on an equal footing with Mother; he could no longer be domineering toward her.

Father's prolonged absence from home must also have had its impact upon him; without doubt, he was very homesick during those long months in Lebanon. When he came back, one of the few possessions he brought me was a present for Mother—a valuable lighter. Mother cherished his gift; she took it with her wherever she went, till the end of her days. While Father lay in the hospital in

Haifa, Mother sat at his bedside to keep him company and keep up his spirits.

The new borders created by the war divided my parents from George and Yussuf, who were at a boarding school in the Jordanian section of Jerusalem; Father and Mother had only me. Henceforward, they shared equally in deciding about my future, showing respect and consideration for each other's views. They now decided that I was to remain at the convent school; observing my concern, they hastened to reassure me that there would be no more separations. Mother would be free to visit me at the convent, and I would spend my vacations with her.

Father and Mother remained on close terms, displaying affection and concern for each other. During his final years, Father drank a great deal. Mother's health was failing, and she feared that, should she die before him, no one would be left to care for him. In the presence of two witnesses, she entrusted a sum of money to the priest to pay for a burial plot for Father.

As she had foreseen, Mother died before Father; this was in 1963. Her death had a terrible effect on him, and he never got over it. A few months later, he, too, died. Being divorced, they were not buried side by side. Mother was laid to rest in Kfar Yassif, her family home; Father was interred in Acre. But this separation was meaningless; during their final years, Mother and Father were linked by ties far stronger than those of marriage.

3

The Path to the Mandelbaum Gate

ON MY FIRST SCHOOL VACATION after the war, Mother took me to her home in Acre. My return to Acre conjured up thousands of memories of my early childhood: sitting at home with Father and Mother . . . watching the sea waves breaking against the rocks beneath my window . . . fishing with my brothers on the shore.

But all that was gone. I clung to Mother desperately, crying on her shoulder while she ran her hand through my hair. Her eyes, too, brimmed with tears—of happiness at regaining me or of sorrow over everything she had lost? Who knows? She spoke to me quietly, her voice trembling yet full of reassurance: "I will never leave you . . . no one can take you away from me. . . ." She sensed my fear of a renewed separation; but, together with that fear, there was an angry readiness to fight the whole world, to prevent such an injustice.

Mother's home was a humble apartment, the only property Father left her at the time of their divorce. She was having to contend with great difficulties. After years of comfort and luxury, she now found herself without a husband, without a rich home, without any means of livelihood. With her characteristic courage and determination, she would not allow objective difficulties to get her down. After some time, she found a job as a social worker, earning enough to support herself as well as paying my school fees and buying my clothes when Father's financial straits made it impossible for him to provide for me.

The Israeli authorities put Mother to work in the villages around Acre, where she soon made herself well known by her helpfulness. When I visited her, she would take me along on her rounds, and I had an opportunity to see how she had rebuilt her social position. Everywhere she went, villagers welcomed her with love and affection, while she proudly showed me off before them. I was so happy. But at the same time, I felt a lingering sorrow for the years that I was deprived of this happiness.

Mother had plenty on her hands. The needs were enormous. The villagers had suffered badly through the war and the upheavals that followed it. Families had been separated, with some members beyond the borders, unable to return home. Many families were in desperate straits because their breadwinners had been killed or maimed in the fighting or had fled the country, leaving their dependents destitute. As though that were not enough, the Israeli authorities instituted large-scale land confiscations, taking farmland from the Arab villages and giving it to newly established Jewish settlements. The villagers did get some compensation, but it was no substitute for the livelihood they had lost. I admired the spirit of these villagers, who faced their trials and tribulations with such steadfast courage and tenacity. Living under Israeli rule, confronted with a new and alien culture and an unfriendly government, they had to fight hard for their very existence and for the right to hold on to the land of their forefathers.

I was in ecstasy during that wonderful vacation with Mother. It was blissful to experience once more her tender warmth and affection. For both of us it was paradise regained.

But the vacation came to an end; sadly and reluctantly, I went back to the convent, where I had to endure a far harsher existence. The nuns were very strict with us, with the full backing of most of the parents. The girls at the convent came from conservative bourgeois families who wanted their children to receive the traditional convent upbringing, with its strong overtones of discipline and Western culture. The nuns, all of European origin, taught us to speak French and English with the correct accents. By their stern example, they instilled us with their inexorable logic and their great willpower. Above all, they taught us to face life with a deep belief in God, with honesty and joy, full of confidence that justice will always prevail in the end.

The regime imposed by the nuns was severe. Every morning we had to get up at five o'clock to attend mass, and every morning was agony as I dragged myself out of my warm bed into the chilly air. Another hardship, of a different nature, was the restriction on parents' visits, which were permitted no more than once a month. But the nuns taught us never to complain, whatever the difficulties. "Life is not a bed of roses," the sisters explained. Knowing our attachment to our toys and possessions, they nevertheless taught us never to protest when such things were taken away. Even if I was unjustly accused, I was to offer the other cheek: "Thus Jesus said . . ."

On Sundays, the nuns would take us out for long walks to visit churches or other holy places. At that time, the Church of the Annunciation in Nazareth was a humble edifice; we would follow Christ's path up to the holy fountain. We trod that route so often it became a part of us. We sometimes passed by 'Ein Miriam (Mary's Well). At one time, this was the only source of water in the vicinity; in modern times, it has fallen into disuse, but every now and then, some woman will draw up a jug of water for a special benediction.

We were taught to love Palestine as Jesus had loved it. All the nuns revered the country with a spiritual attachment that derived from the Bible.

The nuns took us on walks up the gently sloping hills of Galilee, where we admired the splendid views and the beautiful churches. They pointed out the rare flowers that adorned the hills; we picked them carefully, taking them back to the convent to be pressed into books. We learned the names of all the varieties, many of which are unique to Galilee and the Mount Carmel area.

The nuns tried to teach us to meditate, to "listen to the holy voices." I was too young to comprehend the meaning of meditation. But I loved to hear the sounds of wind and water. I had a special affection for the Tabha waterfall.

It was a peaceful life in that convent school in Nazareth, surrounded by green fields and sloping vineyards. In the town itself, the houses were built separately, the spaces in between planted with fig and pomegranate trees and date palms. In spring, the hillsides were thickly carpeted with an abundance of richly colored wild flowers. Nowhere in the whole world is there anything that resembles the colors and scents of the Palestinian spring. From my window at the convent, I could look out over that landscape unchanged since biblical times: the oaks and blossoming plum trees, spaced out between stone fences; the sheep grazing in the open spaces, watched by a shepherd whose flute's lingering Oriental tunes drifted to my ears; the terraced hillside planted with ancient olive trees.

Our people are deeply attached to the olive tree; its fruits are vital to the existence and survival of our villagers. With wheat, bread, and olive oil, a house is always secure from famine, from war, and from catastrophe. Arabic literature mentions the olive tree as the cure of all diseases; in the holy Koran the Prophet Muhammad exhorts us, "Take care of the holy olive tree; from it you will gain your benediction." The olive trees had a special appeal for me, with the mystery of their defiant strength that withstands the ordeals of time by virtue of the long, tough roots they sink into the soil. Like thoughts and memories that sit deep in the mind, deeper than words, the olive tree has its roots in this land since the time of my ancestors, long ago.

The convent sisters taught us to make the most of this life, which is God's most precious gift. We must do good deeds, for which we would be recompensed in heaven. We should learn to suffer, they told us, because through suffering we achieve our own identity, we strengthen our morale and our will, and we attain self-sufficiency. It was necessary to make sacrifices, so that we would be worthy of our first communion.

First communion presented me with a particular problem, for it required me to convert to Catholicism. The nuns taught me that my family's Greek Orthodox faith was akin to atheism; in fact, its denial of the pope's authority was a sin graver than atheism!

I was always running away from the catechism lessons, because I could not accept the teachings of the priest who conducted them. He was continually scolding me: I must obey the nuns, he said, I must eat less chocolate, to teach myself strength of will. He warned me against bad thoughts, but I never comprehended what he meant. I was rebellious and argumentative. My disobedience brought its punishment, with my first communion being postponed several times until I became obedient and worthy. In looking forward to first communion, my motives were less than purely religious. I sensed a coquettish attraction to the idea of parading in front of everyone with my long hair and my beautiful costume, and to feel people's eyes on me as I mounted the altar steps of the Annunciation Cathedral. We were forbidden mirrors, to discourage us from paying too much attention to our appearance; but glancing at my reflection in the window, I would dream of seeing myself all in white, radiant with the joy of my first communion.

My first communion was held in the convent's own church, which was specially decorated with white flowers called Saint-Joseph's-lily. The girls lined up on both sides of the aisle; the organ played a canticle while the choir added "Hallelujah"; and then we marched in two by two, boys and girls; the girls resplendent in white, the boys in their blue costume uniform with a bow tie. As we paced slowly toward the altar, the song of the choir swelled louder and louder, their voices floating out of the church and echoing across the silent mountains.

The girls at the convent school in Nazareth all came from Arab families, Moslem as well as Christian. But in 1952, when I moved to a convent school in Haifa, I suddenly found myself in a totally different milieu. I was the only Arab girl there; all the others were Jewish, most of them from Europe, where they had been baptized during the war so that they'd be saved from annihilation by the Nazis. After the physical danger passed, many of these families retained their Christian ties, giving their daughters a convent education. The Israeli authorities frowned on this tendency; they wanted Jewish children to go to Israeli government schools, where they would receive a "truly Jewish" education. In time, under constant pressure from the authorities, the number of Jewish girls in these establishments declined sharply. But during my schooldays, numerous Jewish girls attended convent schools. They brought with them much of the heritage of traditional European Jewish culture. They were highly gifted, with great talents in music and art and all forms of self-expression. At first, I felt a little overshadowed; I could not compete with their attainments. But the girls were very friendly toward me, never behaving in a superior manner or patronizing me. We soon developed feelings of deep sympathy, affection, and admiration for one another. At the same time, it was exciting for me to imbibe this creative, intellectual atmosphere. I tasted a new freedom, and I enjoyed myself thoroughly.

The attitude of the nuns was quite unlike what I was used to in the Nazareth convent. Here, in Haifa, they were also strict with us, but at the same time, there was a degree of open-mindedness and tolerance for more modern attitudes. I learned that once a week, a nun would take us to the beach, where we were to put on bathing costumes! I was astounded! The first time we went, I felt terribly self-conscious. I could scarcely put on my bathing suit; in Nazareth, we had been taught that it is immoral to expose the body in any way—even short-sleeved dresses were taboo. How could I wear a bathing costume in public?

I was perplexed and confused: How could I reconcile the teachings of the French nuns in Nazareth with the teachings of the French nuns in Haifa?

My salvation came from the Jewish girls. In total contrast to my own angelic purity and innocence, they were very free, open-minded, and, moreover, knowledgeable—and they were very patient and open in sharing their knowledge with me. At first, I could scarcely understand their talk. What was the meaning of their jokes? What were they laughing about? They were my own age, but they seemed so much more sophisticated and experienced. Most of them had boyfriends, whom they went out with during their weekends at home. Returning to school, they always had mysterious and wonderful stories about these boys and what they did. I sat in a corner, listening silently, shocked and fascinated, nauseated and thrilled.

When I met Mother on weekends, I used to seek her help, but I got little from her. For all her progressive outlook, she gave evasive answers to my questions, contenting herself with some vague comment about the bad housing conditions among the Jewish newcomers. Frequently, an entire immigrant family slept in a single room, and my schoolmates often witnessed their parents' intimacies.

As for the nuns, their attitude toward sex was predictable. They tried to repress our desires, but they never quite succeeded. We were healthy young girls, with a healthy curiosity about life and above all about sex. When the sisters went to the chapel for their daily prayers, we were left in the study room, free of their supervision. We were supposed to be doing our lessons, but on occasion, while hymns and chants wafted in from the chapel, one of the girls would walk up to the blackboard and deliver an impromptu lecture about what our fathers and mothers did in bed. The lecture was accompanied by crude but highly explicit sketches illustrating the various poses of lovemaking. At first, I scarcely understood what it was all about, nor why the other girls were laughing so much. When I began to catch on, I felt confused and embarrassed. Then a nun walked in, and we hurriedly thought up some explanation for all the giggling.

One day, a nun took us out for a walk along the seashore. By some ruse, we slipped away from her, and went off in search of adventure. One of the girls noticed a pair of lovers, and the others decided to climb a tree to get a better view. Once again, I felt confused and unsure; I didn't think it was right to spy, but I was afraid to say anything. We clambered up into the tree and held our breath. Down below us, we could see the couple, who did not know they were being watched. For what seemed like an eternity, we witnessed the elaborate ritual of lovemaking.

I gazed, fascinated. I felt a strange and overpowering mixture of curiosity and passion; I shall never forget that sensation. It was as though all my senses were being opened up, as though I had taken a single bound from childhood into adolescence.

When the couple finished, we gave way to a wave of gaiety. Triumphantly, we sang, *"Eize yoffi!"* (How beautiful!) Down below, the startled couple scrambled into their clothes. Suddenly, my mood changed again: I despised myself for helping to humiliate them. But I could not forget what I had seen.

Growing into adolescence, my budding awareness of myself as a woman was given further impetus by an unusual experience. As part of her work, Mother helped to raise money for an ambulance to serve the villagers. When the ambulance arrived, the event was celebrated at a festivity held in Acre, attended by all those—Arabs and Jews—who had helped in the project.

The party was gay and rowdy, quite unlike the restrained, decorous parties I was used to. A naïve, shy fourteen-year-old, I sat beside Mother, trying to make myself as inconspicuous as possible, gazing in wonder as men and women danced together with what I regarded as great immodesty. But it was a colorful, exciting scene, and I was fascinated by the music and the joyful, uninhibited atmosphere.

Suddenly, the master of ceremonies announced that there was going to be a beauty contest. I understood the words he said, but I had not the faintest idea what he was talking about. I had never heard of such a thing. But Mother paid no attention to my bewilderment; seizing me by the hand, she led me to the ladies' room. She quickly ran a comb through my long dark hair and—for the first time in my life—she put some lipstick on me. All around me, I noticed other women and girls similarly engaged in beautifying themselves, and I was quite puzzled. What was going on? Mother hastily coached me on what I was to do. "When your turn comes, just walk across the stage and show off your profile."

The competition began. Suddenly, my number was called. My stomach twisted up, I felt stifled; but somehow I managed to move myself forward, blushing from shyness and confusion. As I walked across the stage, I heard enthusiastic clapping and whistling from the audience, but remembering Mother's advice, I did not turn my head.

It was an elimination contest. One by one, the other contestants dropped out. Finally, I found myself alone on the stage with just one other girl: One of us two was to be chosen as the beauty queen! I was still too confused and bewildered to take in what was happening, but I thought the applause for me was somewhat stronger than for my rival. Perhaps I enjoyed some slight advantage because the Arab villagers knew Mother and me and therefore gave me their support. But Jews were applauding me, too.

At this point, the judges suddenly discovered that I was Arab, while the other girl was Jewish. The outcome was predictable, and, indeed, inevitable: They awarded her the first prize. But this was not the end of the story. When the announcement was made, pandemonium broke loose. The Arabs and Jews seated at the committee table jumped to their feet, shouting and yelling at one another. Fists were clenched, someone lifted a chair, and it seemed that a riot was about to break out.

In the meantime, the audience, too, was protesting the decision, shouting that it was unfair. Within the committee, the dispute was between Jews and Arabs; but in the audience as a whole, most of whom did not know that I was Arab, both Jews and Arabs championed me. The argument raged for a long time, with great fury and bitterness. Finally, a compromise was worked out: The announcer approached the microphone and declared that there would be two beauty queens—one Jewish, the other Arab. The audience received this judgment with great enthusiasm, and the peacemakers were applauded for their political acumen.

In this sudden, abrupt manner, I found myself—shy, unsophisticated, and naïve—exposed to the stares of hundreds of strange men and women, and, incidentally, at the center of something that looked as though it would develop into a further round of the Arab-Jewish conflict. As though that were not enough, the episode had its sequel within my family. My father had known nothing of the festivity or the beauty contest; when he heard about it, he came to Mother's house and furiously rebuked her for exposing me to this "shameful exhibition," which flouted tradition and harmed the family's prestige. Their argument was long and heated, but in the end Mother appeased him; when he had calmed down, she offered him the cake and champagne I had won. In a mellower mood, Father took quite a tolerant and amused view of the whole affair. He told of his astonishment on hearing that a daughter of his had won—of all things!—a beauty contest. Particularly in comparison with Mother's extraordinary beauty, Father considered himself to be ugly; he was always repeating the comment of his headmaster at the Collège Saint-Joseph d'Antoine in Lebanon, who urged him not to take so much trouble over his appearance: *"Ce n'est pas l'habit qui fait le moine!"* (It isn't the robe that makes the monk!)

Summing up his opinion of the whole matter, Father told us rather solemnly, "True beauty is the beauty of the soul!" Although he sounded rather stern and disapproving, I sensed that he was secretly proud of my success.

I was growing into adolescence; in spite of all the restrictions to which I was subjected, I was gradually developing an awareness of myself, a confidence in my capacities as a human being, and a belief in myself as a young woman. One day, when I was fifteen, I penned a poem:

Que le monde ne me confonde
Car je suis toujours la belle Raymonde
Je suis née dans ce monde et pour le monde.

Salut mon beau printemps
Je t'annonce que j'ai quinze ans
Je t'annonce avec un sourire
Que apparait sur ma belle mime. . . .

Shifting from school to school, I came under many different influences. My mother tongue was Arabic, and I was largely formed by my Arabic heritage. But my home also imbued me with a deep affection for Western culture, particularly that of France. Father used to say that everyone had two homelands: his own and France. French was my second language, reinforced by the French nuns at the convent.

I soon discovered the world of books. My romantic soul found its reflection there, mirrored in the works of Victor Hugo, Dickens, the Brontë sisters, and Guy de Maupassant.

No less vivid was my contact with my Jewish schoolmates. I learned their language and their songs. I picked up Israeli folk dances. I grew very close to the Jewish girls. Their religious and national upbringing had given them a profound awareness of their Jewish identity, which was fortified and deepened by their sufferings in Europe. All this rekindled the ancient Jewish dream of a restored Jewish homeland in that Zion the Jews never forgot. The Jewish girls told me what happened to them and their families under the Nazi regime; only miracles had saved them from death during the Nazi Holocaust. They told me terrible stories of what they had endured, and I cried with them as they related these tragic events. These extraordinary accounts, full of brutality and barbarism, had a powerful impact on my young heart. I still lived in a world of ideas; I could not comprehend how human beings could be so cruel.

I read *The Diary of Anne Frank*. The story affected me deeply. "For in its innermost depths, youth is lonelier than old age." Anne Frank affirmed her belief in this saying. "Is it true that grown-ups have a more difficult time than we do? No, I know it isn't. Older people have formed their opinions about everything, and don't waver before they act. It's twice as hard for us young ones to hold our ground and maintain our opinions at a time when all ideals are being shattered and destroyed, when people are showing their worst side, and we do not know whether to believe in truth and right and God."

I showed this passage to one of the convent sisters and asked her opinion about it. She had lost relatives during the World War, and was full of bitterness against Hitler. But she stressed that only God has the right to take life. We must not hate; we must follow Christ's teaching and pray for the souls of our enemies. On the cross, Christ said, "Forgive them, Father, for they know not what they do."

"In this world," she said, "you will see evil people, like Hitler. All your dreams, your ideals, your most cherished hopes will be shaken when you meet the terrible truth. But be like Anne Frank; she still believed that people were really good at heart. She couldn't build her life on confusion, misery, and death."

The nuns showed special compassion and sympathy for the Jewish girls. Contrary to what some Christians had affirmed in the past, the nuns stressed that the Jews did not carry the burden of guilt for the death of the Son of God, two thousand years ago.

In this fashion, my own natural sympathies for my Jewish friends were reinforced by the nuns' teaching. But my compassion for the Jews could not make me forget what had happened to my own people and, indeed, to my own family. My parents had lost everything they owned. The Israeli land laws were very severe, and everyone was affected. Mother showed me some lands that had once belonged to Father; but because he left the country at the time of the 1948 war, he was declared an "absentee," and his property was taken over by the government, which refused to restore it to him when he returned. Others were in even worse straits; the refugees who had crossed the borders were not permitted to return, while their homes and property were taken over by the Jews from the Diaspora. To camouflage this mass plunder, the Israeli authorities referred to it as "the takeover of abandoned Arab property."

Attending school in Haifa, I would have loved to go to visit my aunt's home. But she had fled to Lebanon during the fighting; she thought she was going for no more than a few weeks, but when the war ended, she was not allowed back.

One of my school friends was a Jewish girl named Dvora; she was very sweet, and I loved her. One day, she invited me home, and I went along. When we neared her house, I suddenly realized where she was taking me: Her family now occupied my aunt's house! My shock was redoubled when I went inside and found my aunt's pictures still hanging on the walls; it was on my aunt's piano that Dvora practiced. I even found a doll I used to play with!

It was a shattering experience to renew my acquaintance with a place simultaneously so familiar and so strange. It was now 1953, five years after the war, and I was overjoyed to see all these familiar objects and articles of furniture, all intact, precisely as they were the last time I saw them. But then I realized with despair that the house did not recognize me; it had been taken over by strangers, while my aunt and cousins were far away, beyond the Lebanese border, and unlikely to return.

When I told Dvora, she was as shocked as I. "Take your doll!" she exclaimed. "Let's be friends!" She explained that her family had received this house from the government on arriving in Israel. "We came from Poland; we were also refugees. We lost everything; all our relations died in the concentration camps." Later, she showed me the Auschwitz number tattooed on her mother's arm. "I'm very sorry we took over your aunt's home," she said. "But try to understand—if we hadn't come here, we would all have ended up in the gas ovens."

I bore no resentment against Dvora or her parents. I sensed that they, too, felt the injustice of occupying someone else's home. "Soon, the Arab refugees will be allowed to return to their homes," they reassured me, "and our government will build new houses for us ... and then Jews and Arabs will live together in peace." They were as naïve as I; neither they nor I knew the true intentions of their government. My aunt was never permitted to return, and Dvora's family remained in that house for twenty-five years.

In 1954, I changed schools once more, moving to Saint Joseph's in Jerusalem. Mother used to come to see me there, taking me for walks toward the demarcation line dividing the city. We would stand on the roof of Notre Dame, gazing across the border at the Arab section of the city. She would tell me of the hundreds of thousands of Palestinian refugees who dreamed of returning home one day. She told me of the 1948 exodus, when a torrent of frightened, suffering Palestinians poured north across the mountains of Galilee toward the Lebanese border.

Inevitably, her thoughts and mine turned to her sons—my brothers—only a few hundred yards away, at their school in the Arab section of the city—so near, but so unreachable. Seeking consolation for her loss, Mother would look tenderly at me, the only child remaining with her, while my brothers, like orphans, went to missionary schools in the Jordanian sector. They were alone, with no one to console them; at best, some nun or priest would sometimes smuggle a brief letter or a picture across the border. We walked the streets of Jerusalem, as though we were trudging through the desert, from mirage to mirage; wherever we went, our thirst remained.

I was growing up, nearing the end of my adolescence. More and more, my mind turned to the future. What should I do? Should I continue my studies? Where should I go? As an Arab, did I have any future in the Jewish-dominated state of Israel? Everywhere, we Arabs faced discrimination—in education, at universities, in employment. It was always the same story: "security reasons."

Then the authorities dismissed Mother from her job as social worker. For "security reasons" of course. She had, indeed, committed a grave offense—she had been "in correspondence with an enemy country!" Cut off from normal contact with his family, my brother in Jordan had sent a letter, with a snapshot of himself, to a relative in Europe, who forwarded it to Mother. This letter was enough to brand Mother a "security risk," and she promptly lost her job. Possessing no means of livelihood, Mother looked around for another job. But there was nothing available for a "security risk." Finally, left with no choice, she went to work as a seamstress at a home for delinquent Arab children. I remember how shocked I was when I came to see her and found her sitting at a sewing machine, looking old and tired. I never saw her so sad and despondent, and her depression affected me too. But she comforted me philosophically: "The world turns, and everyone has his turn. Once we owned this land, and now we have to work to survive. Don't cry—it's no shame that I'm sewing. People died in the war, whole villages were destroyed, our friends disappeared. Your brothers are gone too. But perhaps we should thank God there are borders, or perhaps they would be here too," and she waved her arm at the delinquents' home. "These children here are not criminals. They are from the villages that were destroyed: Bassra, Kuweikat, Kabri. All the inhabitants were driven out. And now these boys steal from stores in Tel Aviv or Haifa or get into fights or try to cross the borders. That's their reaction to the repression their people suffer."

In this manner, I learned the anguished, bloodstained history of my people. But then I went back to school, and there I was expected to learn the history of the independent state of Israel.

I developed a fierce hostility against this state that discriminated against us. At the same time, I never despaired of the Israeli people—mainly as a result of the courageous stand of the Jewish leftists and liberals who defended our rights. The Israeli Communists headed the campaign against oppression and discrimination.

Most Israelis have a stereotyped picture of the Arab woman. They associate her with the Bedouin women from the desert. They were always astonished to learn that I came from a cultured background, with a European education. They were even surprised to find Arabs with a fair complexion and light-colored eyes. I was determined to change the Israeli view, to display the Palestinian in a positive light. It was a bitter humiliation for a proud girl like me to find myself looked down upon as an inferior.

One summer vacation, I took a job at the Interior Ministry office in Acre. I helped to fill out forms of application for identity cards. One day, I heard shouts from the waiting room. Running outside, I found an Arab lying on the floor while an Israeli soldier stood over him, kicking him with his heavy boots. Accusing the man of having cursed the state of Israel, the soldier hauled him off to jail.

I was terribly upset by the incident; I burst into tears. The office director, Rami Haber—an Israeli Jew originally from Aleppo, in Syria—took me to his room, trying to comfort me. He was very kind to me, but his kindness could not erase the sight I had just seen: the Arab lying on the floor, screaming with pain, while the soldier stood over him, kicking him. That incident brought home to me what it meant to be an Arab in Israel.

By this time, relationships between Mother and Father had changed beyond all recognition. After the prolonged hostility and estrangement at the time of their divorce, I was astonished to see the reemergence of a powerful bond between them, intellectual as well as emotional. Father used to come to Mother's house for meals on feast days and holidays. In the past, he had refused to tolerate her independence, but now he made no secret of his admiration and respect for her. In this renewed atmosphere of friendship, they discussed my future, showing understanding and sympathy for each other's views. Nevertheless, they disagreed fundamentally. Mother wanted me to remain with her; I was her only remaining child. She was ambitious for me: She wanted me to study and make a career for myself, to become emancipated and independent.

Father's view was quite different. Most of his friends of the cultured Palestinian elite had fled in 1948, and they were now dispersed all over the Arab world, mostly in Lebanon. Sharing the aristocratic, traditionalist view of his class, he looked down on the Arabs who remained in Israel: They were inferior beings, uncultured peasants with whom he had little in common. Mother's more humane and democratic views, and her job as a social worker, had brought her close to these people, and she did not feel isolated. But Father's old-fashioned upbringing had made him into a snob, and there were few Israeli Arabs whom he considered his equal. He dreaded the thought that I might remain in Israel and possibly even marry someone of a lower class. He spoke in glowing terms of the broader horizons of Arab society in other lands, especially Lebanon. He urged me to leave Israel and make my home elsewhere.

Mother held the opposite view. She knew Arab society only too well; she knew what kind of life awaited me as a woman in an Arab country. She tried to guide me in a different direction—to study, to make a career for myself, to be independent.

Torn between these conflicting views, I remained undecided for a long time. But what tilted the balance was my yearning for my brothers. More and more, my mind was occupied with George and Yussuf, my brothers whom I scarcely knew, seeing them no more than once a year, at Christmas, for a few fleeting hours. Now I wanted to be near them, to get to know them at long last.

I was in my last year of high school when I made up my mind. I was going to move to Jordan. When I told my parents of my intention, they began to think along similar lines. With my departure, none of their children would remain in Israel. Consequently, both Father and Mother planned to follow me. I was overjoyed! After these long years of separation, we would all be together again— Mother, Father, George, Yussuf, and I! The prospect made me all the more eager to put my plan into operation. I lacked the patience to wait until I graduated from high school: I wished to leave as soon as possible. I knew that my move was irrevocable: Once I left Israel, I would not be permitted to return. But I did not let that deter me. I signed a paper renouncing my Israeli citizenship and went through all the other necessary formalities.

My feelings were very mixed during those last few weeks in Israel. I was full of eagerness and curiosity about the new life in store for me. My imagination ran riot as I dreamed of a rosy future near to my dear ones. No more separations, no more heartaches, no more yearnings. At the same time, I was depressed at the thought of leaving my parents, even though I hoped that this separation would be brief. How wrong I was!

My parents' mood was in harsh contrast with mine. Mother was very sad at the thought of my imminent departure; she said little, choosing to suffer in silence. But her eyes spoke with a melancholy eloquence. Father, too, was subdued; even though I was following his wishes, the prospect of our separation depressed him.

The days flew by, all preparations were completed. One day in March 1957, Father and Mother accompanied me to the Mandelbaum Gate, the crossing point into the Jordanian sector of Jerusalem. We spoke little. I was silent, torn between excitement and sorrow. Father and Mother, too, hid their feelings in a gloomy silence. We reached the Israeli border post. The moment had come to bid farewell. With a lump in my throat, I turned to my parents. Father was somber; Mother had tears in her eyes. I flung myself into their arms for a last tender embrace. And then it was time to go. The Israeli officer waved me through, and I strode toward the Jordanian border post.

4

Amman:
Into the Gilded Cage

I WENT TO LIVE WITH MY BROTHER GEORGE, in Amman, the Jordanian capital.

Amman was a strange place, totally unlike anything I was used to. The difference was apparent at first glance. Scarcely a woman was to be seen in the streets, which were the exclusive domain of the men. And these men, too, were unlike those I knew: All of them, without exception, wore kaffiyehs on their heads. Even educated men and high government officials wore the kaffiyeh. I was surprised: In Galilee only the villagers still adhere to the traditional Arab headdress, which has been abandoned by the townspeople and the educated middle class.

These externals reflected the character of Jordan in the fifties: a traditional Arab society, with all the traditional Arab mores and restrictions. Even the Palestinian refugees who settled there after 1948 had adopted the puritan morality and stuffy Victorian life-style prevalent in Amman. This was particularly irksome for women, who were expected to follow a strict code of behavior—and dress. Clothes had to be modest, covering the entire body. Short sleeves or low-cut blouses were taboo, and woe betide any transgressor: At that time, Moslem Brotherhood fanatics used to fling acid at women who ventured into public "immodestly dressed."

My brother George was very pleased to have me with him, and he did his best to make me feel at home. But he made it clear, right from the start, that I was to behave in a "fitting" manner. I was not permitted to go anywhere unescorted. Consequently, while George was at work, in the Transport Ministry, I was expected to stay at home and do the cooking and look after the house. When George took me anywhere, he wanted me to conduct myself in a "refined" manner. A girl of my age was supposed to be timid and silent, not speaking unless spoken to; she must not giggle or laugh, so as to avoid a reputation of being "frivolous." Such reserve was foreign to me: I was young, gay, and full of spirit. I could not get used to this repressive "decorum." Whenever I saw something I liked, I would let out a spontaneous cry of *"Yoffi!"* (beautiful!) in Hebrew. George would get furious—as much at my impulsiveness as at my use of Hebrew. "You're not in Israel now!" he would hiss at me, flushed with rage.

Indeed, Jordanian Amman was very different from Israeli Galilee. The Arabs of Galilee suffered severe repression and discrimination from the Israeli authorities; at the same time, we were also profoundly influenced by the modern, open life-style of the Israeli Jews. But living in Amman, I was expected to forget everything I had learned in Galilee; instead, I was to conform to a far stricter code of behavior.

When George took me out anywhere in Amman, I was forbidden to have any contact with a member of the opposite sex. Arab tradition enforces strict segregation between men and women; the vaguest hint of "improper" intersexual contacts immediately gives rise to the most violent reactions, as I had occasion to observe even before finally moving to Jordan. One Christmas, while I was still living in Israel, Mother and I were finally given permission to cross into Jordan for a one-day visit to my brother. We waited an eternity for this precious privilege. That day, when we passed through the Mandelbaum Gate into Jordanian territory, George was there waiting for us. Overjoyed, we flung ourselves at one another in a tearful embrace. Still carried away by the euphoria of our reunion, we got into a taxi, and George and I sat in the back, fondling and kissing one another. The taxi driver observed us in his mirror; suddenly, without any warning, he pulled over to the side of the road and shouted that he would drive us no farther if we continued to behave in this immoral, depraved fashion! Only Mother's earnest explanations that we were brother and sister succeeded in calming the man. This incident is a good illustration of the standards of conduct enforced in Jordan.

Things were not entirely hard and fast. Women's status was undergoing changes; many of the traditional patterns had altered, particularly since 1948. Many families had lost everything they owned; in consequence, numerous young girls went off to work in Kuwait or the Persian Gulf to help support their families. As girls acquired an education, the veil began to disappear. Under the impact of these external changes, customs were undermined; nevertheless, tradition still had a firm hold, and the result was a strangely mixed situation, an interplay of partial emancipation and continued subjugation, and this holds true right up to the present day. Nowhere is this repression more acutely obvious than in the sexual mores imposed on an Arab girl. Reputation is everything. For a girl to hope for marriage, she must preserve her "good name"; in other words, heaven forbid that she conduct a love affair! Even if she arouses no more than a mere breath of rumor—even if some malicious person spreads lies about her—she can lose her "good name," which is a personal catastrophe of the first order. This is no trifling matter: A girl with a "bad reputation" has no hope of finding a husband.

Mother brought me up in an entirely different manner. She never made any objection if I went out with boyfriends. But even she could not ignore tradition. For all her liberal ideas, she repeatedly warned me: "Be careful! If you want to marry an Arab, make sure you remain a virgin!"

At first I was very glad to be in Amman, particularly at being reunited with my long-lost brother. Moreover, I was curious about this new society, so strange and forbidding. It was a fascinating new experience for me, and I enjoyed the novelty. But the burden of restrictions and taboos was too heavy for me, and I was soon bored and irritated by my enforced idleness—especially when I saw how much there was to do all about me. While the bourgeoisie of

Amman—Palestinian as well as Jordanian—lived a life of relative comfort and affluence, the Palestinian refugees were in a sorry plight, suffering hunger and cold in their makeshift United Nations camps. I remember being deeply shocked, that first winter in Amman, on seeing beggars, wearing no more than a few tattered rags, standing in the streets, day by day, in the icy wind and rain, imploring passersby for a few pennies.

Looking for something to do, I went to visit a convent school belonging to the same order as that of my own teachers. On learning that I had a high school education, the nuns asked me to come and teach at their school for a few hours to replace one of the teachers who was absent. Thoroughly sick of my unsatisfactory existence, I jumped at the offer, and George also gave his grudging consent, though he laid down one condition: Under no circumstances was I to go to the school alone; he must take me there and bring me back home. This seemed like an unnecessary burden, but I was still glad of the chance of getting out of the house occasionally and gaining a further glimpse of this strange and unfamiliar society.

Curious as I was about my new environment, I evoked even greater curiosity on the part of Amman society: I had come from Israel, from a land so near and yet so far, so familiar and yet so mysterious. Israel lay behind a kind of iron curtain, with no communication in either direction: The very name of the state was uttered in a hushed whisper. Persons suspected of any kind of contact with the Israelis were tried as spies, and many of them were hanged in public.

Little wonder, then, that everyone was interested in me and wanted to hear at first hand about my life and experiences in Israel. On one occasion, not long after my arrival in Amman, my brother and I were invited to a party by one of Father's cousins, J. Hawa, an officer in the Jordanian army. The party was held at his home, in the camp where he was stationed, and it was attended by other officers and their wives. The guests displayed great interest in me, the "new arrival from Israel." I was showered with questions about Israel, about the lives of Israeli Arabs under military government, about the 1956 Kafr Kassem massacre (due to a misunderstanding over orders, dozens of peaceful inhabitants of this Israeli Arab village were shot by an Israeli internal security unit at the outset of the 1956 Sinai campaign). I did my best to satisfy their curiosity, but their

questions followed one another in rapid succession. Without noticing it, I had become the center of a circle of officers, who were listening to my every word. Most of the questions came from a
distinguished-looking senior officer: This was none other than
Sa'adek al-Shara, the commander-in-chief of the Jordanian army!

I found little difficulty in answering the officers' questions: I was
knowledgeable and far from self-effacing. But as the questioning
continued, I noticed that George was scowling at me. Finally, he
beckoned to me to come to where he was standing with my cousin.
When I approached, both men rebuked me angrily. Why didn't I go
over to the ladies' side of the room? What did I mean by consorting
with a group of strange men? "Look around you—there isn't another woman standing there!" I looked—true enough, the circle
consisted exclusively of men. George and my cousin insisted that I
withdraw from the "men's side" of the room, but I refused. "I am
being perfectly decorous," I said firmly. "I am well brought up. But
I *won't* go over to the ladies!" And with that, I turned angrily and
went back to the officers, coolly continuing my conversation with
them.

George did not take my defiance lightly. A few moments later, he
came over, saluted the officers, and in an icily polite voice, requested
me to come with him instantly. Left with no choice, I obeyed, and
we drove home.

Arriving there, he gave me a furious dressing down on my "loose
behavior." He told me that my misconduct reflected badly on him,
not only on myself. I was a disgrace to the whole family—like
Mother, who had ruined our reputation by divorcing Father. He
called Mother "a scandal to the family." I was shocked by this attack on our mother, and I tried to defend her, but this only made
him more furious.

I should stress that George is not a bad or violent man. He was
acting in a manner he considered right and proper. Having been
brought up in Jordan, he was conforming to the traditional Arab
morals, which hold a man responsible for "his" womenfolk, whose
behavior he is expected to supervise. If he fails to do his "duty" by
punishing the misdeeds of his daughter or his wife or his sister, he is
considered derelict and immoral, just as though he had committed
the offense himself. Consequently, George believed that "disciplin-
ing" me was essential to him. I embodied his honor, and I therefore

had to be "defended"—even against myself. Such is Arab tradition: Whole families have to bear the blame for the misdeeds of individual members, and the sins of parents are laid at the door of succeeding generations. On one occasion, I overheard a cousin on the phone, talking about me: "For God's sake, who will ever marry her? Her mother is divorced!"

Subjected—like all Arab men—to such a heavy burden of "family responsibility," it is little wonder that George reacted harshly to my "misbehavior" at the party. In hindsight, I realize that he was not to blame. But at the time, I could think of nothing but the pain and humiliation to which he had subjected me. I was furious! How I regretted having left my parents! More than anything else, I wanted to go back to them, to Israel.

I found myself in a strange dilemma. In Israel, I would belong to a despised minority and be treated as a second-class citizen. All the same, as a woman, my personal lot would be much better than in Jordan. A difficult choice: humiliation as an Arab or repression as a woman—which is better?

Be that as it may, returning to Israel was not a matter to be arranged overnight, and I did not want to stay in George's home one moment longer. Leaving an angry note, I stalked out of the house and went to seek asylum with a cousin of Mother's.

Although rid of George's oppressive rule, I was little better off with my relatives. They, too, expected me to conform, to behave myself. As for returning to Israel, to my parents—this was, indeed, a grave matter. I cried and begged; my relatives went to the highest officials; they appealed to ministers. But all their efforts were in vain. The Jordanian government would not give permission for anyone to cross into the land controlled by "the enemy." And even if the Jordanians did allow me to go, there was little likelihood of the Israelis permitting me to come back, after having renounced my Israeli citizenship. Once more, my personal desires were checked by oppressive walls.

Glumly, I tried to make the best of the situation. There was little enough I could do. All avenues seemed closed to me. I had no money to study. I did not dare to look for a job: Very few women went out to work in Amman at that time. And when my younger brother, Yussuf, came on vacation from his boarding school, I was afraid to go and see him. I feared that George would subject me to pressure to return to his home, where I would again find myself cooped up. I felt uprooted, frightened and insecure, yearning nostalgically for my parents, my friends, my home.

My relatives sensed my unhappiness. They were kind to me and did what they could for me, but they were powerless to change the society in which they lived. In their view, there was only one solution for a young girl like me: marriage. Every now and then, they would drop broad hints about looking for a husband, but I angrily rejected the idea of offering myself on the marriage market. Exposing myself in the hope of catching a husband—this carried a flavor of prostitution, and I was too proud to contemplate anything of that nature. I wanted to live my own life: to study, to make a career for myself. I had no interest whatsoever in getting married at the age of eighteen.

All this time, I had little with which to occupy myself. Aside from tea parties or family visits, Amman had almost nothing to offer in the way of entertainment or social life—particularly of the kind that women were permitted to join. There was only one exception, the Orthodox Club, founded by refugees from Palestinian towns like Jaffa, Haifa, and Jerusalem, where similar clubs had functioned during Mandatory times. The club was a social and cultural center, with extensive sporting activities. My relatives used to take me there on Sundays and Fridays, when the club was open for social activities.

The club was a very exclusive organization, extremely strict in admitting newcomers; only persons of the highest social status were accepted. The members belonged to the elite of Palestinian society. They were cultured, refined, genteel. Their manners were impeccable, their behavior above reproach. These were the circles my father used to speak of with such esteem and pride, comparing them with the "uncivilized peasants" who made up most of the Arab population of Israel. But although I was deeply impressed, the club was not a social milieu in which I could feel at home. It was a strange world, a kind of relic of nineteenth-century gentility. Family groups sat at separate tables, sipping coffee and making polite conversation. One principal topic was gossip. Whenever someone walked through the door, heads would be bowed as confidential whispers went around: "Who is he? Who's she? Don't you know? That's the son of so-and-so. She's the daughter of X. They are related to Y, who used to own land in Z village. A very genteel family." And so the whispering and flustering ran from table to table, while the newcomer was eyed from head to toe.

The atmosphere at the club was a little more open than elsewhere in Amman, but nevertheless, a strict code of conduct was enforced. We were expected to remain within our family groups; one did not come into contact with strangers. There were plenty of young men at the club, and I was pleased to notice some of them studying me with obvious interest—but heaven forbid that one of them should try to enter into conversation with me! That was unheard of!

All the same, intent glances of this kind could sometimes produce a follow-up. Together with the taboos on contacts between the sexes, there were conventional procedures whereby a man could make the acquaintance of a woman (never the other way around—girls were expected to be completely passive). If a man liked the look of some girl he saw at the club, he would make discreet inquiries about her, her family, status, and so on. If what he heard was encouraging, his next step would be to approach a male relative of hers—if necessary, by way of some mutual acquaintance—and ask to come to call on her. On receiving the request, it would be the turn of the girl's relatives to make similar discreet inquiries; if the man was found to be eligible—financially and socially—permission would be granted for him to pay a visit.

On the appointed day, he would come and be introduced to the family, the girl included. Needless to say, there was no question of her remaining alone with him, but he would spend some time in conversation with the family circle. The girl was expected to be on her best behavior—shy, withdrawn, passive (first impressions are important!). After an hour or two of polite conversation, the visitor would take his leave. If he wished, he could ask to pay a second and even a third call. But after no more than three such séances with the whole family, he was expected to make up his mind. If he approved of the girl, after meeting her in this manner three times, he would then approach the (male!) head of the family and ask for permission to marry her. If permission was granted, the matter would then be put to the girl for her approval. Such was the "romantic" mode of courtship customary in Amman's bourgeois circles.

Various men tried to "court" me in this fashion. They got little encouragement from me. I was in no mood to marry; my ambitions ran in entirely different directions. Any lingering doubts I might have had on the matter were quickly dispelled on meeting my suitors. Amman society adopted a sober view of marriage. Before taking a wife, a man had to show himself to be responsible and well established, to prove himself fit to head a family. Consequently, few young men could consider marriage; first, they had to set themselves up in life, launch themselves into a career, make money. All this takes time. As a result, the men who came calling on me were all in their late thirties or early forties—hardly an age calculated to captivate the passions of a romantic teen-aged girl.

At first, I took no interest in these men. I simply didn't want to get married. But, in time, I began to realize that I had few other options. Despite my tears and entreaties, it was now clear that I would not be permitted to return to Israel. Studying was out of the question, because I had no money. Without qualifications, I had no hope of getting any of the few "respectable" jobs open to women—and therefore had no prospect of gaining financial independence. How long could I remain a burden on my relatives? Apparently, marriage was the only avenue open to me.

Among the men who came to call on me was Da'ud Tawil, scion of a well-known Jaffa family and a prosperous bank manager. Like the rest of my suitors, he was far older than me. But he was polite, sociable, affable. When he came calling on the family—with the express intention of making my acquaintance—he made a good impression. Then he called again! Soon after, he came a third time. A few days later, he approached my relatives and formally requested my hand in marriage.

My relatives notified me that Da'ud had proposed. They asked me to give the matter my consideration.

I thought it over for a few days. Then, I accepted.

The ceremony was held in Amman, in the city's largest Greek Orthodox church. Resplendent in my bridal robes, I stood listening to the bells pealing joyfully. I was supposed to feel happy, but there was a profound sadness in my heart. In spite of the festive atmosphere, I cried for Mother. That day, the Jordanian radio's request program conveyed my greetings to Mother. I asked for the song "Mummy, Don't Cry on My Wedding Day."

After the ceremony, we went to Europe on our honeymoon. It was my first visit to Europe, and there was much to see, many new experiences to savor. Da'ud did his best to help me enjoy myself. But in spite of my excitement, I was subdued and depressed. How I yearned for Mother! Da'ud was very attentive toward me; he must have understood how I felt, because finally, when we were in Vienna, he took a bold step. One day, we went to our hotel room, carefully locking the door and drawing the blinds. Then, in great trepidation, Da'ud picked up the phone and, speaking in a half-whisper, asked the hotel's operator to call Mother's number in Israel!

When the connection was finally made and I heard Mother's voice, I was so choked with emotion, I could scarcely speak. I just sat there, holding the receiver and sobbing broken, incoherent phrases.

Afterward, Da'ud made me swear to tell no one that we had called Israel. If it ever became known in Jordan that we had "made contact with the enemy," we would both be branded as traitors.

5

The Mountain of Fire

ON JULY 14, 1958, Da'ud and I drove into Nablus, to find ourselves in the midst of an enormous demonstration. Our car slowed to a crawl and finally stalled in the midst of that human sea. All around, thousands of people were carrying banners and placards; thousands of voices chanted slogans: "Down with the traitors!" "Down with the Hashemite regime!" "An end to tyranny!" Thousands of flushed and agitated faces, thousands of clenched fists.

I gazed out of the car, bewildered and astonished by these people with their angry, impassioned expressions. It was in the first year of my marriage; little more than a child myself, I was six months pregnant. I had never seen anything that resembled this frenzied mob. Little wonder that I felt terrified. These thousands of agitated individuals, this display of violent passions and unbridled emotions—what was it all about?

The reason did not take long to discover. That day there had been a coup d'etat in Baghdad; the Iraqi monarchy was overthrown, to be replaced by a revolutionary officers' junta of Ba'ath socialist nationalists. The downfall of the Iraqi regime, closely linked by family and political ties to the Hashemite rulers of Jordan, evoked a tremendous outburst of enthusiasm among all those who were sick of the rule of King Hussein. This was especially true of Nablus, traditional center of that Palestinian nationalism that suffered such harsh persecution by the Jordanian government. The whole town took to the streets to cheer the Iraqi revolutionaries and to boo the hated Hashemites.

Lost and terrified, I regarded the enraged multitude. It was a tumultuous welcome to our new home: Nablus, the Mountain of Fire.

Nablus was not our first home. Six months previously, when Da'ud and I returned from our honeymoon in Europe, we headed for Irbid, in eastern Jordan, where Da'ud was to take up his post as manager of the local bank. A convoy of cars was waiting for us when we arrived at El Ramtta: merchants, officials, friends of Da'ud's, all eager to catch a glimpse of the young bride he had brought. Everyone turned out to see us—neighbors, servants, employees of the bank. A sheep was slaughtered at the entrance to our home as an omen of prosperity; Da'ud's mother made the sign of the cross over my head and his, reminding me of the priest who gave communion at church. The bluebird of happiness seemed to be fluttering above us.

I was only eighteen, and I already had everything I could ask for: a prosperous husband, a pleasant home in our flat above the bank, a secure social position. Da'ud did everything to ensure my comfort, his family welcomed me, his friends paid their compliments. Truly, my situation was enviable.

But my comfort had a price: I had to forfeit my freedom. Like Ibsen's Nora, I was a doll—beautiful, pampered—and deprived of my free will. I had entered a society where men dominated everything. My life, my behavior, my future—all these would be determined by my husband. Such were the dictates of an unchallenged tradition.

I entered into a regular, uneventful routine. Every morning, neighbors came knocking at the door, and we would take coffee together. This was more than simple social intercourse: These visits had a double purpose. My lady visitors came to make me welcome in Irbid's middle-class society, but in the course of our chat, they would find some tactful opportunity to ask whether I was pregnant yet. After all, that was now my principal role and task—to provide my husband with children and look after his home and family.

I had passed my childhood and adolescence in Israel, at school with Jewish girls. I had imbibed the freer, more modern attitudes of the young Israelis, who are at liberty to conduct their social life as they see fit. Of course, Israeli society, too, has its repressive traditions, its inhibitions, its taboos. But these are nowhere near as heavy as the irksome restraints imposed on women in Arab society. Remembering my free-and-easy existence in Israel, I found life in Irbid suffocating and very unsatisfactory.

Of course, I did not reveal my rebellious feelings to Da'ud. In all probability, I was not fully aware of them myself. Nevertheless, sensing that life in Irbid was not to my liking, I begged him to arrange for a transfer. I told Da'ud that I missed the atmosphere of Palestine, its climate and landscapes. I hankered after the freer, more cosmopolitan atmosphere of Jerusalem, and I hoped we would move there.

Da'ud saw that I was unhappy and did his best to satisfy my wishes. Soon after, he told me the good news: We were moving. Unfortunately, he had failed to get transferred to Jerusalem, and we would be going to Nablus. But that, too, seemed like a big improvement over Irbid.

Compared with arid Irbid, Nablus was a paradise, a veritable Garden of Eden. I was overjoyed at being back in Palestine. My heart rejoiced at once again seeing this beloved landscape, with its olive trees, the emblem of our land.. I was thrilled by my first glimpse of Wadi al-Tuffah—the Valley of the Apples—with its fruit groves. I feasted my eyes on the fruit peddlers, the women in colorfully striped Palestinian dresses who went out at dawn and brought back fresh figs, pomegranates, and cactus fruits. Then there were the women who sold *liban* (the local yogurt); they came walking gracefully down the street, balancing a box with earthenware jugs full of fresh milk or *liban,* calling the housewives to come out and buy their wares.

Our house was on a hillside, among the olive trees. Sitting on my veranda, I could look down at the sunset and listen to the Angelus pealing, while the sheep trotted down from the hills, with the bells tinkling gently on their necks. Gazing at that beautiful landscape, I could recapture the warm sensation of home.

But home—my hometown of Acre, only an hour's drive away—was on the other side of the demarcation line. I was in Jordanian territory, and my home—my parents—were in Israel, in enemy territory. These were two entirely separate worlds, with no contact between them. Most forms of communication were strictly forbidden; my parents might just as well have been on the moon, for all the possibility I had of reaching them. When I renounced my Israeli citizenship and moved to Jordan, I cut myself off from my parents, from my own past, from my school friends. My step was irrevocable.

As though to symbolize this break with my past, I was not even permitted to bring my Hebrew school books with me into Jordan. The poems of Bialik were "enemy literature." Later, my Hebrew books were smuggled to me, in a roundabout manner, but then I suffered a second disappointment. At that time, the Jordanian secret police began to conduct searches after "subversive books." This was a period of intensive repression against all "dissident" elements—Ba'athists, Communists, Nasserists, and Palestinian nationalists. Houses were ransacked to uncover forbidden literature of any variety, and keeping my books of Hebrew poetry became too risky. In the end, I had no alternative: With my own hands, I had to burn my precious Bialik.

Burning my Hebrew books symbolized my total and final separation from my past in Israel. It was a frustrating feeling, but that was not my only frustration.

Life in Nablus was not very different from what I had experienced in Irbid. Nablus, too, was a man's society; its prevailing ideology was a bourgeois nationalism that aspired to a national renaissance but never envisaged any change within traditional Arab society.

I did not enjoy my existence. I had no work. Our home was cared for by maids, leaving me with time on my hands and very little to fill it with. Our social life was formal and stiff, consisting of an endless round of mutual visits and social functions where men and women were carefully segregated from one another. True, Nablus could boast of some cultural activity. But for women, the only acceptable form of socializing was to join the Arab Women's Union, which conducted extensive—but, of course, completely segregated—events. Seeing that this was the only available outlet, I joined, but it only added to my sense of frustration and suffocation to find myself surrounded exclusively by women. When I expressed my astonishment at this all-female society, one of my friends rebuked me: "Do you come from Paris?" she asked me sarcastically. So different was my background I almost answered "Yes!" In Acre's Quaker center, we used to dance together, boys and girls. In the villages of Galilee, it was normal for men and women to socialize together. Even at the convent school, the nuns would take their senior classes to mixed parties or theater outings. But here, in Nablus, women were kept isolated, so that no man should "misinterpret" their behavior.

Married women were kept under restrictions almost as strict as those imposed on unmarried girls. For example, it was unthinkable for me to travel anywhere unescorted. If I wanted to undertake anything as innocuous as a shopping expedition to Jerusalem or Amman, I had to organize a group of four or five women companions. How could I tolerate such restrictions, when I had been used to traveling freely back and forth between Acre and Haifa?

My repression did not come from some amorphous and faceless "society"; it was my own home and immediate social environment that imprisoned me. As a married woman, I was allowed to attend mixed social events; but this freedom was illusory. The men would gather in one room, while the women congregated in another. The women "chattered" about domestic matters—children, clothes, household—while the men "conversed" about business and finance, or exchanged dirty jokes. At first, I used to stay with the women, as convention required; but soon, feeling suffocated in that petty-minded atmosphere, I would try to approach the men. If I dared to do so, I would catch Da'ud's glances upon me, telling me, "This is not your place!" If I ignored his signals, he would come up to me and expressly request me to return to the ladies' room, lest I become the talk of the town.

Those unfamiliar with Arab society can have no idea how cruelly it imposes its yoke. Its moral code creates an enormous gulf of sexual frustration; inflamed imaginations are a fertile breeding ground for idle and malicious rumors. For both men and women, "reputation" is everything—and much social intercourse consists of maligning persons suspected of "deviant" conduct. Arab men are bad enough, but the women are ten times worse, in spite of—or precisely because of—the repression and restrictions they endure. Women spend much of their time tearing one another's character to shreds. More than anything else, it was this fear of gossip that made Da'ud supervise my behavior. He certainly had no evil intentions in trying to get me to conform. In fact, he was left with almost no choice in the matter. If I talked to men, or even stood near them, I would endanger my reputation and thereby harm my husband's status. Conventional wisdom taught that if he permitted me to behave thus, he would be destroying something essential in himself as a man. He would lose his pride in himself and become a laughingstock. I had no desire to hurt him, but neither could I stand my situation.

Sadly, I would go to my room and read. Simone de Beauvoir was one of my favorites. Her message of freedom was some small comfort, but reading books was an unsatisfactory way of expressing myself. With no one to confide in, I began to keep a diary, filling countless notebooks with my lonely thoughts about myself, my existence, and the world about me: "I seem to contain a kind of spontaneous joy that I spread everywhere. . . . But those around me do not accept this 'frivolity.' . . . As for me, I abandon myself to the present: I grasp at the fleeting moment."

My diary reflected a profound discontent. I was restless and miserable. If convention was my oppressor, dare I flout convention? That could spell ruin! Tradition was powerful, and Mother's fate was a terrible warning of what lay in store for me if I dared to defy it. But this lack of freedom seemed equally unbearable. I was like a bird that has once known liberty; it can never feel at home in a cage. What was right? What was wrong? What could I do?

On October 11, 1958, I gave birth to my first child—Dianna. Childbirth was a great and splendid experience, a great love that was born within me. But at the same time, I sensed a terrible void, which gave rise to a feeling of insecurity. Could I give my baby the love of a mother when I myself was deprived of the love of my own mother, separated from her by the demarcation line that divided Jerusalem?

Lying in Jerusalem's Saint Joseph's Hospital, as the fresh morning breeze came over the hills from the west of the city—the Israeli side—I would turn over, with tears in my eyes, and look at the magnificent Jerusalem landscape, gazing toward the Mandelbaum Gate. At night, I would dream that Mother came and bent over me and my baby, and kissed us tenderly.

The nuns at the hospital were permitted to cross over to the Israeli side of the city. From there, they contacted Mother, and she came from Acre to receive my notes. Sending letters across the demarcation line was strictly forbidden, but the nun—she had once been my teacher—could not care less for the official security regulations. One day, she brought me a most precious gift, a letter from Mother.

What a wonderful surprise! Thank God for his gift, sweet Dianna. Congratulations . . . hoping that you will see your grandchildren also. . . . I feel younger at heart: When I received the news, I could have flown to see her. I worried. I waited to hear news from the radio about you. My heart was at ease, because you are in the care of your kind husband.

Mother was a woman of great feeling, and she made no attempt to conceal her joy and agitation at the birth of my daughter. Of course, her letter carried undertones of sadness; more than ever, she must have wished to be at my side at that moment. At the same time, this message from her reminded me once again of what she always endeavored to impress upon me: She encouraged me to develop, to study, to find fulfillment in my life. She kindled my ambition, she taught me to seek emancipation.

Mother's teachings took on double importance when I returned home with my baby. I was living a kind of dual life. I had my domestic duties, my household, my baby. I endeavored to take care of my family, but I could not help feeling frustrated by my humdrum routine. Traditional Arab cooking is delicious, but many of the dishes take hours to prepare. Other housewives were quite content to pass their days in the kitchen, but I found cooking a bore and preferred to leave the job to the maid. My women acquaintances were shocked to hear of such "unworthy" behavior. How could I permit someone else to prepare the family's meals?! Da'ud, too, lost patience with me. On one occasion, he shouted at me, "You don't know how to do anything, either running a home or cooking the meals!"

This general condemnation added to my depression. My unsatisfactory existence evoked an anger that, for lack of any other objective, even turned on myself. I began to wonder whether I was not in some way abnormal. In despair, I confessed to my diary, "I'm not like the others. I don't converse well. I'm no good in the kitchen, and my linen cupboard is never tidy."

My plight was all the worse because no one seemed to understand my discontent, other women least of all. I have noticed that most women—housewives especially!—deny their oppression. When I confided my frustrations to women friends, they were horrified that I did not find satisfaction in my traditional woman's role as housewife and mother. To them, performing these tasks was the height of creativity. They could not comprehend my discontent, my lack of fulfillment as a human being. "You have everything!" they scolded me. "Go to the refugee camps and see how the women there cope with their poverty and suffering!" I had everything—husband, child, money—and here I was, talking like an irresponsible girl, with dreams of flirtation and romantic love affairs.

What I feared most was that I myself would begin to conform inwardly, succumbing to the pressures from outside and to my own despair. All about me, I saw Arab women digging their own graves, rationalizing their oppression, thus developing contempt for themselves and for one another. We Arab women are taught hypocrisy; schizophrenia is our normal state.

On July 1, 1960, I gave birth to a second child—my son Gaby. I cannot deny that I felt glad on being told, "A son!" I knew that, being a boy, his status would be different. Arab society would be more congenial toward him than it would toward a girl. It was an injustice that began at birth.

The birth of a son—the firstborn particularly—is of great significance for Arab parents. I was now *umm-Gaby,* "the mother of Gaby," while Da'ud was addressed as *abu-Gaby,* "the father of Gaby." But Da'ud's reaction surprised me. The arrival of a male child did not make any great difference to him: Unusual for an Arab man, he rejoiced over Gaby as he had rejoiced over Dianna, and as he was to rejoice over the birth of our other children.

Gaby's birth did not resolve my personal problems. My feelings toward my environment were very ambiguous. As a Palestinian, my nationalist attachment is strong, and it gives me a sense of belonging. But as a woman, I could not feel that I belonged to this society that threatened to dehumanize me into a sex object. I felt like a stranger, persecuted and misunderstood. I did not want to remain a slave, a woman-child; I aspired to develop my personality, and yet I knew only too well how impossible it was to gain experience in the narrow, restrictive world of my home and my provincial town.

I am deeply attached to Palestine—to its hills and fields, its pure air and bright sunshine, its sounds and scents. There is a common language between me and my motherland, an overflowing torrent of love. If trees and stones could speak, they would tell of my tender feeling for the land of my birth. In my childhood I used to lie down in solitary corners, to feel the embrace of the earth, to sense the shadow of the tree branches dancing on my face, to watch a butterfly flit past.

It seems almost unimaginable that anything could come between me and this country to which I sense such a passionate link. And yet, in my frustration with my existence, I began to feel that even the landscape was part of my prison. Nablus lies in a cleft between two hills—Mount Gerizim and Mount Ebal. Looking out of the window, I would see the two mountains towering over the town, enclosing it like gigantic double walls, confining me to a stifling captivity. I was coming to hate the town. In my diary, I wrote, "Where is the enchantment of youth? In this town, age is meaningless—young and old are the same. There is no youth, no love." I was faced with a cruel choice: "In this society, either you are like everyone, or you are broken—or else you 'have to go away.' "

I began to dream of escaping, of going far away. I dreamed of Beirut or Paris or London or New York—of life without strings. Dreams became my refuge. But even as I dreamed, I knew, deep inside, that this was no solution.

In my despair, I thought back with longing for my Jewish school friends. I was the only Arab girl among them, but there were no barriers between us; they felt no hostility toward Arabs, no superiority or disdain; there was a deep affection and respect on both sides. I recalled all the different, conflicting influences I had experienced: the nuns; traditionalist Arab society—whether the fiercely conservative Moslems or the more liberal Christians; I thought of Father and the time-hallowed values of his world, of Mother with the spirit of emancipation and individual liberty she had brought from her native America.

Now, as a young adult, I had to choose among these diverging— often diametrically opposed—heritages. The time had come for me to pick my own path. I could not yet analyze my predicament. I was too young then to display the aggressiveness that later became one of my most prominent traits. But I sensed an instinctive yearning for freedom; freedom became my overriding obsession. I have already mentioned Simone de Beauvoir's *The Second Sex.* The lesson I drew from her book was, Don't cry over your fate; start to change it—right now!

Gradually, my consciousness awakened. I became convinced that I had an important role to play. Busying myself with my home could not fill my inner void.

In my diary, I wrote, "I am too submerged in my conjugal and marital duties—to live, to savor the world and my youth." Despairingly, I cried, "But I am still in my twenties!" I wrote of my yearnings for love, for romance, for tenderness.

But yearnings would take me nowhere. Within me, I sensed a dawning determination to act. Since I could not escape my environment, I had to make it into the battlefield of my emancipation.

In my frustration, I began to search for kindred spirits. Surely I was not alone in feeling as I did? In time my gropings brought me into contact with several other young women who also expressed vague dissatisfaction with their lot. Our conversations were tentative and uncertain. They, too, were at loggerheads with custom and tradition; like me, they felt rebellious, but they had no clear idea of what they were rebelling against. We reflected in each other, finding a sympathetic echo for our needs, our aspirations, and our creativity. At the same time, our views differed even among ourselves, and I did not find complete agreement with my opinions, which the others considered a little extreme. But on one thing we all agreed: We were in need of guidance in finding our way. Here I had the good fortune to encounter a Catholic priest, Father George Habbra, originally from Haifa. Father Habbra was no cloistered cleric; he was fully aware of the poverty and wretchedness of this world, and he tried to better matters by spreading the Christian message of love and hope, to which he devoted his life. We asked him to give us lessons, and he consented. Under his guidance, we studied Saint Thomas Aquinas, Dostoyevsky's *Crime and Punishment,* and Freud. The theme he presented was a rejection of everything that restricts the free will of the individual.

Inevitably, our discussions touched upon the situation of women. He showed us that we, as women, were static, passive, and submissive. He repeated Dostoyevsky's view that when a woman was married without her consent, this was no better than prostitution—a revolutionary concept in our tradition-bound society, where most marriages are arranged. Father Habbra taught us to open our eyes and see our situation in its true light. But there was little he could offer us in the way of practical solutions. On one occasion when I told him of my concerns, he tried to console me by saying, "The external world is vain; try to build up a strong inner life." Teaching that suffering was the path to greatness, he advised us to conform to convention; by sublimation, we would "transcend" our situation.

On December 9, 1961, I gave birth to my third child—my daughter Leila.

That Christmas, Mother was allowed through the Mandelbaum Gate for one of those brief one-day visits. Ecstatic at seeing her, I flung myself into her arms, and we kissed and wept for joy. Those few precious hours together reopened all my old wounds, sharpening the pain of our prolonged separation. Looking at her, I was filled with concern: She had aged greatly since our last meeting and she looked tired and unwell.

Mother, too, displayed mixed feelings—but for completely different reasons. Like me, she was overjoyed at our reunion. She was glad to see Da'ud; she was thrilled to see my children, her first grandchildren. But there was a note of reserve about her, and when the two of us remained alone, she expressed her concern about me and my way of life. She scolded me for conforming with traditional customs. She noticed that at the party we held in her honor I had withdrawn "with the ladies." "Why don't you sit with the men?" she asked sharply. "If you don't insist on your rights, your place will be in the kitchen!" She questioned me about my doings; it did not take her long to learn the full details of my cramped and restricted existence. She was horrified to learn that I did not move about freely.

"I gave you independence!" she reminded me reproachfully. "When you were a girl, you went everywhere—to Tel Aviv, to Haifa. And now—this? How did you permit yourself to be pushed back into such an existence?"

What disturbed Mother most of all was my rapidly growing family. Four years after my marriage, I already had three children. I told her that Da'ud wanted more children, but she brushed away my explanations scornfully. "He's only doing it to keep you at home!" she cried. "Is this what you want?" And she waved an angry arm at the kitchen and the children's cots.

Mother's displeasure pained me deeply, precisely because it pinpointed my own confusion. As much to reassure her as to defend myself, I told her of my discontent, and of my yearnings and aspirations, but I do not believe this was any consolation for her. It was not disapproval on her part; on the contrary, loving me dearly, and with great faith in my gifts, she always had great ambitions for me. Seeing me apparently headed for the traditional role of housewife and mother must have shocked and disappointed her.

When we took leave of each other at the end of her brief stay, this renewed separation grieved me even more than usual. I knew that Mother was leaving me with a heavy burden of disappointment and that by failing to live up to her hopes I was adding to her sufferings.

It was to be our last meeting. The next time I waited for her at the Mandelbaum Gate, she failed to arrive. I never saw her again.

When Mother died, none of her children was at her bedside. Cruel laws and artificial borders prevented me and my brothers from being with her. My grief was redoubled when I recalled our last farewell. I could not help blaming myself for letting her die disappointed in me, her only daughter.

Long after I got over the shock of her death, this sense of guilt stayed with me. I came to feel that I owed a debt to her memory—and that debt spurred me on to challenge my drab, constricted existence.

After many long arguments with my group of women friends, we finally decided on a modest first step. We approached the Arab Women's Union, where we were all members, and proposed that the union sponsor a series of lectures *about* and *by* women—and that, furthermore, the lectures be delivered to a mixed audience of men *and* women! After some pressure, our request was granted; the first lecture took place, and it was a great success. It was addressed by a panel of prominent women—a doctor, a poet, and an education expert. I remember gazing in admiration at these women who had gone ahead and made a career for themselves. Here, I thought, are living examples of women's emancipation—candles to light our way!

The opinions they expressed were not, on the whole, revolutionary. And no wonder! Our request to hold a public lecture had to be presented to the authorities, and the Jordanian governor demanded the most convincing guarantees that the event would be "nonpolitical." Even though we gave all the assurances he demanded, it was two months before the request was approved. Accordingly, the mere fact that the lecture was held—and before such an audience—was a small but significant step forward.

Part of the difficulty lay in the body sponsoring the lecture. The Arab Women's Union was a well-established body when I joined. It was founded in 1921 by Hajja Andalib al-Amad—"the Florence Nightingale of Nablus"—who devoted her life to this work. The union did important welfare work for women, combatting illiteracy and organizing vocational training for girls. In 1947, when fighting began, the union established an emergency hospital for the wounded; this hospital was later enlarged with the addition of a maternity ward, and later a children's ward. Miss Andalib cared for her patients with great devotion and tenderness; she displayed the same traits in relieving the misery of the 1948 refugees. Later, she founded an orphanage for the children of the 1948 war heroes; this grew into one of the largest institutions in the country, where 250 girl boarders were brought up, from kindergarten to high school, and given a chance to lead a decent life.

The Arab Women's Union was not concerned solely with humanitarian projects; it also undertook political action, as in 1947, when it called its members to take part in a mass demonstration against the partition of Palestine. Thousands of women—still veiled—marched in protest, to the utter amazement of the British colonial officials. Later on, in 1966, as I shall relate, the union would sponsor demonstrations against the Jordanian government for failing to prevent the Israeli raid on Samoah.

However, on the whole, the union fell short of being a truly militant women's organization. It was headed by bourgeois nationalists, who rarely took it beyond the traditional role of a women's philanthropic association. Its members came from the well-to-do classes, and it never encompassed poorer women, nor did it extend into the villages and the refugee camps. The union never challenged the traditionalist concepts of women's status in society.

For me, liberation was a personal need. I had to assert myself, and the union seemed to offer the only channel. When I was elected to the executive of the union, I saw my opportunity. I approached the executive, proposing a new form of activity: exchanges with foreign cultural centers, the events presented to mixed audiences of men and women. The proposal did not get a warm welcome—least of all from the union's conservative director, Miss Andalib. Concerned for her reputation, she did not want to risk antagonizing public opinion by such a daring venture. She had two principal objections to the plan: She objected to contact with foreigners, especially Americans, who were the allies of Israel and therefore our enemies; equally, she was reluctant to sponsor anything as radical as a mixed gathering in our conservative town.

The argument raged for months. The opposition was very strong, and I seemed to have little hope of getting approval for my idea. But I was obstinate: I refused to give up, and gradually I gained support. After much debate, the proposal was approved, and we scheduled the first event—a performance by a jazz band from Indiana. Formal approval did not mark the end of the battle. I knew that there could be many snags, and my anxiety grew as the date approached. Would it be called off at the last moment? Would people come? Perhaps the band would appear only to find itself playing to an empty hall.

On top of the open disapproval of conservatives, I faced difficulties at home. Da'ud did not like to see me engaged in activities outside the home, instead of directing all my energies to the family. I should be looking after the children, he said.

On the morning of the concert, a fresh stumbling block arose: Our maid did not come to work. What was I to do? Without her to stay with the children, I could not possibly leave the house. Undeterred, I hurried to the refugee camp where she lived, to learn that she was sick. With some difficulty, I managed to find a replacement. But that was not the end of my troubles.

No sooner was my personal difficulty resolved than I learned of a far graver calamity: That morning, a shooting accident caused the death of a youngster, one of the sons of the al-Masri family, the most prominent family in Nablus. On hearing of the event, various

persons approached me to postpone the concert: It would not be fitting to hold such an event when the town's leading citizens were in
mourning. Miss Andalib called me personally, suggesting that the
evening's concert be put off. Politely but firmly, I rejected these approaches. I deeply regretted the death of the al-Masri boy, but I
knew that once postponed, the recital might never be held. Not only
would all my efforts have been in vain, but we would have had to
start our campaign all over again. I sensed that this was a test case,
and it was vital to establish the precedent. Convinced that I was
right, I took an extremely bold step. When the U.S. cultural attaché
in Amman phoned me to ask whether he should still send the band,
I gave him no hint of the pressures for postponement and told him
firmly that the concert was on!

A few hours later, the band arrived. I went to the hall, full of concern and trepidation. I knew that this evening was a great personal
test for me and for my standing in the town. If the event succeeded,
it would be an important step forward; but if the people of Nablus
boycotted the evening, it would be an enormous failure—my personal failure! Anxiously I waited as the audience came in. At first,
one or two, a couple, a group—and the hall still seemed terribly
empty. I trembled with fear. Then a few more people came, and
some more, and then a larger stream, and suddenly the hall was filling up! It was going to succeed! I felt overjoyed; it was an enormous
boost for my self-assurance.

The concert was generally regarded as a great success—as much a
social breakthrough as a musical event. But the evening was not
without its shadows. The lady who introduced the visitors took the
opportunity to thank me personally for my efforts, but her thanks
contained a note of ambiguity: It was a way of placing responsibility
upon me, rather than on the Arab Women's Union as a whole. This
was no trifling matter. There were many people in the town who resented the visit of an American group, and malicious tongues took
to referring to me as "the American agent." Most of the criticism
came from the traditionalists, who recognized my activities as a
challenge to them; they spared no effort to block any form of
progress, in an attempt to keep matters stagnant.

Later, I ran into opposition of a far more menacing nature. On
one occasion, I applied to the mayor, Hamdi Kna'an, for permission
to use a municipal hall for a recital by a guitarist. Permission was

granted, and the guitarist, sent by the United States cultural center, appeared before a packed hall. The audience thoroughly enjoyed his performance of American folk songs and joined with him in singing the better-known ones.

This success had a sinister sequel: The Jordanian Mukhabarat (intelligence service) rebuked Hamdi Kna'an for allowing me to expose the people of Nablus to "foreign corrupting influences." This intervention by the Mukhabarat could have been a serious setback for my activities and indeed might have exposed me to unpleasant personal consequences. Fortunately, Hamdi Kna'an gave me his full support. Politely but firmly, he told the security officers to mind their own business and showed them out of his office.

To explain how the Mukhabarat could dare to intervene in a matter as innocuous as a musical evening, I must describe the social and political climate prevailing at that time.

As a schoolgirl in Israel, I would often hear of the authorities' persecutions of Palestinian nationalists. On the merest suspicion of nationalist views or activity, Arab citizens of Israel were often arrested at night, taken in for brutal interrogation, and in many cases, without any legal process, placed under administrative detention for months or years. I did not find it surprising that the Israeli authorities repressed every expression of Palestinian nationalist feeling. I hoped and believed that the Arab governments treated the Palestinians differently.

I was wrong.

At this period of the early sixties, Nasser was at the peak of his power and influence. Arab nationalism had become a dynamic political force of worldwide significance. Arab intellectuals argued fiercely and lengthily about the direction and objectives of the Arab national movement. Close attention was paid to the Nasser government's social and economic revolution in Egypt and to the newly proclaimed union between Egypt and Syria.

These developments heightened the dilemma of Palestinian intellectuals. Could a similarly dynamic process be instituted in Palestinian society? Was it feasible under the existing political system? The reactionary character of the Hashemite regime left no doubt as to the answer: To follow the progress of the Arab world, we must overthrow the Jordanian monarchy.

It goes without saying that these notions were debated privately.

Jordan offered little scope for open political discussion, nor were there any democratic freedoms for those who opposed the regime. The clandestine nature of these discussions and the constant fear of denunciation to the Jordanian secret police contributed to the growing radicalization of Palestinian intellectuals, until even the bourgeois nationalists realized that a social revolution was essential for the liberation of their people.

Naturally, there were many differences of opinion. Nasserists argued with followers of the Syrian Ba'ath socialists, and both camps disagreed with the Communists. But as far as the Jordanian authorities were concerned, there was little difference between these groups. Nationalists, socialists, and Communists all suffered the same fate, years-long imprisonment in the El Jaffr concentration camp in the eastern Jordanian desert. While these young students and intellectuals spoke of inspiring the masses with a new revolutionary consciousness, the reactionary Jordanian regime responded with repression, imprisonment, deportation, and terror.

These persecutions had some limited successes. Their main purpose was to teach the young Jordanians and Palestinians that they would do better to shun politics. Indeed, those who showed no interest in political activity led a good life: They received good jobs, they were free to travel. The oil boom had created a great thirst for the skills and abilities of these highly educated young Palestinians, who benefited from the bounty of the Gulf oil sheikhs—but at a price. These sophisticated young people from the modern towns of Haifa, Acre, Nablus, and Jerusalem were forced to conform to the life-style of backward Bedouin tribes. Not only did they have to tolerate the heat and the boredom, but they were also under close police supervision, which made it impossible for them to speak openly or do anything that ran counter to strict Islamic traditions.

When these young men came home for brief visits to their families, I would listen to their stories with great interest. They told how the oil states offered them a mixed welcome: On the one hand, they were rewarded for their skills and education, but at the same time they were regarded with suspicion by the semifeudal rulers who feared that their peoples might be infected by "subversive" notions. And so, the young Palestinians—scientists and doctors, technicians and administrative experts—found themselves simultaneously welcomed and rejected.

They were all homesick in their places of exile. Wherever they found themselves, the Palestinians congregated together, recalling their homes and families, speaking with longing of their homeland.

Listening intently, I found their stories strangely familiar. Where had I heard all this before? Suddenly it struck me: I recalled the stories of my Jewish school friends, who told me how the Jews in Europe were treated with enmity and suspicion, even though they made great contributions with their skills and education; how they were regarded as potential troublemakers, as bearers of "seditious" thoughts; and, above all, how they met among themselves and spoke with longing of Zion. How similar, I thought, what an amazing parallel. Not for the last time, I thought, "We Palestinians are the new Jews."

While numerous young Palestinians headed for the oil states, others opted to remain at home and organize opposition to the regime—even at the risk of torture and imprisonment. They faced a fearsome adversary: The Jordanian secret police did not rest content with spying on domestic opponents. Students attending foreign universities took advantage of the greater freedom in the West to indulge in open political activity, but they soon learned, to their cost, that the Jordanian intelligence services had detailed dossiers on their "subversive" actions. One young doctor was arrested immediately after graduating from a foreign medical school. It was only after months of inquiries that his worried family discovered him in a Jordanian jail.

Many people "disappeared" in this fashion. The authorities did not want to place them on trial, because normal judicial procedure would give them a chance to defend themselves, arousing unfavorable publicity. Consequently, they were kept under detention, for weeks and months—sometimes for years—often without even knowing what they were charged with. Press censorship kept these cases from the public, and it was only when the prisoners were at long last released that their imprisonment became known.

Official persecution did not always achieve its desired effect; in some instances, it backfired. There was the case of Ghassan Harb, arrested in 1966 while taking part in a demonstration of high school pupils in Ramallah; he was fourteen at the time of his arrest. He spent the next four years in prison, but instead of breaking his spirit, jail became an excellent school. Helped by his fellow prisoners, many of them highly qualified intellectuals and teachers, he had little difficulty in completing his secondary education. Moreover, being imprisoned together with leading Marxist intellectuals like Dr. Zayaddin, Ghassan became a fervent Communist with a thorough grounding in revolutionary ideology. Within a short time of his release, he went off to the Soviet Union to continue his education.

In spite of such "setbacks," the Jordanian government maintained its pressure, endeavoring to kill the spirit of resistance and struggle and to stifle the awakening of a critical consciousness among the younger generation of Jordanians and Palestinians. Some resigned themselves to the situation; afraid of the personal consequences of political involvement, many intellectuals turned their fear into submissiveness; they became afraid of freedom. For those who persisted in their allegiances, the constant fear of denunciation made all political activity conspiratorial in character.

On July 17, 1963, I gave birth to my fourth child—my daughter Suha.

I loved my children. Then—as now—they were a major part of my life. I was a devoted mother when they were small; they were my first priority. I was always available to them. I nursed my firstborn, Dianna, till she was nine months old, never leaving the house until her first birthday. I fussed and cosseted her, and the other children too. Spock was my own private oracle.

All the same, there were complex undertones in my attitude to motherhood. In a way, I clung to my children—and to the task of caring for them—as a kind of defense against myself. The children could not recompense me for my frustrations. My discontent found its only outlet in yearnings and dreams, nourished by the books into which I flung myself, particularly the classic romances. Filling my head with my favorite heroines, I identified with Anna Karenina and Madame Bovary; I comprehended their tragic plight and sympathized with their desperate struggle for love and freedom. Their heroism inspired me, but I could not help seeing their tragic fate as a warning of what lay in store for me if I permitted my romantic inclinations to carry me away.

All this gave me a further, almost furtive, reason to welcome the birth of my children. In them, I saw a way of protecting myself from my own tempestuous nature and overcoming my dangerously romantic dreams. Bearing children in rapid succession, I went from one pregnancy to the next, glad to find myself bloated and unattractive. Deep within me, I entertained the secret hope that I could fill my existence with the burdens and responsibilities of motherhood, which would carry me safely past the "dangerous age"—the age of life.

Flinging myself into motherhood was made easier because this was—and remains—the approved role for an Arab woman. Society and convention demanded it of me, and I earned honor and respect by "doing my duty." In any case, I had little choice in the matter: I knew nothing of contraception, and there was little hope of learning such things in conservative Nablus.

On September 12, 1964, just fourteen months after the arrival of Suha, I gave birth to my youngest daughter, Hala.

Still only in my midtwenties, I was the mother of five small children. But I was deeply aware of the futility of my existence. I had achieved little—nothing! Now, bound by my maternal duties, I seemed to have few hopes of doing more. But even though I was largely confined to my home, I would not allow myself to be shackled.

The cultural events I had sponsored were a bold innovation in Nablus. I now launched myself into a field of activity no less unconventional. Always deeply influenced by my reading, I now supplemented my identification with romantic heroines by imitating the famous hostesses of eighteenth-century France. I resolved to turn my home into a "salon" for literary and social gatherings, choosing my guests from among the most prominent figures in the town's social and intellectual circles. At the time, I had no clear objective in mind, nor did I foresee what these gatherings would develop into. My immediate purpose was to find a way of asserting myself, some channel for my ambitions and aspirations. I hoped that these meetings would give me an opportunity for broadening my intellectual horizons.

Conducting these "salons" was no light undertaking for me. For one thing, my education fell far short of that of most of my guests. I had not gone beyond high school. Was it not presumptuous of me to preside over gatherings attended by intellectuals and scholars? As a relative newcomer to the town, could I extend invitations to its leading citizens, members of its most illustrious families? But it was precisely the difficulty of it that made the challenge all the more exciting and attractive. Through these people, with their experience and knowledge, I hoped to get to know the world.

I adopted bold tactics: I would extend invitations not only to prominent citizens of Nablus but also to visitors from Jerusalem, including foreign diplomats. This was a radical departure from local custom, provoking considerable criticism and censure among the more conservative circles in Nablus. Hitherto, it was quite acceptable to invite the consuls who represented the Arab countries. But to "purist" Nablus, the center of Moslem and Arab nationalist feeling, it was a totally different matter to invite British, French, or American diplomats. These men represented countries deeply resented in nationalist circles. The British were remembered as the country's former colonial rulers, the French were detested for their deeds in Algeria, and the Americans were hated for their support of Israel. The presence of Western diplomats led to the functions in my house being dubbed "espionage gatherings"—and this was no laughing matter. I was doubly exposed in undertaking such invitations, for I belonged to the Christian minority in predominantly Moslem Nablus. Ever since the Crusades, Moslem Arabs have associated Christian Arabs with the West. Even now, Christians are sometimes regarded with suspicion as "representatives of the imperialist powers."

Furthermore, how dare I, a woman, flaunt myself in this manner? Rumors went about the town that these "salons" were just a pretext for me to surround myself with admirers and conduct affairs with strangers. These venomous tongues did not remain content with mere gossip; various acquaintances approached Da'ud and urged him to "curb" me and put me in my "proper place."

Da'ud was not too happy with my activities, and he was doubly discomfited by these pressures to "assert himself" and prove himself "master of his own home." But I stubbornly ignored his reproaches. This was very daring on my part—Arab women are expected to respect and obey their menfolk.

My "salons" were highly successful. Beginning as purely social events, or "literary evenings," they soon turned into an arena for serious political discussion. In the atmosphere of fear created by Jordanian repression, it was a risky undertaking to conduct political arguments in the presence of dozens of guests. But lacking any other channel for free debate, leading intellectuals and prominent political figures flocked to my "salons," which often witnessed highly dramatic confrontations. One evening, I invited Mr. Wilson, the U.S. consul; in the course of the conversation, the PLO was mentioned, and Wilson criticized its leaders for their lack of realism with regard to Israel—whereupon he was confronted by Hikmat al-Masri, the Speaker of the Jordanian parliament, who was then also deputy chairman of the Palestine Liberation Organization. Al-Masri rejected Wilson's views, telling him in no uncertain terms that the United States should stop interfering in the Middle East, halt its supply of arms to Israel, and leave the Arabs and Israel alone to work things out between themselves: "And then we'll see who is the strongest!"

The success of these evenings gave me great satisfaction. Aside from the gratification of overcoming my own doubts and confounding my critics, there were also direct personal benefits for me. One of the "salons" was attended by Mrs. James Berkart, the wife of the director of the American Friends of the Middle East. Mrs. Berkart wrote the editorials for the *Jerusalem Star,* and while we were chatting, she suggested that I write a column about Nablus affairs. I was very excited about the idea of launching a career as a journalist, and I took up the offer with great enthusiasm. The column was supposed to deal with social matters, but I soon began to branch out into cultural and political topics. On one occasion, I wrote some unfavorable comments about U.S. intervention in Vietnam, and this led me into a fierce argument with the American cultural attaché.

My work for the *Jerusalem Star* brought me one highly prized fringe benefit: I could take an occasional trip to Jerusalem—unaccompanied! But this privilege was severely restricted. One day I returned at six o'clock in the evening, provoking Da'ud's violent condemnation of my "shameless behavior!"

There were other unexpected complications stemming from my journalistic activities. For one thing, I occasionally conducted interviews with various men. Even though I would always invite their wives to be present at the interview, several of these ladies were highly upset at my presumption in daring to approach their hus-

bands. My contact with Mrs. Berkart also led to another confrontation with the Jordanian security services, which showed great displeasure at my links with "that Jewish woman," as they referred to
her.

Directly and indirectly, my activities gave me an excellent schooling in public affairs. On the face of it, I was dealing in trivialities:
social gatherings, cultural events, an occasional newspaper column.
But in pursuing these activities, in organizing support for them,
in overcoming the obstruction of the traditionalists, I was gaining invaluable political experience. Indeed, several years later, a
Nablus Communist gave me what was, for him, the supreme compliment. Commenting on my activities in his town during the sixties,
he said, "Raymonda, what you did in Nablus was a real social revolution!"

I had launched into these activities partly for personal reasons, to
satisfy my own ego. Under similar circumstances, an American or
European housewife has a chance to go to a university or find her
independence some other way. I, too, needed to assert myself, to
break out of the stifling confines of my home, to prove myself, to be
more than a housewife. But aside from my desire to advance and
break out of traditional feminine roles, I was deeply interested in
public affairs. Political issues were no mere abstract concern. The
tragedy of the Palestinian people is the story of my own life and that
of my family. I had spent my childhood and adolescence with
barbed-wire fences dividing me from my brothers. As a young
woman, I found myself no more than an hour's drive away from my
parents, but the frontier was sealed, depriving me of any chance
of seeing them. Other relatives were scattered all over the Middle
East, many of them impoverished after losing everything they
owned. How could I remain unaware of these restrictions and injustices?

I flung myself into public affairs with all my energy, ignoring the
protests of my conservative environment, which condemned me for
"neglecting" my children and husband. Da'ud, too, made no secret
of his resentment about my "unladylike" behavior. "In the whole
town, you are the only woman who goes out of her home like this!"
he scolded. But I defied his reproaches. "You go out—why
shouldn't I?!" And I continued my activities, regardless of his
objections.

In time, I set my sights higher, becoming more daring and ambitious.

My work for the *Jerusalem Star* gave me invaluable opportunities during 1966. In my status as a journalist, I covered the visit to Nablus of the wife of the new Soviet ambassador to Jordan. She came to address an audience of Nablus women on life in the Soviet Union. Obviously, this was a social and political event of great importance, and I endeavored to give it the coverage it deserved.

Later, a group of Arab diplomats and PLO leaders toured the villages along the Israeli border. The purpose of their visit was to highlight their criticism of the Jordanian policy for leaving the frontier undefended, abandoning the unarmed villages to Israeli attacks. A group of Soviet diplomats undertook a similar tour. On both occasions, I covered the visit for my column, giving me an opportunity to extend my political and diplomatic contacts.

That same year, my membership on one of the Arab Women's Union committees gave me the opportunity to attend the PLO conference in Jerusalem. My role—like that of the other women delegates—was that of passive listener. Only one woman, Issam Abed al-Hadi, addressed the conference; the rest of us were carefully segregated from the men delegates.

My growing political involvement was not to the liking of some conservative and nationalist circles in Nablus. They treated me with suspicion because of my contacts with Western diplomats; they found it presumptuous on the part of a woman to "push herself forward." At times I felt quite isolated, an outcast almost. But I did not give up. As the scope of my activities grew, as I gathered the support of a group of like-minded women who shared my dissatisfaction with the present state of affairs, I was simultaneously—perhaps without being fully aware of it—preparing myself for a far more active political role.

The turning point—and my "baptism of fire"—came in November 1966, following the Israeli raid on Samoah.

One night in November 1966, Israeli troops raided the West Bank village of Samoah. According to the Israeli contention, the raid was in retaliation for attacks on some of their settlements. The Israeli historian Walter Laqueur wrote that the raid was "planned as a punitive action of limited scale against a local terrorist base ... [but] developed against all planning into a full-scale battle with the Arab legion which lasted four hours and caused many deaths." Laqueur adds that the raid was criticized "also within Israel."*

Be that as it may, the raid confirmed our worst fears. There had long been dissatisfaction with the Jordanian government's policy of leaving the border unprotected and denying the outlying villagers arms for self-defense. The Samoah raid, in which scores of civilians were killed or wounded and dozens of houses demolished, provoked deep anger all over the West Bank. As much as our indignation was directed against the Israelis for perpetrating the raid, it also turned against the Jordanian government, which did nothing to protect us. "Yesterday it was Samoah," people said. "Tomorrow it could happen in Jenin, or Nablus!" People feared for their lives, and for the lives of their families and children. In addition, there was a feeling of humiliation, of helplessness: We had nothing to defend ourselves with, because the Jordanian government feared arming the Palestinians.

Spontaneous protests erupted all over the West Bank. Demonstrators went out into the streets to denounce the raid and to demand action from the authorities.

The Jordanian government, indeed, took action—but not of the kind we demanded. As the demonstrators marched through the towns of the West Bank, they were attacked by armed troops. King Hussein sent in units of his faithful Bedouin, whose soldiers came from Transjordan, from the East Bank. Most of them are backward and illiterate, stemming from the nomad Bedouin tribes, which despise and resent the far more advanced and better-educated Palestinians. Given a free hand by their officers, the troops behaved ferociously, beating demonstrators mercilessly and firing into unarmed crowds.

In the past, such tactics had succeeded in silencing West Bank protests; now, however, resentment was running at such a pitch that these repressive methods only succeeded in fanning the flames of discontent. Further demonstrations protested the brutality of the army, but this time the demonstrators found themselves facing a

* In *The Road to War*, p. 72.

new and dreaded adversary: One day we saw the red-uniformed cavalry of the king's own bodyguard, men notorious for their fanaticism and cruelty. The soldiers proceeded to live up to their reputation. They charged into the crowds, flailing about them with their whips. I saw one of these horsemen grab a girl by the hair and whip his steed into a gallop, dragging her, helpless, beside him on the ground.

The government adopted the most extreme repressive measures. Hundreds were arrested and taken off to the dreaded El Jaffr concentration camp in the eastern Jordan desert. Nablus notables, such as Hikmat al-Masri, were placed under house arrest. A curfew was imposed throughout the West Bank, and the inhabitants were forbidden to leave their homes.

It was a terrifying time. No one could feel safe, even inside his or her own home. On one occasion, Da'ud saw a Bedouin soldier about to shoot a fourteen-year-old girl who dared to stand on the veranda of her home. It was only with the greatest difficulty that Da'ud persuaded the soldier not to fire.

One day, I was bending over the crib of Hala, then two years old. Suddenly, I looked up to find myself staring down the barrel of a gun. A Bedouin soldier was standing outside, brandishing his weapon, with his finger on the trigger.

The situation grew worse. The curfew went on for weeks, and people were only allowed an hour or two to go outside to buy essential provisions. The poorer families were in terrible straits; with the men confined to their homes and unable to work, they had no money left, and they found themselves literally without food for their children.

We even ran out of water; there was no piped supply, and since we were unable to replenish our water tanks, the tanks soon ran dry. The authorities sent water trucks, and we were allowed out to receive an allocation. On one occasion, while I was waiting to fill my water jugs, I fell into conversation with a Bedouin soldier, reproaching him for the way he and his fellow soldiers were treating us. He was shocked by my scolding. He was combatting the king's enemies, he said; these people were criminals. . . . I explained that our protests were just as much on his behalf. After all, Jordanian soldiers were also killed and wounded in the Israeli raids. But my arguments fell on deaf ears.

During the curfew, even the phones had been cut off, to hinder communication among the population. In the brief time that the curfew was lifted, we had too much to do just to ensure the basic necessities of existence. I had a neighbor, Sahar Khalifeh, who remains a close friend to this day. Sahar was married, like myself, and the mother of two young daughters. We had been closely associated, both in Father Habbra's classes and in our activities in the Arab Women's Union. Sahar is an intense and sensitive person, a gifted writer, and, like myself, deeply resentful of the restrictions she has to face as a woman in Arab society. And, indeed, Sahar was to take what is for an Arab woman the extremely unusual and brave step of divorcing her husband and bringing up her daughters alone, while not neglecting her own development. She went back to university to complete her studies and has recently published her second novel, which enjoyed considerable success. Whenever we had an opportunity during the curfew, she and I would discuss what could be done. We felt doubly repressed and frustrated. Like the rest of the Palestinian population, we were powerless to halt the Jordanian government's repressive acts. To make matters worse, it would be unthinkable for us women to take any initiative. But the situation was intolerable, and finally, after much soul-searching and uncertainty, we summoned up our courage and decided to take action.

One day during the hour-long break in the curfew, she and I set off to canvas members of the executive committee of the Arab Women's Union. We ran from house to house, ducking behind trees and down alleyways to evade the military patrols and guards posted everywhere. We ran along with beating hearts, because the soldiers were quick to shoot at any sign of "illicit activity," and anyone could see that we two were not engaged in shopping. Fortunately, we were not detected, and we managed to reach the house of Mrs. Kamal, a prominent member of the Arab Women's Union, to whom we presented our demands, which were backed by other executive committee members. We urged that the Arab Women's Union take action. At first sight, our demand may seem obvious and unexceptional. But in fact, it was an unusual and daring step. It was simply unheard of for a women's organization to take the initiative in matters affecting the whole community. Nevertheless, it was the only avenue open: Most of the men leaders of Nablus—as in the rest of the West Bank—were in prison or under house arrest. In fact, the sole body whose organizational structure remained intact was the Arab Women's Union.

Sahar and I were successful in our mission: The executive committee decided to act. The plan was passed by word of mouth all that day, into the night, and the next day, during the break in the curfew, the authorities were taken by surprise! Thousands of women—many of them wearing black in mourning for the victims of repression—formed up and set off toward the governor's office. We marched through the streets, chanting slogans:

"Arms for self-defense!"

"An end to the brutality of the army!"

"An end to the curfew!"

"Release the imprisoned intellectuals and political leaders!"

The authorities were at a loss what to do. If this had been an ordinary political procession, led by men, the government would not have hesitated to send in the troops to disperse it at any cost. But even at the height of the repression, the Jordanian officials hesitated to apply their usual brutal tactics against a demonstration of unarmed women.

The army was ordered not to molest us, and we reached the governor's office, where a delegation presented our demands to the governor, requesting him to transmit them to the king. The governor received the delegation in his office. He was clearly astounded and upset—so much so that he reproached us for not requesting his permission for our march.

A few days later, the Jordanian government suspended the curfew. The authorities also proclaimed the introduction of universal military service, to indicate that they were taking thorough measures to defend the country (though this was not meant seriously, being no more than a sop to satisfy Palestinian opinion). Gradually, the repressive measures introduced during the emergency were relaxed, and matters returned to normal.

I do not know how far the Nablus women's demonstration was instrumental in persuading the Jordanian government to end its repression. But the fact that the demonstration had taken place at all, the fact that women had taken the initiative in going out into the streets to press political demands and had therefore entered the political arena on a scale and in a manner never dreamed of before—

this was a big turning point in the social and political history of Palestinian society.

As matters turned out, it was not to remain an isolated event.

A few months later, in June 1967, the third Arab-Israeli war erupted.

6

June 7, 1967

JUNE 7, 1967. In the early morning we see the Jordanian tanks withdrawing from Jenin and Tulkarm.

Why are they pulling back? We wonder. It seems incomprehensible.

The radio gives no clue. Radio Amman continues to broadcast patriotic songs and military marches. The Israeli radio announces: "We have taken Ramallah, Jenin, Tulkarm, and Kalkilya. Our troops are approaching Nablus. The enemy forces are surrendering." We smile in disbelief at these bragging Israeli lies, and continue to trust the Jordanian radio.

Our house is on the outskirts of the town. We sit outside on the veranda, gazing at the unusual sight. Israeli planes are raiding the nearby Jordanian camp of Deir Sharaf. We watch the aircraft dipping and diving, and the scream of their jets reaches our ears.

We can see the flames and smoke as they pound the camp with bombs and rockets.

The maid serves coffee.

A group of Israeli planes swoops down over Wadi al-Tuffah—the picturesque Valley of the Apples—where the retreating Jordanian tanks have taken up positions. The planes release their bombs; we see smoke and earth erupt among the fruit trees.

The Jordanian soldiers are very brave; they fire their machine guns at the diving planes. But it is a one-sided battle, and the outcome is a foregone conclusion.

All around, we hear the sounds of exploding shells and bombs, and the rattle of small-arms' fire. We feel very exposed.

Da'ud decides that we had better go down into the shelter. The children are panic-stricken. The little ones are in tears.

Seeking reassurance, they shower me with questions.

"Mama, what's happening?"

"Mama, will we die?"

"Mama, what do Jews look like?"

At eleven o'clock in the morning, people run through the streets of Nablus, shouting joyfully: "The Algerians! The Algerians are coming!"

We know that an Algerian force has arrived to help in the fighting, and citizens line the streets to welcome the saviors who have come to protect us from the Israelis.

A column of military vehicles enters the town from the direction of Tubas. The citizens wave and cheer.

Suddenly, there is a burst of fire. Only now do people grasp their error. It's the enemy.

The Israelis are in Nablus.

Two days before, we young women had been given "military training." Our instructor was a Jordanian officer who enjoyed being in command of women because it gave him a feeling of superiority. Our "training" was purely theoretical: The only weapons we saw were rusty old British rifles. We marched in full view of enemy airplanes that flew overhead. Nevertheless, we enjoyed the training because of the khaki uniforms and the feeling of adventure, which satisfied our passionate desire to be Palestinian militants.

Our enthusiasm did not last long. Later, we took boxes of fruit, cigarettes, and sweets and went to visit the wounded soldiers in the hospital. Their morale was high, but one of the doctors was pessimistic. "The war is over," he said. While we were talking to him, trucks arrived with wounded people. Doctors and nurses were rushing about. We saw nothing but blood and corpses. They were civilians hit by napalm and bombs.

Somebody screamed. I felt as though I was about to faint. I could not stand the sight.

The Israelis had taken Jenin and Tulkarm, someone said.

My heart beating, I hurried home to my children: Were they still alive?

In the shelter, we listen to the radio. King Hussein is speaking. "My beloved people, I am with you wherever you may be—in the fields, in the army camps, or in battle. Defend yourselves tooth and nail!"

There is an old man in the shelter with us. He tries to keep up our spirits by telling jokes. After the king's speech, he says, "My false teeth are barely sharp enough to eat a sandwich." Turning to the radio, he pretends to be addressing the king: "Bite 'em with your own teeth!"

The king wants us to use our bare teeth against Mirage aircraft. After the Israeli raid on Samoah, His Majesty's army opened fire on patriotic Palestinians who dared to demand arms to defend ourselves. For two months, His Majesty placed the West Bank under curfew, while thousands were imprisoned by His Majesty's secret police.

And now, His Majesty says, "Defend yourselves tooth and nail!"

At five o'clock in the afternoon, everything suddenly falls silent. The guns cease their barking, the whine of the jet planes seems to have receded.

We sit in the shelter, straining our ears, but there is nothing to be heard.

What is happening?

We hear sounds from outside. Voices, footsteps.

Da'ud says something about Dir Yassin. Memories of 1948, when

Jewish forces captured the village and massacred most of its inhabitants. Is this the fate in store for us? I am terrified.

I have lived among the Israelis, I know them. I remember my school friends, my neighbors. Such people do not massacre unarmed civilians. But how do Israelis behave in wartime?

All I remember of the 1948 war is people running, soldiers shooting. Corpses. Panic-stricken people fleeing for their lives. The sad stories of the refugees carrying their few possessions as they trudge toward the haven of the Lebanese border.

The children cling to me in fright. Hala, the youngest, doesn't leave my side. They are all about me, caressing my cheeks, playing with my hair. Hasn't all this happened before?

Memories of Haifa, 1948. Outside—shooting and explosions. Inside the house, my cousins and I cling to my aunt, seeking comfort and reassurance.

Memories of Nazareth, 1948. I am sitting in the shelter with the other children and the nuns. There are people from the town who have come to take refuge in the convent, under the flags of France and the Vatican. All about me, I see tense, frightened faces. I want my parents, but they are far away. Terrified, I cling to one of the nuns, and she strokes me, to reassure me. The nuns intone "Ave Maria," and the response comes back, "Grazia Plena."

Now, sitting in the shelter in Nablus with my own children, I sense their bewilderment. Like my aunt in Haifa, like the nuns in Nazareth, I am only too well aware of my own helplessness.

I try to reassure the children, but they are too young to understand anything except their fear. They continue to cry.

In an effort to take our minds off our present fears, the old man launches into yarns and reminiscences about 1948. "Jewish friends concealed me in their homes," he recalls. "I escaped death the first time, but now—I shall be glad to die in such charming company."

Suddenly, he recognizes a familiar voice; his son has arrived. The young man returned to Nablus only two months ago, after seven years in a Jordanian concentration camp—the price for expressing his nationalistic views.

Eagerly, we inquire for news. The young man has witnessed the battle from his home. "The fighting is over," he says dejectedly. "The Israelis have taken the city."

This is unbelievable. It can't be true. Never in our worst dreams could we have imagined such a calamity.

We are stunned.

We decide to leave the shelter and go home.

Outside the house, we hear a loudspeaker. An announcement, in literary Arabic: ". . . The town has surrendered. We will not harm you if you put up white flags. Anyone who goes outside does so at the risk of his life! The mayor of Nablus requests you to surrender. . . ."

Like the mayor of Nazareth in 1948. Like the loudspeaker in Nazareth. Like the surrender in Nazareth.

Is this the same voice? The same officer? In Nazareth, too, the announcement was in literary Arabic.

What has become of my confidence in an Arab triumph? My dreams of returning home to Acre?

We are in the hands of the enemy. We are defeated! The glory of the Arab world, the banner of Arab unity, the ambition to reconquer our homeland—all our aspirations—all come to nothing.

I feel an uncontrollable urge to cry, to shout, to curse everything I hold dear. I sit numbly, broken and dejected. All around me, the children continue to whimper.

There is no electricity. We go to bed in the dark.

The night is silent, uneventful.

When I first came to Nablus, I soon got used to the set speeches that were made on every social occasion. "The usurped lands"—that meant Israel, where I had spent most of my childhood and adolescence.

There were beautiful poetic words. "The liberation of Palestine." For me, that promised fulfillment of a personal dream: I would go home and see my parents and dear ones.

There were frightening words: The Arab radios spoke of "the destruction of Israel." That made me terrified. It meant the destruction of my parents, of my Arab acquaintances in Nazareth, Haifa, and Galilee.

At that young age, I did not yet comprehend that these were

nothing more than verbal threats. I did not understand then that the Arabic language contains many, many words. . . .

At the beginning of June, after the closure of the Strait of Tiran and Hussein's flight to Cairo to exchange a fraternal kiss with Nasser, people's spirits rose. Nasser made a speech welcoming the imminent war, and the Arab radio stations assured us that victory was at hand. We were overjoyed. A wave of euphoria swept the West Bank. There were mass demonstrations in Nablus. The reconquest of our homeland seemed imminent.

I saw a friend crying at the sight of the joyous crowds. He knew the Arab world, and foresaw future events.

Another friend said, "We've walked into a trap. Are we a nation that is ready for war?" he asked. "The Jordanian army exists to defend the palace and the king. But the people do not have arms."

For twenty years, the Palestinians had not been allowed to carry arms. But that morning, a truckload of weapons was brought to the city. Many young people hurried to take arms. An old man said, "Isn't it a crime to give arms to people who don't know how to use them?"

On the morning of the previous day, June 6, the Egyptian radio, Saut al-Arab, announced that Egyptian military targets had been attacked, and that enemy aircraft were flying over Arab territory. "Our forces are continuing to fight valiantly!" the announcer repeated over and over again.

There was something disturbing and incomprehensible about the news. Our euphoria gradually gave way to tension and perplexity.

The hospitals were full of wounded from the frontier villages. We organized a blood donation service. Throngs of donors stood in line.

On June 6, there was a meeting at the Nablus town hall to discuss what was to be done if Israeli forces entered the city. Should we put out white flags?

The young people, enthusiastic nationalists, were violently opposed to capitulation; it violated their aspirations, their ideology, their morality. It was their mission to restore Palestinian dignity. Surrender, they said, would prove that we Palestinians are ineffectual; they refused to consider such a thing.

The older men are equally patriotic, but more experienced. They talked of saving the city.

The morning after the occupation, we awake to find our house an island in a human sea. Astonished, I gaze out of the window at one of the most amazing, horrifying scenes I have ever beheld. Outside our house, in the road, in the olive groves, there are literally thousands of people—old, young, families with children, pregnant women, cripples. In their arms or on their backs they carry bundles with a few possessions. Young women clutch babies. Everywhere, the same exhausted, broken figures, the stunned, desperate faces.

It is like a nightmare. What can this mean? Who are they? What are they doing here? What has happened to them? I hurry outside, dismayed and shocked. I ask them, but they seem unable to speak coherently. When they see me, they beg for water ... water ... water.... Da'ud hastens to the garden and gives out water to hundreds of people who throng about him. I run around under the trees. People are sitting there weeping from misery, horror, and despair. Parents beg bread for their children.

At last, I find one woman who seems a little more coherent. "We are from Kalkilya," she tells me, resigned and bitter. "We were forced to leave. The Israelis—they brought everyone to the mosque and ordered us to get out of the town. Immediately."

My mind goes back to 1948, and the mass exodus of Palestinians. My God, I think, is this going to happen again?

Seeing the refugees has unnerved me. I am filled with fear. Is the same fate in store for us and our children? Will we also be forced to take our possessions and flee into the hills?

I will not go. I will refuse to leave. Let them do what they want! Better to die in my own country ...

A woman screams. She has been wounded, and she is bleeding profusely. I hurry over to give her first aid.

Sahar and other neighbors are also outside, offering what help they can. Da'ud is still giving out water, surrounded by hundreds of outstretched arms. He is worried; he says that our water supply is running low and there won't be enough left for our own use.

I go over to talk to Sahar. With the best will in the world, the provisions in our homes will never suffice for all these people, I tell her. What we have is a mere drop in the ocean. We have to go to the military authorities and explain the situation; we will demand permission to open up the storerooms of the Social Welfare Department, where emergency stores are kept.

Sahar is a brave woman, but my suggestion is very daring. It is highly daring for a woman to approach strange men, doubly so when these men are officers of a hostile army. In addition, she is afraid to approach the Israelis. She has never encountered a Jew face to face. Trying to fight down my own fears, I tell her there is nothing to be afraid of. "I know the Israelis. . . ."

The day before, Sahar's husband painted a red cross on his car in order to take two wounded Jordanian soldiers to the hospital. We decide to use the same car. We take two men along with us—a young teacher and the mayor of Kalkilya, Haj Hussein Sabri, whom we found among the refugees. Haj Hussein, a member of a proud and wealthy family, exercises all his iron will and remarkable self-control to hide his torment as he sees the catastrophe that has descended upon the people of his town.

Driving slowly through the crowds of refugees, we head for the home of the director of the Social Welfare Department. The director refuses to accompany us. He is afraid of being shot by the Israelis. "I have children," he pleads. "I am not going to my death."

I point out that we are protected by the Red Cross emblem, but in my heart, I can comprehend his fear. Yesterday I saw an ambulance from Jenin that had been shot up—the same could happen to us.

Nevertheless, I conceal my doubts and assure him that the Israelis will not shoot him. Somehow or other, we shame him into doing his duty. He has the keys to the food stores.

We drive into Nablus. Everywhere we see tanks, roadblocks, barbed wire. Some houses are on fire.

Every few yards, armed soldiers stop us. The three men are plainly terrified. My heart pounds hard each time we are halted.

Soldiers come up to our shiny new car. In the streets of the apparently deserted city, we must seem like beings from some other planet. They show their astonishment, but they are totally amazed when I say, "Shalom!" and address them in Hebrew.

"Are you Jewish?" they ask, delighted. With unconcealed admiration, they ogle Sahar and myself.

"*Eizeh chatichot!* (What broads!)" they exclaim.

Suddenly, I feel furious. These men are jubilant, triumphant; they feel lighthearted and relaxed—while we, defeated and humiliated, forage for food for thousands of homeless refugees. I want to yell, "Why did you come here, you murderers?" I choke down my rage.

Their victory is our disaster, and it is that disaster we must deal with now.

At the next roadblock, a soldier again exclaims: *"Eizeh chatichot!"* How strange—ordinarily, my feminine vanity would be flattered by such a comment, however vulgar. But from a victorious army, it is an insult.

Outside the office that formerly served the Jordanian governor, two tall, blond Israeli officers receive us. Like their soldiers, they are astounded by our appearance, and even more so when I speak to them in Hebrew.

In response to their questions, I inform them that we are "volunteers." I say the word proudly, remembering that my mother used it to describe herself during the 1948 war. In the thick of the fighting, she collected the wounded in Acre and helped the doctor perform emergency operations.

Mother rests in peace in the cemetery of her native village, not far from Acre. And now it is my turn to be a "volunteer." An officer comes out of the military governor's office and asks us what we want. He is astonished by our request. "Such activity is forbidden!" he says. "The situation in Nablus is unclear." He seems worried about possible pockets of resistance in the town.

Another officer hears me speaking Hebrew. "It's hard to believe that you learned the language before 1948. You don't look *that* old." Another compliment? He strides up and down the corridor in his military gait, speaking to us from time to time. He inquires where I learned Hebrew.

Suddenly, he approaches me again and asks me my name. "I remember someone with that name!"

He knew my father before 1948. The tension leaves his face. "In memory of your beloved father, I am at your disposal. You'll get your permit."

This is my first introduction to Moshe Fish.

Later, Moshe Fish asks me about some of his Arab acquaintances from before 1948. Bitterly, I tell him that none of them are living in their former homes. All are refugees. He listens, silent and pensive.

"That's sad," he says slowly. Suddenly, he becomes aggressive. "But you wanted war! Nasser wanted it. Shukeirg [head of the PLO] certainly wanted it. You wanted to kill us. Your slogan was 'Kill! Kill!' "

I think of the corpses I saw yesterday. What can I say? My people have been forced into exile; the tragedy is ours. But I am too dazed and shocked to answer him.

At long last, we conclude the entire procedure. Loading our car with food from the UNRWA (United Nations Relief and Works Agency) warehouse, we drive back, escorted by an Israeli officer.

Near our house, we see the throngs of refugees, waiting impatiently for food. We also encounter neighbors out in the street; suddenly, I notice that their expressions are furious. Livid with anger, they stare at the Israeli officer and then turn accusing looks at Sahar and me.

Some of these people are very extreme in their nationalist views, and they are clearly offended to see two young Arab women in the company of an Israeli officer. We explain that we had no choice in the matter, that the needs of the refugees had to be met. Our explanations fall on deaf ears.

"Talking to the enemy is collaboration!" someone says furiously.

Sahar loses her temper. "We have suffered enough from slogans and ideologies!" she cries. "Ba'athism, Marxism, and all the rest. Now we have thousands of mouths to feed, hundreds of wounded to care for. We've talked enough! Now let's go to work and save what we can of the Palestinian people!"

We go to work, cooking up wheat in large pots, preparing tea and milk for the children, handing out medicines for the sick. It's a long job, and we stay up most of the night.

The refugees seek places to sleep. Although it is June, the night is chilly. We ransack our homes for blankets.

Da'ud rebukes me for giving away all our blankets.

"What about your own children?" he asks angrily. "Don't they deserve blankets?"

I remind him that our children are sleeping inside a warm house and not outside in the cold night air. Da'ud is not mollified, and we argue bitterly.

But he is not hardhearted; a few moments later, he goes into the house, brings out our brand-new embroidered eiderdown and gives it to a refugee family.

The Israeli soldier guarding the Kalkilya refugees is a university student. He comes from Morocco and speaks French. He is upset and angry when he sees the homeless families huddling beneath the trees. With a look of pity on his face, he gives the children his own rations. He does his best to help us, helping me to take care of the wounded or find an ambulance.

Bitterly, he mutters: "*Ça, c'est la démocratie et l'humanité du peuple juif.*" He shows me his rifle. "Believe me, madame, I didn't use this rifle, and I will not use it. I saw them kill boys like me. I won't use my rifle. *Croyez-moi, madame.*"

In the darkness, I hear moans and cries. Those with nothing to cover themselves with are shuddering audibly.

Suddenly, a woman's voice cries out: "For God's sake, help me, I'm dying!" I go over; she has been shot in the kidneys. Her children stand around, crying.

Finally, all is silent.

We finish our work and go off to snatch a little rest. I lie down on my soft bed, ashamed to be sleeping in comfort.

Two days after the occupation of Nablus, the American consul in Jerusalem, Mr. Wilson, came to see us. Eagerly, we asked him to tell us what had happened in Jerusalem during the fighting. His report was both depressing and encouraging. There was the depression of knowing that the city had been occupied, but we were heartened by his descriptions of the brave defense of the city. He told of the Jordanian soldiers who, lacking sophisticated arms, had fought in hand-to-hand battles in defense of the city, until they were overrun.

Quietly, we listened to his account. Unlike previous meetings, we were too depressed to engage in political arguments with Wilson. I could not help recalling his argument with Hikmat al-Masri, when the latter criticized the Americans for supporting Israel. We knew America was our principal enemy, and I had not changed my views of U.S. policy. At the same time, I wondered whether there was some way we could mobilize American humanitarian aid.

We asked Wilson about the situation in Kalkilya. His face grew grave. "The town is seventy-five percent demolished," he said softly. We were dumbfounded. "Impossible! Unbelievable!" We thought of the wretched refugees outside our windows, squatting under the olive trees, hoping against hope that they would be allowed to return to their homes. Where would they go? This was the second time they had lost their homes. In 1948, they were driven out of their former homes, now the site of the modern Israeli town of Kfar Saba. With blood and sweat and determination, they had built Kalkilya into a second home, making it into a flourishing township surrounded by orange groves. Now they had lost their home for the second time. Could we tell them of this new catastrophe? We decided that it would be too cruel and resolved to leave them in ignorance for the time being.

Not that the refugees did not have any inkling of the fate of Kalkilya. Some of them asked a couple of Israeli soldiers when they would be allowed to return home.

"What home?" answered the soldier bitterly. "Ask Dayan if you have a place to go to. There is no Kalkilya! Finished!"

"Go to Hussein!" said the second soldier.

The first soldier turned around to him and said angrily in French, "*Fermez la gueule!*"

The rumor quickly spread among the refugees, but most of them refused to believe it.

I was nearby, standing over the wood fire, cooking wheat and heating milk for the children. I pretended not to understand the mixture of Hebrew and French in which the two Israelis continued their conversation.

"You people don't have a heart!" said the one who spoke French. "Don't you have a home, a family? Is this Judaism? You ought to remember Auschwitz!"

The other one, speaking a better Hebrew, said, "Shut up! These people endanger our dream of *Eretz Yisrael* [the Land of Israel]."

His friend was not convinced. "Who brought me to this awful country?" he said sharply. "The land of our ancestors, the land of the prophets. Like Dayan, the great prophet!" He broke into a string of curses in French slang.

I listened and said nothing. As the refugees heard of the fate of their homes, the old people were silent too. But the young people cursed and muttered, their hot blood unable to contain their misery. I watched the women fold one hand over the other in the traditional Arab gesture of grief and mourning. The sheikh of Kalkilya, Sheikh Sabri, tried to console his people. "Prayer," he said slowly, "prayer is always a consolation in difficulty or danger. In Islam, God tries his followers."

When the curfew was lifted for the first time, the people of Nablus hurried out to find friends, family, acquaintances. The town is like a single tribe, everyone related to everyone else.

Some of our friends lived at the entrance to the town. Fortunately, they were not at home during the fighting. When they went to see their house, they found it riddled with bulletholes.

Our friend stood looking at his home and at the homeless refugees roaming about. His face pale and tears in his eyes, he said, "I would have preferred death rather than live through this humiliation."

With Sahar and some other friends, I tried to take advantage of the two-hour break in the curfew to collect blood for the wounded refugees. The stock of plasma at the hospital had all been ruined, because with the conquest of the town, the electricity supply had been cut off and the hospital refrigerators stopped functioning.

We walked into the cafés—usually the exclusive preserve of the men, but this was no time to consider decorum or traditions. "Come to the hospital," we urged the men sitting there. "Come, we need blood urgently!" There was no response. They were still in a state of shock; there was a terrible wordless apathy. On the eve of the war, long lines of blood donors queued outside the hospital; but now, no one budged. Who cared about the dying, the wounded? With sullen expressions on their faces, the men rebuked us women for our presumption in flaunting ourselves in their cafés. The atmosphere was heavy with defeat, depression, indifference.

By now we were desperate. Ignoring conventional propriety, we took a letter from the doctor at the hospital and hurried to the military governor's office to demand blood. Our mission was urgent; the doctors could not perform operations for lack of plasma, and people were dying in their beds.

At the entrance to the municipality, we were halted by a sentry.

He refused to let us in. I insisted, but he threatened me with his Uzzi submachine gun. *"Yalla!* [Get out of here!]" he shouted. Desperately, I screamed at him in Hebrew. "We're trying to save lives! Don't you understand?"

"No!" he shouted back. "There's a war on, people are dying everywhere!"

As we were shouting, Moshe Fish appeared. Moshe led us inside, and we presented the letter to a young officer, who raised his head and gave us a searching stare. Addressing us in French, he said: "You look like intelligent modern girls. What would you have done if we Israelis weren't here? Where would you have demanded blood?" He wanted to impress us with Israeli superiority, to prove that we were backward and helpless without them. I was infuriated. "Any fool could answer that!" I shouted. "There are hundreds of people in the hospital injured and dying with napalm burns! Would that have happened if you Israelis hadn't come? You cut off the electricity and ruined the plasma stocks—don't forget that either! And don't forget we're under curfew and we can't collect blood from the population!"

He was silent. Finally, without answering, he said: "Please come with me."

We hesitated. He was inviting us to ride with him in an Israeli military jeep. Urgent as our mission was, we did not want the townspeople to see us in an enemy vehicle. "No," I said, "we'll wait for you in the hospital."

On our way to the hospital, we passed Sahar's mother, who was talking to another woman. We told the two women that we were on our way to try to save a woman in the hospital with a bullet in her kidneys.

The two older women looked at each other silently. Then one of them said, "There's a rumor going around that you two are joyriding around the town with young Israeli officers in a military vehicle."

The woman with the bullet in her kidneys died. She left seven young children, under the olive trees. How were we to tell these innocent young creatures that they had lost their mother?

The bereaved husband got hold of a donkey. The smaller children rode on the donkey, the older ones walked. The sad little band set off, walking toward the Jordan bridge. The father wanted to leave the occupied territory and cross over to eastern Jordan.

I begged him not to go. "How will you go with these children?" I asked.

"God will help," he said wearily.

I never knew how God could protect so many suffering human beings.

The Israelis were sending buses for some of the refugees, taking them to the Allenby Bridge and dropping them off there, abandoned, bedraggled, with their few miserable possessions, whole families with men and women, old people, children in arms. Silent and dazed, the columns of refugees made their way across the bridge, half-destroyed after having been blown up by the Jordanians. They knew they were heading for an uncertain, homeless future; at best, they could hope to begin life again in yet another improvised refugee camp.

In many cases, families were separated, with one part being taken by bus to the bridges while the others came to Nablus, where they squatted under olive trees. When those in Nablus discovered that their dear ones were on the other side of the river, they too set off, trudging down to the Jordan Valley. Whatever happened, the family had to remain together.

As the refugees crossed the river, Israeli soldiers forced them to sign statements that they would not return. This included people who were crossing to withdraw money from their bank accounts in Jordanian banks. When they later came to the bridge and asked to return, they were not permitted to come back.

It was a new Mandelbaum Gate.

A French TV team arrived in Nablus. As I spoke French, I accompanied them. I took them to the refugee centers in schools, in camps, under the trees, and by the roadsides. Hundreds of people gathered around us. I translated their stories while the cameras turned. The tales were hair-raising: children who had died by the way, husbands who had disappeared, people who were shot before their eyes, and those who were taken away—God knows where.

I spoke in front of the cameras, making an appeal to the conscience of the Christian world. While I was speaking, a woman fainted.

For the second time in one generation, Jordan opened its gates to a flood of Palestinian refugees. The people of Jordan and its government gave all the help they could, generous and unstinting. But the Jordanians did not have enough to give, and contributions came in from all over the world.

Little of the foreign relief was getting through to us, on the West Bank; most of the supplies were needed in eastern Jordan. We only had enough to give out one small loaf of bread per person every twenty-four hours.

That night, Moshe Fish brought the military governor of Nablus, Zvi al-Peleg, to our house. Taking them to the kitchen, I opened the door, and they stepped outside to look at the refugees.

The two officers stood there for a few moments in silence, surveying the scene. Then, wordlessly, they stepped back inside our house.

After seeing the two Israeli officers emerging from our door, the refugees were suspicious of us, convinced that we were collaborating with the enemy.

The next day, Zvi al-Peleg sent trucks full of bread and milk to distribute to the refugees.

The mayor of Kalkilya and Sheikh Sabri went to Jerusalem and called on the United States consul, Mr. Wilson. In response to their appeal, Wilson cabled Arthur Goldberg, the U.S. delegate to the United Nations, begging him to intervene with the Israeli government on behalf of the Kalkilya refugees.

The American pressure soon had its effect.

Later, Moshe Dayan was interviewed by BBC Television, and he declared that the destruction of Kalkilya was the greatest mistake of the war.

After two weeks, the refugees were permitted to return to the town. On top of the rubble and ruins of their former homes, they put up tents.

Mr. Wilson came to visit us. He arrived in his official limousine, which bore the American ensign.

The neighbors—Ba'athists, left-wingers with strong anti-American views—stared angrily. Was it not enough that our people had been killed with American arms? Had this man come to gloat over our downfall? For the masses of our people, Zionism was equated with U.S. imperialism. Anti-American feeling, strong enough before, had increased tenfold.

At the time I could not reveal that it was Wilson's help that had brought some salvation to the people of Kalkilya. Being a diplomat, Mr. Wilson was forbidden to express his own personal views; instead, he had to defend the position of his government. Later, in his book *Jerusalem: Key to Peace,* he finally expressed his own opinions—for which the Israelis accused him of being pro-Arab, while the Arabs accused him of being pro-Israel. In fact, he was pro-justice.

Perhaps it was my upbringing that made it easier for me to comprehend the mentality of foreigners and explain our predicament in a manner they could understand. I may have learned this as a child in Israel, mixing with my Jewish friends. I am from Galilee, where people are more outgoing—unlike the proud reserve and withdrawal that characterize Nablus. My openness toward outsiders was unique among the people of Nablus. There were times when I wanted to scream: "For God's sake! How can we gain friends if we reject all foreigners? I know they reject us, but if we don't learn how to approach them, how can we explain ourselves?"

But all around me, people only cursed the Americans and other foreigners. "They are only blind because they wish to be. They deliberately ignore truth, reality, humanity," people said.

Full of bitterness against the outside world, they withdrew into their shells, and condemned me for my contacts with the outsiders.

Finding myself regarded with suspicion, even hostility, by my own people because of my contacts with Israelis and Westerners, I could not help thinking back to my mother's predicament during the 1948 war. Her actions at that time incurred similar suspicions—and worse!

After the Israeli capture of Acre, Mother was horrified by the events she had just witnessed. And with the Acre carnage fresh in her mind, she set out for her native village, Kfar Yassif. Without any means of transportation, she walked the whole way. On the road, she encountered families of refugees fleeing northward, away from the advancing Israelis. These sights further heightened the urgency of her mission.

Arriving at Kfar Yassif, she hurried to the mayor, Yani Yani, and related everything she had seen: the fighting in Acre, the hospitals full of dead and wounded, the flow of refugees toward the Lebanese border. She knew that the people of Kfar Yassif lacked arms, and she urged Yani Yani to surrender, to save the village from the fate that had overtaken other Palestinian villages. The villagers gathered around to hear her story, which made a deep impact. Shocked and grieved, the villagers debated what to do. It seemed unthinkable to submit to the Israelis. But the village had few arms, its people had no military training—they would be no match for the well-armed and well-organized Israelis. After long consultations, the villagers decided to take Mother's advice, surrendering to the Israeli forces.

The news of Mother's actions reached the local Arab commander, an Iraqi officer. Scenting treason, he promptly ordered her to be executed. Mother did not panic; courageously she confronted the officer and told him what she had told Yani Yani. She explained why she advised the villagers to capitulate. The Iraqi listened to her explanation, and although he was in favor of fighting on, he comprehended Mother's patriotic and humanitarian motives for doing what she had done. The officer sent a messenger to his headquarters at Tarshiha, canceling the execution order.

In the days of the June 1967 fighting, 180 young people from Nablus were killed in the mountains around the town, trying to fight with the arms they had received just two days before the war. They had no military training to speak of, and the guns were rusty.

On learning that Da'ud was a bank manager, the military governor asked him to go around the town and bring the other Nablus bank managers to him. He gave Da'ud a permit to move around during the curfew.

I came across an old man, sick and helpless, stranded in one of the houses. He begged me to get him to his son's house. But it was curfew—how could I do anything for him?

In the end, I asked Da'ud to take advantage of his curfew pass. We drove the man to his son's house and carried him inside. Then, on the way back, we ran into an Israeli patrol.

"What are you doing outside during the curfew?" their officer asked gruffly.

We explained that we had been carrying a sick old man to his home.

"Who gave you permission to move around during the curfew?" the officer shouted angrily. Da'ud showed him the curfew pass; the officer snatched it out of his hands and ripped it into shreds. Then he ordered Da'ud to take the car to the military headquarters and leave it there.

Da'ud had no choice but to obey. When he got home, he was furious with me for talking him into taking such a risk.

Foreign journalists were beginning to arrive, curious to find out how we were living under Israeli occupation. The older people received them resignedly, patiently explaining that the "Holy Land" has never been holy—it has always thirsted for blood. Many conquerors have come here: There were the Crusaders many centuries ago; there were the Turks, and then there were the British. "We have survived them all. We'll survive the Israelis too."

The younger people mostly refused to speak to the newspapermen. They were still in shock after the downfall of the June War. Some of them expected an Arab army of liberation to come and free them. Later, Abdul Nasser was to coin the slogan "What was taken by force will be restored by force!" But we did not see that force would ever be a true solution for our problems. Hitherto, force had not gotten us very far.

The news of Nasser's resignation came as another terrible blow, on top of all the other setbacks and humiliations we had suffered. Abdul Nasser, the giant, the symbol of Arab nationalism, had fallen.

When the news came over the radio, many people burst into tears.

A friend, Dr. Feisal, stood in front of our house weeping. We were all depressed, our confidence shattered even further.

The regional manager of Da'ud's bank came from England to see how the bank was faring. He arrived in Nablus, accompanied by the managers of two of the Israeli branches of the bank. As it happened, both of these Israelis used to be friends of my father, during his days of prosperity. Now, when they recognized me, they greeted me most warmly, kissing and embracing me.

A friend of mind, E., was visiting our home at the time of their arrival. On seeing the warm welcome I extended to these two Israelis, she was enraged at what she considered "treason" on my part.

I was in the kitchen preparing drinks for the visitors when E. stormed in through the back door, blazing with fury.

"Aren't you ashamed?!" she shouted. "The French people closed their doors to the Germans!"

She left, vowing never to come to our home again.

Almost immediately after the war, Israel annexed eastern Jerusalem. At first, we West Bankers were not allowed into the city. Then gradually the restrictions were lifted.

The first time I went to Jerusalem, it was to make contact with the foreign consuls. I went to report on our situation and our urgent need for help from the Red Cross. Our delegation consisted of the head of the Arab Women's Union, Hajja Andalib al-Amad; the vice-president, Issam Abed al-Abdi (later imprisoned, together with her daughter, and deported by the occupation authorities); the vice-president of the Red Crescent, Rashda al-Shaika, sister of the mayor of Nablus; and the writer Mrs. Faiza Abed al-Megid, of the Children's Welfare Association.

The consuls—representatives of the United States, Britain, and France—received us warmly. They did not know much of what was happening on the West Bank, and they listened very intently to our reports. Our immediate concern was to bring in the Red Cross, which was excluded from the occupied territories; the Israelis insisted that all help be channeled through their own aid association, the Red Magen David.

Coming to Jerusalem was an unforgettably painful experience.

For us, the city had been a militant Arab emblem; it was a shock to see it under occupation.

What we found in Jerusalem was new, unfamiliar, hostile. The Israelis were jubilant over the annexation of eastern Jerusalem. They called it reunification of the city. Seeing these strange, rejoicing faces and these circles of young Israelis dancing the hora, I relived the tragedy that had been the dominant feature of my youth.

Standing there, I once again faced the Mandelbaum Gate, the Gate of Tears, where I, too, had shed my quota of tears. My link with that spot was close: This was the incarnation of the tragedy that divides families, that divides the present from the past. The gate symbolized my own lack of identity.

When I crossed over into Jordan in 1957, my brother George was in Amman. Knowing that Mother would be accompanying me to the Mandelbaum Gate, George flew to Jerusalem especially to snatch at the rare opportunity of glimpsing her. Unfortunately, his plane was delayed, and he arrived late. Mother had not been permitted to linger in the frontier zone; when George hurried up to the Jordanian side of the border, she had just departed. Desperately, he asked where she was. The Jordanian officer in charge was used to the tragic dramas enacted at the Gate, but he had not been hardened by the suffering he witnessed. Gloomily, he pointed at a tiny figure dwindling into the distance on the Israeli side of the border.

"Do you see that shadow? That is your mother."

My brother's eyes brimmed with tears and he began to weep hopelessly. He had been deprived of everything—home, family, country. His grief even overshadowed his joy at being reunited with me. Though he could not know it then, that fleeting view of Mother was to be his last sight of her.

Accursed Mandelbaum Gate! How many young people paid with their lives for daring to cross over to the other, forbidden side, in search of mothers and fathers?

How many times had I looked at that oppressive, merciless gate that perpetuated the injustice of separation?

How I wanted the Mandelbaum Gate to open then! My unfulfilled hopes, as I waited for the impossible, created a bitterness that is one of the principal memories of my childhood.

Our deepest wishes and desires were linked to that gate. We

wanted it to be opened, so that we could enter our homeland. When I was at boarding school in Jerusalem, I longed desperately for it to open, so that I could run to my brothers.

But no one dreamed then that it would be opened in this manner, under occupation.

During that first visit to Jerusalem after its "reunification," I went to the New City, where I had gone to school. I walked in the streets, searching for my childhood.

I strode along, gazing in astonishment at the overflow of Israelis from all over the country who had come to celebrate the fulfillment of the prophecy of Jerusalem's reunification. Cars, trucks, buses, even motorcycles—all bringing in Israelis, young and old, men and women, miniskirted girls embracing handsome young men in paratroopers' uniforms—a joyful, triumphant throng, celebrating their victory, their conquest of Jerusalem. They rejoiced in their free, uninhibited fashion, kissing in the streets. . . . What an irony—we were under the domination of a free society.

We walked the streets, subdued, humiliated, defeated, and powerless; in silence, we surveyed this new reality, these new dimensions of our tragic situation. I looked at these strange faces, Israelis of every color and hue, European Jews and newcomers from the Arab countries, townspeople and kibbutzniks. I watched them singing and dancing the hora, and I remembered how I used to love dancing the hora with my Israeli friends. I remembered the Hebrew songs. I thought of my Jewish friends who had come from the Diaspora, who had survived the Holocaust and wished only to live in peace, the girls who showed such comprehension for my plight and my suffering. I wanted to shut my eyes and ears, to keep those dear personal memories from mingling with the images of the Israeli soldiers, killing and destroying. What I saw was no longer the Jewish people fighting for their survival—I was witnessing a Jewish conquest of our land. Were these military parades the fulfillment of their dream?

The other ladies with me, more conservative than I, were quite intimidated by this display of euphoria; the intoxicated Israelis were behaving in a way quite foreign to Arab traditions. We felt like strangers in our own city.

I thought of the city's past, of the desert caravans with their merchants who passed through the city, of the European nobles who left their homes to fight for it, of the pilgrims who came from all over the world to see the sacred relics. Walking past the tractors and bulldozers that were busy altering the city's borders, I listened to the calls of the muezzin from the al-Aksa Mosque. Once again I heard the noontime Angelus bells, which I used to hear at school. This was Jerusalem, the center of the three great religions that share a faith in the dignity of human life.

During the British mandate, the city had its own special charm; Arabs and Jews lived side by side in a multireligious community. With its missionary institutions, its international schools and hospitals, with people from all the countries of the world—Russia, Britain, France, Germany, Austria—Jerusalem was cosmopolitan, a city of the world. After 1948, the Israeli sector of Jerusalem became purely Jewish. My father, who remained in the Jewish section of Jerusalem, said that after 1948, the divided city, once proud but now humiliated, appeared to him like a noble lady forced to wear shabby clothes.

And now, in 1967, I watched the tractors erasing the remnants of the gates and barbed-wire fences that once divided the city.

All over the world, it seemed that the masses were celebrating the Arab downfall. What a feeling of pride there was in Europe and America; Israeli sympathizers sang and danced, celebrating the fulfillment of the prophecy. Their sympathy was for Israel, the underdog—but now we were the underdogs. Israel was strong, Dayan was a superman, the other Israeli leaders were heroes too. At one stroke, Israel erased the memory of Nazi persecution, freeing the Europeans of their guilt for what befell the Jews during the Holocaust. The world loves the strong; "might is right," it seems. No longer were the Jews homeless refugees; they had a powerful state of their own.

The place of the Jewish refugees was taken by the Palestinians. Before the 1967 war, the Palestinian refugees were sick and tired of their situation. It was not aid they wanted, neither welfare assistance, nor UNRWA rations and blankets. They wanted a home, they wanted a new status of dignity. But now their previous tragedy was repeated and compounded: There was a new flow of refugees, new displaced persons, new tragedies.

7

Occupation and Resistance

WITHIN A RELATIVELY SHORT TIME after the end of the June War, the Israeli authorities gradually lifted some of the restrictions they had imposed at the time of the occupation. The curfew was shortened and then suspended; we were allowed to move about the West Bank, even though our movements were hampered by military roadblocks and police identity checks. In time, it became possible to cross the old demarcation line into Israel. I seized on the first opportunity to request permission for a short visit to my hometown, Acre. I had a deep yearning to see once more the environment in which I grew up, the beloved home of my childhood, the familiar fields and villages. In addition, there was a sad purpose to my trip: This would be my first chance to visit the graves of my mother and father.

I began the journey with a great sense of eagerness and impatience. Driving along the coast road, I again admired the landscape of my childhood. The orange groves, the jasmine, and the fresh sea breeze transported me back to that time. I gazed at the flowers, remembering how my father used to explain the characteristics of each variety: Violets are humble, he used to say, but roses are proud.

Anyone who has ears to hear the seductive call of nature can comprehend the wistful love aroused by a land to which one is attached.

At last I arrived in Acre. The town's gates were open, those same gates that had been closed to ward off the onslaughts of invaders—Napoleon, Ibrahim Pasha, the British. I thought back to 1948, when the Israelis took the town with relative ease. I know my people fought. They did not have tanks or planes or artillery; all they had were their primitive guns, but they fought as long as they could until they were forced to surrender.

In ancient times the town's inhabitants had never fled, because the gates were closed; they lived or died within their own hometown. I wish those gates had been closed in 1948, I wish the people had been prevented from fleeing. Over and over again, I asked myself: Why did they run away? Didn't they know that they would not be allowed to return? That their places would be taken by newcomers—Jewish immigrants or dispossessed Arab villagers from the surrounding countryside?

How glad I was to be back in Acre, within its ancient walls; back home, with all the bittersweet memories, the haunting voices of the past, the faces of dear ones long departed. And yet I was filled with sorrow as I walked the cobbled alleyways.

I reached the street where I had lived as a child. Everything was so familiar and yet so strange. I looked beyond the promenade on the seashore, tears forming in my eyes. Suddenly I had to see my old house. I hurried to the familiar door and knocked furiously. I expected it to open for me again as it had opened so often in the past. I expected to see Mother's tender smile, to feel her arms embrace me. I expected to hear Father's grave voice welcoming me. I knocked again and again, but there was no reply, no sound, nothing but the awful throbbing in my temples that echoed the bitter truth of reality. I slumped down on the steps, sobbing helplessly as I covered my face with my hands. I thought of Father and Mother, I thought of their lonely deaths while I—only a few kilometers away—had not been permitted to cross the armistice line to comfort them in their last moments. And now they were dead; they were dead and gone; our home was empty; they would never come back. . . .

As I sat there, a group of tourists suddenly appeared, pushing and shoving to buy tickets. Bewildered, I did not understand what it was all about. Who were these people? What did they want here? Then the door of the house opened, and at the same time, a man thrust a ticket into my hand, demanding ten lira. Suddenly, I understood what had happened: My old home had been turned into a museum, a place for tourists to visit! I was horrified! How could they do that to my beloved home?

All the same, shocked as I was, I could not resist the urge to go inside. What did I hope to find? Was I just seeking some contact, some lingering touch of the past? Unsure whether this was dream or reality, I followed the guide inside, gazing about me in fascination.

But I was soon brought down to earth. My reverie gave way to anger and bitterness. As the guide led the visitors around, he explained blandly that this house, our home, used to belong to an eminent Jewish family. What a humiliation! I felt my blood rise. In my fury, I wanted to shout: "Don't believe him! He's lying to you! This is my home, this house belongs to my family! This is where my own father was born."

But I said nothing, listening in stupefaction as the guide pointed out the arched Eastern architecture, the walls hung with paintings, the floors of Italian marble. "Look at that grand piano," he said enthusiastically.

I crept out on tiptoe, hoping that no one would look at me too closely. My eyes were again filled with tears—but this time, tears of fury. I do not know what angered me more—the sad fate of my family's home or the pitiful untruths the guide was pouring into the ears of the visitors. I wondered what would happen if I were to push forward to silence him and tell them the truth about this house. Would they all look at me with pity? Or would they think I had taken leave of my senses, that my demented mind had made up some fantastic tale of the departed glories of my family? What would they say if I told them that the grand piano had been imported from Damascus for my grandmother, who came from a noble Syrian family that had enjoyed an eminent position during Ottoman times? That my grandfather had once been the honorary British consul? What would they say if I told them that the books of poetry, literature, and philosophy that filled the library were the property of my father?

I thought of my father. A widely educated man, he attended college in Lebanon, then studied law in Alexandria and France. He became a grain contractor to the British navy. But he was a nonconformist, with a hankering for a bohemian life-style; he had inherited a taste for intellectual pursuits, and he loved to travel.

The Israelis would never believe me if I told them of my father. To them, we Arabs were no better than a mass of Bedouin nomads. That was the stereotype.

Sadly, I slipped out of the house, with its phantoms of the past. Hurrying through the streets of Acre, so familiar and yet so strange, I too felt like a phantom. Then I headed back to Nablus.

After the first few weeks and months of Israeli occupation, life in Nablus gradually slipped into some kind of "normalcy." The Israelis conducted a population census and issued new identity cards. After the ending of the curfew, people moved about more or less freely, although it was a long time before we were permitted to leave the town. Israeli soldiers patrolled the streets and conducted identity checks. At first, this was largely a matter of routine. It was only later, as the fedayeen of the Palestinian resistance stepped up their activities, that the security checks became strict and irksome.

After the trauma of the war, which began with such high expectations and ended in bitter humiliation, people were still numb. It was difficult to grasp what had happened—and even harder to accept it. Seeing Israeli troops and military vehicles in the streets of Nablus was still a shocking experience; like a wound that refuses to heal, it has remained a source of pain. The only things that helped to pull people out of their dull apathy were the exigencies of everyday life. Urgent necessities and constraints left little time for melancholy thoughts. The need to find food, to earn money, to repair the damage caused during the fighting, to reorganize our lives for the single, stark purpose of survival—all these spurred people into action.

The situation was grave. Nablus had known hard times under Jordanian rule too, but the war and the Israeli occupation had largely paralyzed economic activity. After a few weeks, the wheels began to turn again as merchants opened up their shops, farmers began bringing in their produce to the city markets, and transportation started up again. But this recovery was only partial; while some people went back to work and made a livelihood, many of the citizens of Nablus were in desperate straits. Building and similar projects ground to a halt, and the laborers were left without jobs. Many families had depended for their livelihood on remittances that came from sons or husbands working in Kuwait or the Gulf; the money used to be transferred by way of Jordan, but links with Amman being cut by the Israeli occupation, whole families were left with nothing with which to buy the necessities of everyday life. In such situations, people drew on their savings, but here, too, there was no salvation to be found. The banks in Nablus are all branches of Jordanian banks; following the Israeli occupation, the local branches were closed, and depositors were unable to withdraw their money. Just before the war, the Jordanian government authorized the West Bank bank managers to issue small sums, but these did not last long.

With the closing of his bank, Da'ud—like all other West Bank bank employees—was left without employment. Although he has been paid his salary as though he were still working, he has been living in enforced idleness ever since—over ten years without work. (At times, Da'ud has wanted to follow the many other bank employees who moved to Amman or to the Gulf states, where he would be able to work and make money. But I have always resisted the idea: I feared that we would not return to Palestine. What is the use of making money if we live abroad and if our children are brought up far from Palestine? The choice was between wealth in exile and the sufferings of occupation. I preferred the latter.)

During the early period of the occupation, when people were desperate for money, Da'ud did what he could to alleviate their suffering by countersigning their checks, to confirm that they had money in their accounts. These checks were then taken by young men who slipped across the Jordan River and cashed them at Jordanian banks, bringing the much-needed money back to their families. In slipping across the border, these young men risked their lives, for if they encountered an Israeli patrol they could be shot. Indeed, many of them never returned from their perilous missions. To help those hundreds of destitute Nablus families, the municipality collected money from relatively well-to-do families and organized allocations of food for the most needy cases. It was a sad sight, that long line of women, children, and old men who queued up outside the municipality every day, standing patiently for hours as they waited for the meager rations—a loaf of bread, a little rice and sugar and beans.

As I passed that line one day, something strange caught my eye:

Many of the women were wearing veils! Prior to the war, the veil had largely disappeared, at least in Nablus and other large towns. Only the older women from the most conservative families still maintained the tradition of never going out unveiled. And yet, here, I noticed that most of the women were once more wearing their veils. It took me a moment to comprehend the reason: Humiliated at having to beg for food, they were literally hiding their faces in shame! They were people with a strong sense of pride and self-respect—and suddenly, a calamity had befallen them, and they were now dependent on charity to remain alive.

The sense of disgrace was not merely personal, there was also a collective feeling of humiliation. Even those who possessed the basic material needs of life—food, clothes, a roof over their heads—they, too, had lost something; they, too, felt ashamed and degraded. The defeat in the June War was not some abstract political setback; it was a personal blow for each and every one of us. There was a general air of depression over the city.

When I saw my people's defeat and humiliation, I felt a strong urge to run far away from this place where every moment reminded me of our downfall. When I heard the Israelis speaking with that arrogant self-confidence of victory, there were moments when I wished I wasn't an Arab. Like others, I sensed a rejection of everything Arab; I had lost my faith in the Arab leaders, in the whole Arab people. Having lost our confidence in ourselves, we were left with nothing but a deep feeling of self-hatred.

The women of Nablus wore their dejection like mourning; they used no lipstick or other makeup. At a time when women the world over were flaunting miniskirts, Palestinian women went back to long dresses. I followed the general trend. Before the war, I went about in brightly colored dresses and short-sleeved blouses. But now, although I did not go to an extreme, I, too, began to wear more modest, conservative clothes; I, too, found that it fitted my depressed and subdued mood. It wasn't just a matter of my own personal preference; it would have been unthinkable for me to walk the streets all dressed up.

The modest, almost drab appearance we presented was in striking contrast with the flamboyant exhibitionism of the Israelis. Within a short time after the occupation, the West Bank was opened up to a veritable flood of Israeli tourists. In trucks and buses, in cars and jeeps, Israeli civilians flooded into the West Bank by the tens of thousands. Noisy, gay, colorful in their dress and uninhibited in their behavior, they soon showed that they considered themselves at home. They roamed through the town, staring curiously at the peasants in their traditional costumes, brandishing cameras in all directions—I think they were surprised to find we didn't live in tents. They flooded the markets and shops, hunting for bargains and curios; those who spoke Arabic entered into conversation with the shopkeepers; others made do with gestures. The Israelis snapped up any imported products, which were far cheaper in our stores than in Israel, where there are heavy taxes. (Later we, too, were forced to pay the heavily inflated Israeli prices.)

Our people watched this new "invasion" with reserve. The shopkeepers and merchants were glad enough to serve these new customers—they were a godsend at a time when business was so bad. But for most of the people, they could never forget for one moment that these "visitors" had come in the wake of an army of occupation, and the attitude toward them was therefore one of polite reserve, mixed with some curiosity about these strange beings who, for the past nineteen years, had lived so near and yet were so remote and unfamiliar.

In the second half of 1967 and in the winter of 1967–68, despite the relief efforts of the municipality and various voluntary agencies such as the International Christian Committee, the situation in Nablus was very acute. Conditions were especially hard in the working-class districts of old Nablus, where the families of unemployed laborers suffered want and deprivation. The men hunted for work, but in vain—there were no jobs to be had. In despair, many of the men left the country in search of employment in the Gulf states, from where they hoped to be able to provide for their families.

As winter approached, and with it the orange-picking season, there was talk of work being available in Israel. The first reaction was one of shock and anger: Did the occupation authorities truly believe that any self-respecting Palestinian would cross the border and go to work for some Israeli employer? Certainly not! Imagine— some of our people might even find themselves working in fields or orange groves that had once belonged to them!

But the employment situation was bleak, and it was not long before workers from Nablus began to board the early-morning buses that took them to work in Israeli orange groves and factories. The nationalists were extremely angered by this breach in the instinctive policy of noncooperation with the Israelis.

At this time, Eric Rouleau, Middle East editor of *Le Monde,* came to see me, and I invited some friends to meet him. In the course of the conversation, one of my guests violently criticized the laborers working in Israel. "The idiots!" he cried. "They work on construction sites in Jerusalem, putting up Jewish apartments at strategic points in the city. They're helping the Israeli economy, building their own jail, digging their own graves!"

Another guest reacted violently to this onslaught. "It's all very well for you bourgeois to sit in your salons and criticize the workers. But what are the workers supposed to do? There are no other jobs available. How are they supposed to feed their hungry children— with nationalist slogans?"

Rouleau listened to the angry exchange with great interest. "It was far worse in France during World War II," he recalled. "Hundreds of thousands of French workers were taken to work in Germany. Thousands of trainloads of French workers taken off to staff German munitions factories."

The controversy over laborers taking jobs in Israel was not the only issue of its kind to engage our attention during the early months of Israeli occupation. The June War took place at the end of the school year, and the schools remained closed throughout the summer, as usual. But as the time approached for the schools to re-open, fierce disagreements arose. The Israeli authorities exerted pressure on the schools to change their curriculum and adopt the one in use in Arab schools in Israel. The Israelis wanted to censor the school books, rewriting Arab history to suit Israeli views. There was a great fear that our children would be subjected to the kind of brainwashing that is the lot of Arab children in Israel, who are forced to learn all about Jewish history and literature but grow up knowing very little of their own national and cultural heritage.

Not that we were overcontent with the existing Jordanian curriculum. The Jordanian Ministry of Education introduced a study program aimed at making our children "Jordanians," while stressing little of our own Palestinian identity. One day, while we were still under Jordanian rule, I saw the geography book in use in Dianna's school. Astounded, I glanced through it and found that our children were expected to learn the minutest details about Transjordan, about its hills and deserts, its Bedouin tribes and villages, while there was scarcely a word about Palestine. I flung down the book in anger. "What do I care about their desert?" I shouted. "Why should my children learn all this? We are from Jaffa and Acre, from Palestine. Why don't they teach the children that!"

This bias was no mere accident; it was part of a deliberate Jordanian policy of playing down our Palestinian identity. There was almost no mention of our history, no glorification of our heroes. Instead, there were great and elaborate celebrations of Jordan's national holidays, of Hussein's "Jordanian revolution." Our own rich and splendid folklore was thrust aside, and great stress was placed on the Bedouin traditions of Transjordan. Not sufficient that our Palestinian identity was camouflaged by Jordanian citizenship and Jordanian passports; they wanted to give our Palestinian children a Jordanian soul.

But now, after the occupation, this Israeli attempt to interfere in our schools was far worse. Whatever our disagreements with the Jordanians, whatever the resentments we bore against them—and they were many!—the Jordanians were still Arabs. And while we disliked the Jordanian authorities' intervention in our schools, the present Israeli attempt to dictate the curriculum was intolerable.

The reaction among many Palestinian teachers and parents was fierce. "Under such circumstances," they said, "it is better not to send our children to school at all! Better that they should grow up to be ignorant laborers rather than see them alienated from their people!" This view had numerous proponents, the most prominent being Yussra Salah, who was a senior inspector for the Jordanian Ministry of Education; with such vigorous objections, it seemed clear that the schools would not be reopened.

While public opinion in general was quite in agreement with this decision, many parents were worried about the fate of their children. Would they then be allowed to grow up without schooling? The extremists answered with a clear and ringing "Yes!" citing the example of Europe during World War II where many children missed years of schooling as a result of occupation and resistance. But however satisfactory this was as a political answer, it did not allay the anxieties of parents. Those families that could afford to do so arranged for their children to go to school in Jordan or Lebanon. There were even some parents who sent their children to boarding schools in England or other parts of Europe.

I, too, faced the dilemma. My eldest daughter, Dianna, was eight; she needed and deserved to go to school. Could I deprive her of this right? And for how long? On the other hand, the idea of sending her off to boarding school at such a young age was a horrifying thought. I could not help remembering the tragic circumstances under which I, too, had been sent off, as a small child; I thought of my suffering and loneliness, far from my beloved home and parents. How could I do the same thing to my own daughter? But what choice remained? In the end, with great reluctance, I had to face reality, and Dianna was registered for boarding school.

When it became known that the wealthy families planned to send their children abroad—with the rest of the population, of course, unable to afford such a luxury—there was widespread resentment among middle- and lower-class families. The decision not to reopen the schools had been adopted as a general consensus, but when it came to implementing the decision, the poorer people were left to carry the burden, while the rich could afford to protect their children from the effects of the boycott. This blatant unfairness altered the climate of public opinion, making it possible for other voices to be heard.

Right from the start, the decision not to reopen the schools had found a most distinguished opponent: Kadri Tukan, a former Jordanian foreign minister and at that time the founder and director of Nablus' Najah College. Shortly after the 1948 debacle, Tukan published a remarkable book that tried, honestly and frankly, to analyze the reasons for the Arab downfall. The book came to the clear conclusion that the Jews were a modern, well-educated people with an extensive mastery of modern technology, while we Arabs were ignorant and backward, with little or no access to modern thought and techniques. His conclusion was clear: The Arabs would never gain or maintain their rights unless they moved into the modern era— and for this, the prime requisite was good education for our young people. It was this view that motivated him in founding the college he directed; and now, following the same line of thought, he spoke out most forcefully and eloquently against the decision to close the schools. His view was backed by Hamdi Kna'an, the mayor of

Nablus. Both men urged that the schools be reopened, making every effort to prevent, or at least minimalize, Israeli intervention in the curriculum.

The debate was fierce and angry, but gradually opinion shifted in favor of reopening the schools. The Israeli authorities, anxious to show that the situation was returning to "normal," seemed ready to withdraw their more extreme demands. After some long and stubborn arguments with Israeli officials, the military government agreed to permit the schools to follow the Jordanian curriculum as before; as for the textbooks, it was finally agreed to withdraw one or two—more as a face-saving gesture for the Israelis than because they really found these books so objectionable. The schools were reopened.

This debate was a good political lesson for us. It showed that even under Israeli occupation, we could continue a normal way of life, without surrendering our national pride or groveling before the occupation authorities. But while the majority of public opinion in Nablus saw the whole affair as having reached a satisfactory and even victorious conclusion, there were some diehards who remained unreconciled, terming the reopening of the schools a "surrender." Yussra Salah, who had been so prominent in the campaign, refused to accept the decision; she left her post as school inspector and has never returned to her former educational work.

One day not long after the war, I heard a knocking at the door early in the morning. When I looked out of the window, I was frightened: Outside our house stood a car with Israeli plates. I did not know whether or not to open, but in the end I plucked up my courage and went to the door. It was my first cousin, Amel, from Kfar Yassif in Israel, who had come to Nablus with her husband to see whether I was safe. I welcomed them into the house, but even my pleasure at seeing them again did not allow me to forget that my neighbors would draw their own conclusions on seeing an Israeli car parked outside my house. My forebodings proved correct. Once again, I encountered hostile glances from people who suspected me of "treason" and "collaboration." There was worse to come.

One day Hamdi Kna'an told me that an Israeli officer had inquired about me. There were several other people present when he told me of this, and I caught their angry, suspicious glances fixed on me. It was not hard to guess what they were thinking: If Israelis are asking about Raymonda, that probably means she's a spy! As I sensed this unspoken accusation, I blushed in confusion, but then Hamdi Kna'an told me the name of the Israeli, and I forgot myself sufficiently to let out a shriek of joy. It was Mishka Fuchs, the director of the Acre Museum, a man I knew well from my childhood. I was so pleased to hear from him and to know that he had inquired after me that I forgot for an instant that this was an enemy, an officer in the Israeli army of occupation that had taken over Nablus. Then, when I saw the looks on the faces of those around, I realized that I had blundered—but it was too late.

Such incidents placed me in a difficult, or even a dangerous, situation. Walking the streets or engaged in philanthropic work with the refugees and the destitute workers of Nablus, I saw the hostile glances being thrown at me, and even without being told, I could guess what was being said about me behind my back. Daily, I received visits from Israeli friends, Jews and Arabs; but whenever an Israeli car stopped in front of my house, I knew that it would bring me both joy and pain—the joy of greeting old friends whom I had not seen for ten years and the pain of knowing that the visit would be misinterpreted by my friends and neighbors in Nablus, who could not comprehend why I was "welcoming the enemy." At one time, there was even a rumor making the rounds of Nablus that I had held a party for Israeli officers! My status and my relatively prominent social position in the town made me a prime target for such attacks.

One day we found a letter in our mailbox. It was brief and to the point. In harsh words, the letter condemned me and my family for our contacts with the occupation authorities, for receiving Israelis in our home, and for going on a visit to enemy territory—namely, Acre. The text was crudely written, in a schoolchild's writing; but the signature was ominous: Fatah!

It was frightening to receive such a warning—even though I am not sure to this day whether it was, indeed, sent by the Palestinian resistance. But together with my fear, I also felt a deep anger. What the hell do these people think?! Didn't they know that Acre is my own hometown? As for my contacts with the Israeli authorities, they were made primarily to ensure bread for the refugees. Should I have left them to starve?

Da'ud was upset by the letter. He is a peace-loving man, and the warning made him lose his nerve. "This is the reward for all your activities! Your help to the refugees has brought us disaster! What if something happens to us? We have small children to look after!"

"But I had to do something, didn't I?" I countered.

"Why can't you behave like the others?" Da'ud asked. "Sit still, keep quiet! What about all these women all around? Why didn't they go to the Israeli governor on behalf of the refugees? Now we are the 'traitors' and 'collaborators' because of your behavior! Take care of your own children. Charity begins at home!"

The letter and Da'ud's panic-stricken reaction, coming on top of the general hostility I sensed around me, placed me in a serious dilemma. On the one hand, I feared that something might happen to us. But on the other hand, I did not think that I was doing anything wrong. I remembered my mother's behavior under similar circumstances in 1948, and I resolved to follow her example. If I could save a life by speaking with an Israeli officer or making use of his car, then a soul was gained and humanity strengthened. I remembered Pearl Buck and her story of the Japanese family that received an American soldier while fighting was in progress. I was deeply affected by this story, which fortified the Christian ethics I had received from my French nun teachers.

But my attitude was not well received by my acquaintances. "Occupation is occupation!" they declared flatly. "We should take the path of passive resistance and reject the occupation. If an Israeli says 'Good morning,' we should not respond! That is the correct way to behave."

Ever since then, there have been two schools of thought. I continued with my approach, believing in dialogue, even with enemies and adversaries. But there were those who opposed any contact: "The Israeli with whom you want to make dialogue is in uniform and carrying a gun!" they used to taunt me.

But that was only one of the many questions that arose in connection with the Israeli occupation.

While the intellectuals debated how to face the challenge of the occupation, some of the young people found a clear answer: armed resistance. The guerrillas, the Palestinian fedayeen, were already in action. The first group crossed the Jordan River in June, and there were soon clashes with Israeli troops. As the news went around, it boosted morale. After the disastrous humiliation of our defeat in the June War, when Israel had crushed the Arab armies, we lost all hope, all confidence in ourselves. The fact that after the Arab defeat Palestinians had taken up arms restored our sense of dignity and self-respect. We did not care which groups they belonged to— Fatah, Popular Front, or Jabril—for us, they were all fedayeen, and they earned our love and esteem.

The Israeli response was prompt and vigorous. Israeli troops and police conducted extensive hunts for the fedayeen, demolishing houses where they took shelter or hid their arms. The occupation authorities imposed severe punishment on anyone who offered help to the fedayeen, trying to intimidate people so that they would refuse to open their doors to the guerrillas. But the Israelis overlooked Arab tradition, which makes it unthinkable to refuse food or water to a passerby in need, even if he is an enemy. The Israelis themselves benefited from our hospitality. For example, they established a checkpoint near our house, and I myself often brought the astonished Israeli soldiers tea or coffee.

But there was an even more striking example. Early one morning, there was an accident outside our house. I awoke to the children's screams and hurried outside in my dressing gown. It was a misty morning, and an Israeli military car had collided with an electricity pylon. I hurried over to the damaged vehicle and asked the soldiers if they were all right. Did they need any help? Da'ud brought them first aid to care for their injuries. They were not badly hurt, but our response seemed to cause them as great a shock as the accident itself. I could see them thinking: "These people are our enemies, and yet they come out to help us!" Thanking us, they went off to find help, leaving one of the soldiers to guard the car. We invited him into the house, gave him breakfast, and plied him with tea and coffee. The hours passed, and the others did not return. Clearly, the nervous soldier did not understand what we were up to; cautiously, he asked several times whether we were, indeed, Arabs. I spoke to him in Hebrew, to reassure him—but it was a long time before he overcame his fear. In the end, I picked up the phone and called the military governor, Sha'ul Giv'oli, telling him of the plight of the soldier. Giv'oli, too, was astonished by our behavior. "I have no words to express my thanks," he said in wonder. "You have been leading strikes and protests against us, and yet you looked after one of our soldiers." Later he sent one of his officers to thank us personally.

Such was our attitude toward Israeli soldiers, who were enemies, a foreign army of occupation. How, then, did the Israelis expect a Palestinian to refuse his help to the hunted fedayeen? All the same, whenever the military authorities found someone who had helped the guerrillas, they did not hesitate to demolish his house in reprisal, even if he had done nothing more than offer a man a glass of water.

All our sympathies lay with the guerrillas. They emerged at a time when our morale was low, when we had lost our self-respect. My Israeli Arab friends told me that prior to the June War, when Israeli Jews feared their country was about to be overrun by the Arab armies, there were some Jews who asked Arabs whether they would shelter them in their homes in such an event. But now, after the Arab defeat, they were ashamed to be Arabs, because the Israelis looked down upon them. In the Israelis' everyday language, the word *Arab* became a synonym for everything inferior or worthless. In my first contacts with Israeli Jews, I was deeply aware of the humiliation of belonging to a defeated nation, while in their faces I read the pride of triumph and victory. How I envied them!

In this atmosphere of gloom, the fedayeen were our only hope, the only ray of light that encouraged us and restored a feeling of our own worth. There were some people who cast doubt on the value of the fedayeen's operations inside the occupied territories. If the Arab regular armies failed to stand up to Israel, what hope was there that the guerrillas could do better? They pointed to the heavy losses the fedayeen suffered inside the occupied territories or in the Israeli reprisal raids on guerrilla camps in Jordan. But even the skeptics and pessimists were convinced when they saw how the Israelis were concerned by the fedayeen attacks, how they had to bring in large forces to cope with them, and how much trouble they took in defensive precautions.

I have never made any secret of my sympathies for the fedayeen. Why, then, didn't I join the underground? There are a number of reasons. Most of the fedayeen were young—men and women in their early twenties or even teen-agers. Unlike them, I had to consider my responsibilities toward my children; could I risk depriving them of their mother? This was not the only hindrance: I had deep moral scruples about violence. I know that in the face of oppression, acts of violence are unavoidable; they are necessary or even laudable. But nevertheless, I found it hard to contemplate actions that would cause bloodshed. But with all my dislike of force, there were numerous occasions when the behavior of the Israeli occupation authorities aroused me to fury. Angered by their acts of repression—the arrests, the torture, the demolition of houses, the land confiscations—I would gladly have seized a bomb and flung myself at the enemy, regardless of the cost.

One of the high points of the fedayeen operations was the three-day battle that raged in Nablus. Underground members launched grenade attacks on Israeli patrols and fired at them from points of ambush. In retaliation, the Israelis brought in large forces to hunt down the fedayeen. Tanks patrolled the city, firing in all directions to intimidate the population. The shooting went on all night; we slept on the floor for greater protection, with the children crying for fear. It was terrifying: At any moment, we expected a tank to fire into our house and bring the roof down over our heads.

The following day, the enraged population of Nablus took to the streets to protest the behavior of the military forces. The mayor of Nablus threatened to resign if the Israeli troops continued their acts of intimidation against the civilian population. "We civilians are not responsible for the actions of the guerrillas!" the mayor said when Moshe Dayan came to the city that day. The protests did no good: That night, the Israeli forces continued their patrols, again firing indiscriminately whenever they thought something was moving.

The clashes went on for three days. It was rumored that Yassir Arafat was himself in Nablus, personally commanding the fedayeen unit. In the end, the Israeli forces tracked down the guerrillas. These included the Hawash brothers: They were killed in the fighting, and the next day their home was demolished in revenge for their attacks on the Israeli forces. In memory of the Hawash brothers, that clash was referred to as the Hawash Night. Even though the guerrillas suffered a tactical defeat, their daring in taking on the vastly superior Israeli forces made a deep impression on the population of Nablus.

The fedayeen's operations had a powerful impact on the population of the occupied territories. It was more than a tonic to restore our national pride and self-respect—the fedayeen organizations jolted Palestinian society out of its conservative attitudes of mind. In the first fedayeen attack inside Israel after the occupation, a young Palestinian nurse from Kalkilya threw a hand grenade into the Zion

Cinema in Jerusalem. She was caught and sentenced to life imprisonment, but her deed inspired many young people to join the fedayeen. She was followed by many others, most of them girls from bourgeois families.

For a Palestinian woman it was a revolutionary act to join actively in the armed struggle. Weapons are man's monopoly; war is his domain—and women have no business with either. But under the shock of the occupation these young girls—many of them teenagers—threw off the modesty and submissiveness that are the conventional virtues of Arab women. In taking up arms against Israel, they were simultaneously rebelling against our own society and its repressive traditions. Arab conventions were suddenly confronted with a new and splendid image of a genuinely emancipated woman. The Palestinian revolutionary organizations put forward a program for sexual equality, and that was more than a mere scrap of paper: Equality of the sexes became a reality in the ranks of the resistance. I myself saw young men of the fedayeen, on trial before the Nablus military tribunal, stand up and give a military salute to their leader, a girl. Such a tribute symbolized the revolution that was shaking the very foundations of our society. This was a change of a most far-reaching and fundamental nature, and it was hard to imagine that Arab society could ever be the same again.

It was not the resistance alone that revolutionized the status of Arab women. Before the June War, we used to believe that progress would come to the Arab world by way of industrialization and socialism. Unintentionally, the Israeli occupation also brought about considerable progress. The sharp change in the status of Arab women came, above all, by virtue of the prominent role they played in the resistance organizations, but we should not forget the women who went to work in Israeli factories. The Palestinian women did not enjoy the full rights granted to Israeli women workers; they worked hard for low wages, and they had to put up with hostility and even humiliation. Nevertheless, they were working in a society that does not despise work; inevitably their own self-esteem rose. Although their Israeli bosses exploited them, they also gave these women the feeling that they were productive and even indispensable. Most of these women came from refugee camps; they were under the domination of their menfolk—fathers, brothers, or husbands. Previously, if they went out to work at all, it was as domestic servants, where they were, again, misused and exploited in undignified labor. But now, many of these women told me that working in the Israeli factories gave them a new sense of their own worth. In many cases, they were the only wage earners in their family, and it was precisely this new role as breadwinner that imposed a great responsibility upon them and at the same time gave them a feeling of dignity that undermined the old patterns of male domination and female submissiveness.

Of course, old habits die hard, and the social and economic changes encountered resistance from the traditionalists, with their hidebound notions. I know of a girl who worked in an Israeli factory; while she was there, she had an affair and became pregnant. Arab tradition is extremely harsh with a young woman who "loses her honor." In this case, the disgrace is not hers alone—her whole family is brought into disrepute, and it therefore falls upon the family to expunge its dishonor by killing the miscreant. The terrified girl knew only too well what was in store for her: Consequently, she delivered secretly and immediately killed the newborn baby. Her deed was discovered, and she was tried and sentenced to imprisonment. A friend of mine, a social worker, who visited her in prison, told me that the girl's principal concern is for what will happen to her when she completes her sentence. Prison, with all its rigors and confinement, is a sanctuary for her; she fears that when she is released, her relatives will kill her so as to redeem the family's honor.

But this case and others of the same nature, however painful, could not reverse the general trend toward emancipation that was speeded up by the new conditions after 1967. The status of women used to be an academic debating point, little more. But now, under these new circumstances, the time for talking had gone. In the past, I saw men as being domineering and powerful, but the defeat of 1967 was, to a large extent, the defeat of Arab *men*. Now, for the first time, I saw men humiliated and powerless. I saw them during the exodus that followed the war, men trudging dejectedly while the women followed, carrying their babies. Watching this dismal sight, I thought how powerless we humans are. Only God is strong; human beings should not flaunt their strength.

Men dominate our society. But they should remember that their strength derives from money, power, fame. Now the Arab defeat had stripped men of their power, demolishing many of the barriers between the sexes. Men and women faced one another, naked and undisguised.

In the past, men had tried to teach us women how to behave, in accordance with their version of the traditions of Islam and Christianity. Others had expressed seemingly more progressive views, but they, too, were tainted with the stereotypes of male-dominated Western liberalism. Whatever their views, whether conservative or "progressive," I have often noticed men's fear of women's emancipation. Even the most highly educated man seemed to fear the moment when his wife would throw off his yoke and liberate herself.

The Israeli occupation changed many things; even though it was a new form of external domination, it came as a symbolic break with the internal social repression of the past. We found ourselves at the collision point of two dissimilar civilizations. The culture and traditions we shared with the rest of the Arab world were confronted by Israeli culture, which we rejected as alien but which affected us nonetheless. Even though our girls did not immediately follow the example of the Israeli girls, who flaunted their miniskirts in our streets, the free, uninhibited behavior of the young Israelis, both men and women, in the long run made a deep and lasting impact on our social mores.

Ever since 1948, there had been a great upsurge in women's education. Even in villages and the more conservative towns, there was a greater awareness of the need for education, and girls in the thousands left to study at foreign universities. Leaving behind the traditional passivity of the Arab woman, these girls went off—with the consent of the most conservative families—to undertake vocational training, to pass their exams and qualify as teachers or in other professions. The process did not end there. In the emancipated and relatively liberal atmosphere of Beirut, where many of them studied, these girls learned many new things: new fashions and customs, new ways of behavior and a new, freer culture. After throwing themselves into the intellectual and political activities of foreign universities, they came home with new ways of thought, new ideologies. Imbibing new revolutionary theories, they were deeply impressed by the wave of self-criticism sweeping the Arab world. They read the book of Dr. Sadek Jalal al-Aze, who criticized the Arab policies that had led to the defeat of 1967. On their return home, they sought ways to express their revolutionary creativity. Some women voiced their opposition to occupation in speeches and writing. The local newspapers began to publish what was, in effect, a women's resistance literature.

But for many women, words—whether spoken or written—were not enough. One day, a schoolgirl came to our door collecting money for a needy family. She was seventeen years old with a very striking appearance: Her green school apron set off her golden blonde hair and large turquoise eyes. Such types are rare among our people. Much taken by her looks, I asked her name. She was Miriam Shakshir, the daughter of a wealthy Nablus merchant. I was soon to hear that name again: Miriam joined the resistance, and undertook a dangerous mission. She placed a bomb in the library of the Hebrew University. In the resulting explosion, two Israeli students were killed, and others were wounded. Miriam was arrested and sentenced to life imprisonment. In prison, her health broke down. According to latest reports, she now weighs less than eighty pounds. She is literally dying by inches. Appeals for her release have come from all over the world, but the Israeli authorities have rejected them all.

Recently, a friend of mine visited Ramleh Jail, where Miriam is imprisoned. After seeing the girl's state, she appealed to one of the jail officials to procure her release. "Let her at least die at home!" she urged. The official showed compassion: "I want to see her released, believe me; it hurts me to see her suffering." But another Israeli official, at Nablus Jail, was quite unmoved by the account of Miriam's agony. "Let her be punished every day, and then those whose children were killed in the explosion will have their revenge." Two Israelis—two entirely different attitudes.

The prominent role played by women in the resistance made a strong impact on Palestinian society. I made it a regular habit to attend the sessions of the Nablus military court, where the Israelis tried young resistance fighters; I witnessed many unforgettable scenes. One of the striking aspects of the trials was the attitude of the families, especially when the accused were girls. In the past, an Arab father's principal concern was for his daughter's "honor"—in other words, for her virginity. When a friend of mine, Rada al-Nabulsi, was brought to court, she told the judges how her interrogators had tried to rape her. She spoke openly and without equivocation, even though she knew that her family was sitting in the courtroom and listening to every word. In the middle of her description, her father stood up and hurried out of the courtroom, crying bitterly. Her mother and sister remained in their places; they, too, were weeping. It was a horrifying description; even strangers were shocked.

In using such methods, the Israeli interrogators were obviously relying on the Arab woman's traditional obsession with her feminine honor and virginity. They knew that this was a potential weak point, and they would threaten a woman prisoner with "disgrace" unless she consented to answer their questions. But these unscrupulous tactics were no longer as effective as they had been in the past. For example, the interrogators believed that Rasmiyah Oudeh knew the whereabouts of an ammunition store, and in trying to force her to reveal what she knew, they threatened to rape her with a metal rod. The threat—fortunately, it was not carried out—failed to break her spirit, and she refused to divulge her secret. It was not she alone who suffered—her house was demolished, and her family was turned out into the street.

Throwing aside conventional thinking, the families gave their full moral support to the young girls in the resistance. Fathers cared more for their daughters' strength of character in facing the ordeals imposed by the occupation authorities than for the old concepts of "honor" or "disgrace." Honor lies in defending the motherland, and fathers were proud to have daughters in the resistance. Some families, previously unknown, gained honor and respect by virtue of the courage of their daughters. "These girls are the spirit of the revolution," said one sheikh whose niece was a resistance member. Even when it became known that boys and girls were training together in the same camps, there was no criticism, though such a thing would have been considered taboo a few years previously.

The Israelis did not comprehend this change in our mentality. Their propaganda tried to depict the girls of the resistance as "prostitutes" because they had disregarded traditional Arab conventions. But Palestinian public opinion did not fall for this trick. On the contrary, it boomeranged. I was pleased to see how furiously people reacted against such stories.

Not all women took an active part in the operations of the resistance. But the example of Rasmiyah Oudeh and heroines of her caliber radicalized all Palestinian women; this new revolutionary consciousness overshadowed the differences between men and women, sweeping away hidebound traditions. We encountered far less male antagonism against women taking an active political role. Men who had previously opposed all progressive ideas now made no secret of their admiration for our struggles.

The first large protest action by women took place in 1968, after the Israeli authorities arrested a large number of resistance members, including some thirty women, mostly girls in their late teens or early twenties. The women were brutally tortured under interrogation.

The detainees included Issam Abed al-Hadi, vice-president of the Arab Women's Union and president of the PLO's women's organization. She was arrested together with her sixteen-year-old daughter. When the Israeli interrogators failed to break the mother's resistance, they subjected her daughter to torture. Unable to bear her daughter's sufferings, Issam Abed al-Hadi flung herself forward, offering herself to be tortured in her place. One interrogator hit Mrs. Abed al-Hadi over the head, and blood poured down her face.

The Israeli authorities did not confine their vindictive behavior to the detainees. Israeli patrols roamed the streets of Nablus, brutalizing passersby, beating them indiscriminately, to "teach the population a lesson" for its continued opposition. At the same time, orders were issued to demolish the homes belonging to the families of the detainees. Among those arrested were three Nabulsi sisters, who belonged to a prominent and wealthy family that owned a beautiful mansion in the center of Nablus. The Jordanian government had planned to make it into a museum, and indeed the house was a veritable showpiece, featuring exquisite Oriental architecture and mosaics. It had ten rooms in each of the three stories, and they were full of Louis XIV furniture. But the authorities disregarded aesthetic values: This house, too, was destined for demolition, along with some twenty others. The Israelis placed guards all around while the furniture was carried out in preparation for the demolition.

Under the impact of these dramatic events, public opinion in Nablus was in an uproar. Stories were leaking out about the mistreatment of the prisoners. On top of that, the impending demolitions would make many families homeless. Enraged by the heartless attitude of the military authorities, there was a widespread call for action of some sort.

Most of the girls arrested belonged to middle-class families; their mothers and aunts were of a generation whose women had never taken any active political role. But now, with the awareness of what was happening in the Israeli interrogation centers, these women were prepared to do almost anything for their daughters and nieces. In the same way that these women were politicized, the women's philanthropic organizations, previously nonpolitical welfare associations, now suddenly became the focus and principal channel of protests. This is not to be wondered at: Overt political organizations had always been banned, under Jordanian rule too, and the women's charitable groups were among the few public bodies that were large, well-organized, and cohesive. Under the pressures of the occupation regime, these groups now took on tasks they had never dreamed of before.

The prime mover in organizing the protest was Haula Abed al-Hadi (one of the founders of the Sons of the Martyrs, a society that aided the dependents of fallen resistance fighters; the society was later banned by the Israelis). She called on me to help her, asking me to take on the task of contacting the Israeli and foreign media representatives, to ensure that our protest would be heard. Thrilled by the opportunity to make my contribution, I flung myself into the task with all my energy.

I had long been in contact with foreign journalists; even before 1967 many of them visited my home. Formerly, my "foreign connections" had been frowned upon; now, however, they were to prove invaluable. I picked up the phone and began calling up acquaintances in Jerusalem. One of my first calls was to Mr. Sutherland, the new United States consul. When he grasped what I wanted—I asked him to send Western newsmen to cover our protests—he was furious at me for asking him to undertake an active political role, which could give the Israelis a pretext to ask for his recall. But the newsmen I contacted were more forthcoming, and many of them promised to come to Nablus and send eyewitness reports to their newspapers and radio and TV stations.

I did not rest content with calling up Western newsmen. I felt bound to make an appeal to the progressive and liberal elements in Israeli public opinion too. Surely some Israelis must oppose the brutal policies of their government! And it was vital to mobilize their support, first and foremost by bringing the facts to their attention. At that time, my relations with Israelis were of a personal, haphazard nature; I had few contacts with public figures or people connected with the media. But as I racked my brains, two names came into my mind: Abdul Aziz Zuabi and Uri Avneri.

Zuabi was a prominent Israeli Arab, a member of the leftist Mapam party. Other Arabs often criticized and attacked Zuabi for belonging to a Zionist party, but he was following his own convictions, and he utilized his position inside Mapam to fight for the rights of the Israeli Arabs. I had met him when I was a child; he had been very helpful, first to Mother and later to me, when I wanted to leave Israel in 1957. I now renewed my contact with him, asking him to come to Nablus. He listened carefully and promised to come.

Uri Avneri was well known to me by name and reputation. Wounded in the 1948 war while serving in the Israeli army, the editor of the *Ha'Olam Hazeh* weekly had long made a name for himself as an inveterate opponent of the Israeli establishment. Adopting unorthodox tactics and making the most of his flamboyant, sometimes sensationalist weekly, he uncovered abuses and injustices in Israeli society, nettling the authorities with his well-researched and embarrassingly accurate revelations. In 1965, Avneri stood for election to the Israeli legislature, the Knesset; running as an independent, he succeeded in getting himself elected, and he continued his antiestablishment campaign, almost single-handed, inside the legislature. When I contacted Avneri at the Knesset, he, too, listened carefully to what I had to say. Then, speaking very clearly and distinctly, he promised to come to Nablus the next day, at nine o'clock in the morning.

In addition to Zuabi and Avneri, I wanted to contact the Israeli Communist party. I had great respect for the Israeli Communists, for their prolonged and heroic defense of Arab rights. But I did not contact them at this time because I knew that this would provoke the most violent reaction on the part of the Israeli occupation authorities, who hated and feared the Communists.

While I was busy phoning, news of the projected protest spread around Nablus. It was decided to make this an action by women alone. This was done to reduce the risk of bloodshed, and also because, in many families, the man was the only breadwinner—if he were to be arrested, his dependents would face disaster.

At the appointed time, seven hundred women entered the Nablus municipality and settled down for an all-night vigil. There was an air of excitement and tension, an exhilaration and a fear of the un-known. The protest of the population of Nablus was being spear-headed by *women*. How daring! But how would the military government respond to our challenge? Hitherto, the Israelis had dealt firmly and brutally with any signs of defiance. How would they react when they encountered nonviolent resistance on this scale? Would they be more considerate with us because we were women?

I stayed in the municipality until late in the evening, but I decided not to spend the night there. At that time, my youngest daughter was still small, and I decided to sleep at home. Bidding farewell to my friends, I went home and made some more phone calls. Finally, late at night, agitated and exhausted, I lay down to sleep. At five o'clock in the morning, there was a knocking at the door. A messenger had come from the municipality, sent by Haula Abed al-Hadi. "Come quickly! Uri Avneri has arrived with a whole group of journalists and photographers."

8

Confrontation and Dialogue: Encounters with Israelis

HALF ASLEEP, I dressed and hurried to the town hall. When I got there, I found Uri Avneri, together with several other journalists and cameramen—some from his own paper, others foreign newsmen who had accompanied him. One of the *Ha'Olam Hazeh* journalists was Iraqi-born, and he served as interpreter while the journalists interviewed the women, who were not slow to take advantage of their sympathetic ears. Dozens of women crowded around, each one eager to tell her story. Some told of the ill-treatment of their imprisoned sons and daughters; others had their own personal sufferings to describe, after the rough behavior of Israeli military patrols in recent days. One of the journalists—John Wallace of the *Daily Telegraph*—was talking to me when, suddenly, he uttered a cry of astonishment. "Look!" he whispered to me, "those women are lifting their dresses right up to show the bruises on their bodies—and they've completely forgotten that they're veiled!"

Everyone tried to make the journalists understand the urgency of the situation. We took Avneri and the others to see the houses that had been marked for demolition; they went inside, listened to our explanations, took pictures, and made notes.

The morning dragged on. Then, shortly before nine o'clock, Israeli soldiers appeared and threw a cordon around the town hall. When we asked their officer what they were doing, he told us they had been sent to "prevent Uri Avneri from entering the town hall." By this time, Avneri, having completed his visit, was seated in his car, about to leave the town. When he heard the soldiers explain their mission, he winked and smiled at me imperceptibly. Now I realized what he had done. Automatically assuming that his phone was tapped, he informed me that he was coming at nine—and then arrived four hours ahead of time, giving him a chance to slip through before access was blocked. Which goes to show that official wiretapping can be turned to an advantage at times.

Although Avneri himself left the town, he left behind some of his staff, and other journalists and media representatives began to appear. Despite the military cordon, we managed to make contact with them, and I was busy for hours on end, explaining why we were protesting, telling of the tortures and the projected demolitions of houses, answering journalists' questions, and guiding them around. The newsmen—both Israelis and foreigners—appeared shocked and surprised. But previous experience had taught me that the media in Israel and the West were far from friendly to our cause, and I wondered how much of what the journalists heard and saw would be published.

The sit-in went on all day, and the stream of foreign newsmen also continued unabated. Realizing what a bad effect this might have on public opinion, both abroad and within Israel, the Israeli military authorities showed signs of growing nervousness. Finally, in the afternoon, an officer approached the town hall and ordered us to leave. We argued with him, but he was adamant; we had to leave the building. Since the sit-in was originally planned for only twenty-four hours, we did not offer too much opposition. At the same time, we did not want to end our protest by what could be interpreted as a humiliating capitulation. Accordingly, we told the officer that we would leave the building on condition that he withdrew his men who were surrounding it. Eager to get the matter settled as quickly as possible, the officer consented, and the Israeli soldiers pulled back.

This was our opportunity. We left the building, but not—as the officer probably imagined—with the intention of dispersing quietly to our homes. Instead, we marched out en masse and strode down the street, where thousands of additional women swiftly joined our ranks to produce the biggest protest demonstration held in Nablus since the occupation. We marched through the streets of the city, chanting Palestinian national slogans, clapping, and singing. It was a mighty sight, and I sensed a great feeling of pride when I looked around me at those women who only a short time ago had been submissive, meek housewives and students, and who now, before my eyes, had turned overnight into the proud, militant champions of our people's dignity and freedom.

Although we experienced a great exhilaration as we strode along in our thousands, we knew that the Israeli authorities would not allow the march to continue. We had won a brief tactical victory when the soldiers withdrew from the town hall, but the military authorities would surely strike back as soon as they overcame their surprise. As the Israeli response would probably be violent, I hoped there were media representatives present who would be able to give an eyewitness account.

We reached the main square of the city, and I was not surprised to find large numbers of soldiers with shields and clubs sitting in jeeps waiting for us. As the marchers filled the square, a loudspeaker blared above our chanting, ordering us to leave immediately: "If you do not disperse, we shall shoot!" There was no time to think about heeding the warning. Without giving us a moment to obey, the soldiers leaped out of their jeeps and flung themselves at the marchers. Swinging their clubs, they beat everyone who stood in their path, kicking and trampling women who fell to the ground. Although we outnumbered the soldiers, they were armed and organized, and we found ourselves defenseless before the onslaught.

It was an awful scene. The yells and curses of the soldiers mingled with the cries of women. Unarmed as they were, some of the women tried to grapple with the soldiers. One of them, Samoa Toukan, was arrested and later tried for assault.

Near me, a woman fainted. I went to help her up. While I bent over, I felt a violent blow on my back as a soldier brought his club down on my back. The pain ran through my whole body, bringing tears to my eyes. But outrage was greater than the physical discomfort. How dare they! How could they send armed soldiers to beat women!

This use of force was on personal orders from Israeli Defense Minister Moshe Dayan. But the episode was not one of his more glorious victories. Although our demonstration was broken up, we did not consider ourselves defeated. The next day, newspapers all over the world carried eyewitness reports from the journalists, who described our protest and gave prominent coverage to our grievances. Photographs showing the soldiers beating women demonstrators sharply altered the generally favorable view of Israel's "chivalrous" army. The whole episode considerably tarnished Israel's reputation in world public opinion and was an important step in bringing about an awareness of the Palestinians' plight.

I had my personal gratification too. In the past, my "foreign contacts" had brought me under criticism from nationalists who considered me wanting in patriotism. Now, I had my vindication: These very contacts had proved invaluable in furthering the Palestinian cause.

The message also got through to Israeli public opinion. The following issue of Avneri's weekly, *Ha'Olam Hazeh,* gave a detailed account of our protest, accompanied by pictures of Israeli troops beating demonstrators. Avneri himself had good reason for his sympathetic coverage: Several years previously, he personally was mishandled by the police while protesting the Israeli government's repression of its Arab citizens, as well as during demonstrations against discriminatory religious laws. His paper was the first to present Israeli public opinion with frank and undistorted reports of what was happening in the occupied territories, and his revelations were to have a major impact on liberal and progressive Israelis.

Avneri did not remain content with his journal's disclosures. Taking advantage of his position as a member of Knesset, he voiced his protest in the Israeli legislature. He was particularly eloquent and indignant on the issue of demolitions. Speaking of the Nabulsi mansion, he warned that its demolition would leave, in the center of Nablus, a mark of disgrace that would overshadow all hopes of future cooperation and peace between the two peoples.

Avneri was not the only Israeli Knesset member to offer his help. While we were still in the town hall, before the protest march, news was brought to me that Abdul Aziz Zuabi had arrived in Nablus and was at my home. I invited him to come to the municipality, but he declined the invitation; this was occupied territory, he told the messengers, and he, as a member of the Knesset, refused to come to the town hall. There was nothing to do but send a delegation of women to my house, where they answered Zuabi's questions and gave him full details of our demands. Zuabi promised to present our case to the Ministry of Defense, and he kept his word. As a member of Mapam, backed by Mordechai Bentov, a leading Jewish member of the party, Zuabi succeeded in getting Mapam to use its influence to moderate some of the more blatant excesses.

Avneri's group and Mapam were not the only Israeli political groups to champion our case. The Israeli Communist party, Rakah (the only Israeli party with a significant number of Arab members), has a long and proud record of standing up for the rights of Arab citizens inside Israel. The party was tireless in defending Palestinian rights and always took a courageous stand on our behalf, which did not increase its popularity with the Israeli public. In consequence, the military authorities barred Rakah members from entering the occupied territories, and we therefore had fewer chances of direct contact with Rakah. Rakah's Arabic-language paper, *Al-Ittihad,* was also prohibited in the occupied territories. Palestinians who received *Al-Ittihad* from Israeli friends were punished by the military tribunals. Despite these obstacles, we made the acquaintance of Rakah by way of the defiant works of the poets Tufik Zayyad, Mahmoud Darwish, and Samih al-Kassem. Their poems, smuggled through to us, were soon on everyone's lips, raising our morale and fortifying our resistance. Later, the military authorities reduced their restrictions on Rakah in the occupied territories, and we established close contact.

As a result of the publicity we generated by our protest, the Israeli government was subjected to various internal pressures from prominent political personalities, from the media, and from progressive Israelis, as well as their counterparts abroad, to moderate its repressive practices in the occupied territories. There was no fundamental change in policies, which remained anti-Palestinian and expansionist, but some of the worst aspects were toned down, at least for a time. There was a reduction in demolitions and some improvement in the treatment of the imprisoned patriots. This taught us a most important lesson: that not all Israelis support their govern-

ment's policies in the West Bank and that, under appropriate circumstances, Israeli public opinion could be a valuable ally to our
cause if we could break through the iron curtain of total noncom-
munication dividing us from the people of Israel. This curtain had
been erected by both sides. I myself had encountered this deliberate
policy of intellectual boycott when crossing from Israel into Jordan
in 1957: The Jordanian authorities had refused to allow me to bring
in my books of Bialik's poetry because they were in Hebrew. Bialik's
works expressed the Jewish will to live and the longing of the exiled
Jews for their homeland. He wrote lyrical poems of great beauty
about the Judaean mountains and my own beloved Galilee. But
they were written in Hebrew, and for that reason the Jordanian authorities banned them.

This deliberately erected wall of ignorance was largely demolished by the 1967 war and the subsequent Israeli occupation of the
West Bank. For months after the occupation—in some cases, right
up to the present day—many Palestinian nationalists refused to
meet with Israeli Jews in any social context and declined any political discussion with them. Although there was great curiosity about
Israel, people from the West Bank generally preferred to satisfy
their interest by questioning Israeli Arabs. Many of these meetings
were held at my home.

In time, however, this artificial distinction became blurred. Under
the impact of the war, the occupation, and the direct face-to-face
confrontation with Israelis, there was a drastic shift in the Palestinian view of Israel and of the Israelis' will and ability to maintain
their independence. In the past, we all believed in the destruction of
the state of Israel. I remember a visit from a British member of Parliament, who heard a young doctor—a supporter of George Habash—proclaim that he would accept nothing less than the
destruction of Israel. The M.P. listened carefully, but he rejected the
notion, warning that proposing such an idea would harm the Palestinian cause itself. "Politics," he reminded the young man, "is the
art of the possible."

And indeed, with the progress of time, there was less talk of the
destruction of the state of Israel. The PLO put forward the slogan of
a "secular democratic state," in which Christians, Moslems, and
Jews would live together. This idea in turn is now being modified,
with growing support for the idea of a Palestinian state to be estab-

lished alongside the state of Israel, with the two sovereign entities seeking ways of peaceful coexistence and close cooperation; one day, the two states might merge into a federation of some kind, opening up the way for a nonviolent reunification of the whole of Palestine.

This change in views was far from easy. Under the frustration and sense of impotence evoked by the Arab defeat of 1967, and the aggressively expansionist policy followed by Israel since then, there was a widespread and deep-seated fear that Israel would try to fulfill the biblical prophecy of an empire stretching from "the Nile to the Euphrates." While the Arab states adopted the "three no's of Khartoum" (no negotiations, no peace treaty, no recognition), there was a similar mood of intransigence among the Palestinians of the occupied territories. Some of our people undertook shopping expeditions into Israel and frequented Israeli resorts or places of entertainment—to the glee of Israeli propagandists, who made much of the fact to enhance Israel's "benign" image. But public opinion in the West Bank generally condemned anything that smacked of collaboration with Israel. The general consensus was that our rights could be recovered only by force, and anyone who talked of a political settlement of the conflict was considered to be a traitor to the Palestinian cause.

A similar tangle of changing and conflicting attitudes existed—and exists to this day—among Israelis. Even Israeli liberal and leftist circles display many contradictory trends. I have already mentioned how Abdul Aziz Zuabi and Mordechai Bentov induced Mapam to use its influence in restraining the excesses of the military government. On one occasion, while with Zuabi at the Knesset, I met Me'ir Ya'ari, Mapam's venerable founder and leader. During our conversation, I waved my arm at the Knesset building and said, "How I wish we Palestinians could have a Knesset of our own!" Ya'ari put his arm around me and said, "Golda Meir denies the existence of a Palestinian people. At one time, the whole world denied the existence of the Jewish people. But we Jews fought and struggled, we didn't give up. And now we have a state of our own. If you Palestinians want it—if you believe in yourselves, if you wish it—no one can stand in your way!" He reminded me of the famous saying of Theodor Herzl, the founder of the Zionist movement: *"Im tirtzu, ain zu agada"* (If you wish it, it will not remain a fable).

I was deeply touched and affected by Ya'ari's understanding for our cause. But other members of his party displayed a rather more ambiguous attitude. For example, the military governor of Nablus at that time was Sha'ul Giv'oli, a member of Ya'ari's own Hashomer Hatzair kibbutz movement who adhered to Mapam. Early in the occupation, Giv'oli wrote an article for the Mapam newspaper. The article was translated into Arabic, and we read it with interest bordering on astonishment. In his article, Giv'oli described an incident in which he was driving along a road in the occupied territory when he came to an Israeli military checkpoint. A long line of Arab vehicles was parked before the barrier, waiting to pass, while the soldiers charged with manning it were besporting themselves in a neighboring orchard, stealing fruit from the trees. Giv'oli wrote that, on seeing this, he instantly gave orders for the barrier to be removed, and all the cars were allowed to proceed without further harassment. He concluded his article by writing that the Palestinian people had lost everything; the only thing left was their pride. If that pride, too, is taken from them, it should surprise no one if they succumb to rage and violence.

We were amazed to read such views from the pen of a man serving as military governor of an occupied town. Giv'oli frequently uttered similar liberal sentiments; on one occasion, I remember a young woman flinging at him, "I hate you! I don't want a mild military governor who smiles at us. I want one who behaves harshly, so that people learn to hate you!"

But Giv'oli's liberal talk was in flagrant contradiction to his deeds. As military governor, he loyally executed his government's policies, including deportations, imprisonment without trial, and the demolition of houses of suspects, some of whom were subsequently found innocent of any acts of violence.

Two days after the women's demonstration, I was called to Giv'oli's office, where he warned me to desist from my "inflammatory" behavior. I reminded him that Israel was a democratic country and that when I lived there, I had taken part in protests that were perfectly legal. "This is not Israel!" he retorted. "This is occupied territory!" He warned me to refrain from making contact with Israeli oppositionists, specifically mentioning Uri Avneri.

I decided not to take this "warning" passively. "Sha'ul Giv'oli," I said, "are you the same man who wrote that wonderful article in the newspaper? How do you explain the fact that you gave orders to your soldiers to beat women? I don't understand. I wish I hadn't read your stories; then I would be able to think of you as just another army officer, a 'man of iron.' "

He looked confused. "Those were orders from the minister of defense," he said stiffly.

"Do you have to obey blindly?" I persisted. "In that case, what is the difference between you and Dayan?" There was little he could say in reply. In effect, he could not deny that, with all his pleasant manner and his concern for our pride, he was a loyal tool of Dayan's policy.

Despite this argument, and many others that followed it, Giv'oli continued to pay routine visits to my home. In a way, his visits followed the precedent established by the previous Jordanian governor, who paid courtesy calls on prominent Christian families at Christmas and on Moslems at Ramadan. But that did not make them any more pleasant for us. As a representative of the army of occupation, I had no desire to have him as my guest. His visits were an imposition; he came uninvited, taking our hospitality for granted. Arab tradition made it hard for us to tell any caller that he was unwelcome. But later, when Giv'oli's successor, Segev, followed up a violent argument with me by declaring that he would never again visit our house, I rejoiced at being rid of this burden. As long as these visits persisted, they provoked repeated confrontations. We seized on every possible opportunity to protest to Giv'oli about the arbitrary arrests, the torture of detainees, and the continued demolition of suspects' houses. During one of Giv'oli's visits, one of our guests addressed him in a very frank and sincere manner.

"You and I," he said, "we're the same age, of the same intellectual level. We could be friends—if we were to meet on an equal basis. But you hold the gun, and I don't; you wear a uniform, and I don't; you were given the chance to defend your homeland—a unique privilege—I wasn't. Where is the justice? Last week, you and your government deported my best friends. Why? What have they done? They didn't use explosives, they only talked—about our destiny and our future. Your men gave me a warning too—for talking! How can I talk to you all when you hold the guns, you are my judges, free to judge me according to your whims and moods."

The debate raged back and forth. Giv'oli admitted that he did not wish to be doing his present job, he did not want to be part of an occupation army. "But we were forced into it!" he declared defensively. "We didn't declare war, the Arabs did. We had no alternative!"

If Giv'oli, the Jew with leftist pretensions, found himself in an untenable position in his arguments with Palestinian intellectuals, the situation was ten times worse for Abdul Aziz Zuabi, an Arab who nevertheless was elected to the Knesset as one of the representatives of a Zionist party. I first encountered Abdul Aziz when I was a young girl and enlisted his help in gaining permission to cross over into Jordan. Earlier, he had intervened on behalf of my mother when the Israeli authorities dismissed her from her post as a social worker on the grounds that she was a "security risk." After 1967, I ran into him again by chance in a Jerusalem restaurant; he was now well known, a member of the Knesset, but I was reassured and flattered when he recognized me, though he had last seen me as a teenage girl ten years previously. I must have made quite an impact on him, I thought coquettishly.

Following up on that chance encounter and on his sympathy during the women's demonstration, I invited him to Nablus, where I held a banquet in his honor. It was the least I could do to express my gratitude to him. In extending hospitality to Zuabi, I also offered the hand of friendship to his colleagues of Mapam and the periodical *New Outlook*. He brought his friends to our house, where we introduced them to leading citizens of Nablus. What began as tentative, cautious discussions soon developed into an extended dialogue, all the more fruitful because it was unofficial.

On one occasion, there was a direct confrontation between Zuabi and Hikmat al-Masri, a prominent Nablus politician and former Speaker of the Jordanian parliament. Al-Masri challenged Zuabi, asking him how he, as an Arab nationalist, could belong to Mapam, a party that is avowedly Zionist and, moreover, belongs to the ruling alignment and supports the Israeli government. "How can you consent to support a government founded on denying the rights of the Palestinian people?"

Zuabi was not shaken by this onslaught. Replying coolly, in a diplomatic fashion that testified to considerable political experience, he pointed out that Mapam is a left-wing party.

"What kind of 'left' is it when you are Zionist and support the state of Israel, which usurps Palestinian rights? You are a free-thinker—how can you convince yourself that justice can be transformed into injustice? That is the essence of Zionism."

Another guest asked Zuabi to explain the meaning of the term *Marxist-Zionist.* "Your party is represented in the Jewish Agency; Mapam kibbutzim are established on Arab land!"

Zuabi defended his party, pointing out that it protected the rights of Israel's Arab minority. But his defense, however eloquent and logical, could not entirely conceal his own inner confusion and the conflict of loyalties between his Arab nationalism and his Israeli citizenship, as expressed in his adherence to Mapam. Zuabi told of the struggles he and his Arab colleagues waged, of their endeavors to enlist the support of their party for Arab grievances. Not content with remaining on the defensive, he bitterly described how the 300,000 Arabs living in Israel had been abandoned by the Arab world. At best, they were forgotten, at worst, denounced as traitors. He told us of the hatred he encountered from Arabs when, on missions abroad, he defended the right of the Israeli people to self-determination.

The exchanges with Zuabi were often heated, and there were wide areas of disagreement. However, in the course of time, even if our positions remained far apart, we gradually began to comprehend each other's point of view. Despite our arguments, we all came to value Zuabi as a human being; later, when he became deputy minister of health, he made great efforts to help the West Bank population, and he earned widespread respect and love. When he died recently—still a relatively young man—his death was widely mourned on the West Bank, as well as by Israelis—Arabs and Jews.

In another meeting, when Zuabi was accompanied by Bentov and by Eliezer Be'eri, Mapam's "expert on Arab affairs," one of my friends got into a heated argument with Be'eri, condemning Mapam for its support for the aggressive Sinai campaign of 1956, for denying the rights of Palestinian refugees to repatriation, and for opposing Palestinian self-determination. "You are very clever in depicting Zionism with a liberal image," he said scornfully. "You meet foreign intellectuals like Sartre, Simone de Beauvoir; you present Arabs like Zuabi and Muhammad Watted as examples of Israel's democracy and socialism." Mapam, he pointed out, "supports the self-determination of peoples, opposes American intervention in

Vietnam; you even demonstrated against the military-government regulations imposed on Israeli Arabs—and yet you establish your kibbutzim on Arab land!"

Be'eri's response was rather patronizing, whereupon his adversary shouted: "You're not talking to the illiterate *mukhtars* [village heads] of the twenties! We are a new generation of Palestinians, equal to you in education and civilization and intellect. You're not talking to a colonized people! You can't make us forget our rights to our land!"

Although there were many sharp exchanges of this nature, the discussions continued. Aside from their value as a direct dialogue— however extreme the disagreements—there were many incidental benefits to these meetings.

The review *New Outlook* exercised a strong influence on progressive intellectuals all over the world. Visiting my home, foreign sympathizers of the periodical heard our criticisms of Mapam, listening carefully to our case. While we paid tribute to the actions of individual Mapam members like Bentov, Zuabi, Watted, Latif Dori, and others, we condemned Mapam's positions. To the credit of the *New Outlook*'s Israeli directors, they gave us a fair chance to present our opinions to their foreign visitors, thereby opening up important channels through which we could make our views known abroad.

My home became a unique center for informal dialogue. I hosted a constant stream of personalities of worldwide renown: Herbert Marcuse, Eric de Rothschild, Guy Penne (the personal assistant of Mitterand), university professors, scholars, writers, politicians, and members of parliaments of many lands, as well as socialist and progressive groups. My talks and discussions with these people provided me with an unusual opportunity to extend my political education.

At the same time that I was meeting these intellectual challenges, I was still subjected to criticism for my contacts with Israelis and other foreigners generally regarded as hostile. On top of all that, I was beset with my own doubts. Still laboring under the depression and heaviness of heart left by the Arab defeat of 1967, every day's news brought us new sorrows. There were daily clashes between the fedayeen and Israeli patrols, with young men maimed and killed on either side. These reports saddened me; my heart bled every time I heard of young Palestinians who had fallen in battle, and I found no consolation when the Israelis, too, paid with the blood of their young men.

Altogether, in spite of my profound admiration for the heroism of the fedayeen, in spite of everything my people have suffered at the hands of the Israelis, I harbored no vengeful or bloodthirsty feelings. A former military governor of Nablus, Segev, was later injured by a bomb explosion; his injuries led to the loss of a leg. When I heard the news, I exclaimed, *"Haram!"*—the Arabic call of grief and regret at a calamity. My companions were surprised and critical. Why did I express sorrow for this man who was—and remained—an enemy? During his period of office in Nablus, he had ordered arrests and carried out deportations and demolitions, as well as other acts of repression. I was well aware of all his evil deeds; at the same time, I could not forget his help when we were making efforts to acquire an artificial-kidney machine for the Nablus hospital. As long as he was in uniform, he was an enemy—but inside the uniform, he remained a man nonetheless. Time and time again, I encountered the same conflict—how to relate to an enemy as a human being? How to relate to a human being as an enemy?

If there is an experience designed to dehumanize us and obscure the "humanity" of the Israelis, it is crossing the Jordan bridges into Israeli-controlled territory. In itself, it is a bitter humiliation for a Palestinian, returning to his own home, to be forced to apply for a "permit" from the Israeli military authorities. As Palestinian "visitors," we find ourselves welcomed by some soldier or customs official, a Jewish newcomer from the Soviet Union speaking broken Hebrew, who wishes the arrivals "a pleasant stay in *our* country."

By the time we reach the Israeli side, we have endured an hours-long wait on the Jordanian side, in the blazing sun, without water or shade. At times, bureaucratic delays cause a holdup of several days on the Jordanian side, and a whole family can spend several nights sleeping in the open air so as not to lose its place in line. There have been numerous cases of newborn babies who, unable to endure the conditions in line, died in their mother's arms.

Irrespective of social class or the purpose of their journey, everyone has to stand in line while the Israelis conduct security checks. These are more than a mere formality: The arrivals are closely scrutinized and their names checked against detailed lists provided by the Shin Bet (Israeli intelligence). A person appearing on the list may receive permission to enter—and then promptly be taken off to spend his "holiday" in an Israeli jail, in retribution for his political activities in some Arab country. All too often, some long-awaited visitor—a son or brother returning after years of absence in the Gulf states—fails to arrive at the home of his family; and his worried relatives, after painstaking inquiries with the authorities, discover that he has been taken straight off the bridge and imprisoned for some "security offense" committed thousands of miles from Israeli territory.

Every time I cross the bridge, I witness the same kind of harassment: An old woman comes, bringing presents for her children; the Israeli official orders her to pay a sizable sum in customs duty. "I have no money, sir," she pleads.

"If you haven't got any money," shouts the soldier, "leave your goods here and go away!"

Despite all these sufferings and humiliations, we are expected to take it all silently and patiently, without uttering a word.

True, at the bridge there is a sign in Hebrew and Arabic advising those with complaints to direct them to the officer in charge of the bridge. But an old woman mutters an Arabic proverb, "A complaint that is not to God is a humiliation," and another chips in bitingly with another saying, "To whom should one complain when the ruler is a despot?"

We squat in a circle, under the supervision of Israeli soldiers with guns, waiting for our turn for a body search. Each time someone is called, the whole circle picks itself up, and everyone moves along one place, in a routine that is repeated countless times as the hours drag by. "God is with the patient," someone sighs nearby. I know that saying: My mother used to extol the virtues of patience as the hallmark of great and courageous people. But I have always hated this proverb, with its undertones of surrender and submission. And my patience is truly exhausted by the time I reach the hut where the searches are conducted.

The search is a very elaborate ceremony; not only do they comb through our clothes and belongings with great thoroughness, but we are also obliged to strip naked. Each time this happens, I argue with the women soldiers conducting the search, but they insist. Later, I complain to the officer in charge of the bridge, who apologizes, claiming that the soldiers had misunderstood their instructions.

After one such shouting match with the Israeli women soldiers, I submit a written complaint about the manner in which I have been dehumanized and humiliated. To the officer on duty, I shout, "You'd better put a gynecologist on the bridge. Those women aren't allowed to poke into such sensitive and intimate places!" The officer laughs at my anger and sneeringly offers to act as my gynecologist.

Arriving home, I contact Nablus mayor al-Masri. Al-Masri, angered by my account, complains to the military governor, Giv'oli, who investigates the matter. The Arab Women's Union also takes action, sending a petition to Dayan.

To justify themselves, the military authorities contended that a body search on a woman militant revealed detonators concealed on her person. Dayan responded to the petition, saying that the military authorities were entitled to conduct such body searches if they had grounds for suspicion.

The protests had little effect; nor did the Israelis take much notice of humorous articles and letters in our newspapers, which ridiculed the body searches, presenting them in a facetious light. One was entitled "Strip Tease on the Bridge," and another invited applications to join the "new nudist club."

On one occasion while crossing the bridge, my patience gave out after waiting for many hours. I demanded to see the officer, but I was refused. Unable to contain my anger any longer, I yelled at one of the soldiers, screaming at him in Hebrew to go and get his officer. ("What's the matter—is he God?" I shouted provocatively.) After a brief argument, he consented to go and call his superior.

A very handsome young Israeli captain named Ronni appeared and asked for the "troublemaker." When I stepped forward, he asked me what I was complaining about. I told him that four busloads of men had been searched and allowed through, while we women were left waiting. He went away for a moment, to look into the matter; he must have been told that my complaint was justified, because he came back and promised to rectify the situation.

Having settled the most pressing matter, Captain Ronni now looked at me curiously. "You were quite right," he conceded, "but why did you shout?"

"I had to," I replied, "otherwise no one would have listened to me."

"Tell me something," he said. "Of this whole long queue of women, how come that you are the only one to complain? The others have babies, they are suffering more than you."

I turned to the other women and translated his question. The women—poor peasants for the most part—replied, "You speak in our name!"

When I translated their words into Hebrew, Ronni looked astonished. "What about them?" he asked in wonder. "Why don't *they* complain?"

The women explained that they had been grumbling all the time, begging the soldiers to speed up the procedures, but no one paid any attention. "You screamed, you spoke to them in their own language," they told me.

Again I translated, and the captain turned defensive. "Anyone can complain and criticize," he said plaintively. "What would you do in my place? Make some suggestions!"

"Very well," I said. "Look at this woman with the submachine gun. She's too busy flirting with the soldier over there, and that's why she's so slow. Why don't you replace her, or bring someone else to help her?"

Grudgingly, he conceded that I had a point; he made arrangements for the searches to be speeded up and then went away.

Finally, after another prolonged wait, it was my turn to be searched. When I went in, the woman in charge—she was an Oriental Jewish woman with a blatant inferiority complex that made her rude and aggressive—addressed me angrily: *"Yalla, yalla, bechlah culu!* [Get a move on, undress completely!]," she shouted at me.

"I won't undress!" I shouted back.

She was shocked. Again she shouted, *"Yalla,* I don't want any problems. I want it all out!"

"Nothing out and nothing down!" I flung back. "I want to see the officer in charge. You have no orders to undress me!"

I was brought to Captain Ronni again. When he saw me, he cried out in exasperation, "What, *you* again?!" He led me to his office, shouting: "There are a thousand women out there. Why is it *you* that's making all these difficulties?"

I yelled back, "If we don't complain, you think everything is all right. I complained fifteen times, and there was no result! The others have resigned themselves, they have given up complaining—but their sons and daughters join the fedayeen! Is that what you want?"

We continued to shout at each other for some time, but then he calmed down and apologized for raising his voice. He ordered coffee for us, and we continued talking. I noticed that his manner was still agitated and nervous. In the course of our talk, he tried to call Jerusalem several times. "I'm worried about my wife," he admitted. "There was an explosion in our neighborhood supermarket this morning, and I can't find her at home." He seemed near hysteria. "And then you complain about us undressing you to search for explosives!" he shouted. "Why should I be patient with you?"

"It's you people who are to blame," I retorted, "you and your occupation. That's what makes people lay bombs!"

"It's cowardly to kill women and children in supermarkets!" he bellowed self-righteously.

"And what about the Israeli bombing raids on refugee camps?" I challenged. "Aren't they acts of cowardice against women and children? Are our children any different from yours?"

In the midst of this exchange he received a phone call from Jerusalem; it was his wife. Reassured, his manner grew more relaxed as he put down the phone. All the same, he said, sighing, "I'll end by divorcing my wife. She screams just like you!"

Before allowing me to go, he asked me not to write about the incident. I gave him a half-promise, but in the end I did write to the papers, giving a detailed report of my treatment.

This incident had a sequel later. It was in the course of a day of strikes and demonstrations in Nablus. I was on a tour with two journalists—Michael Adams and Eric Marsden. We were halted on the outskirts of the city, and the soldiers would not allow us to proceed. I argued with them, explaining that we were from the media, but they did not relent. In the end, I demanded to see their officer. To my surprise, it turned out to be the handsome Captain Ronni. He strode up to us and reiterated the ban: Foreign journalists were not being allowed into the city that day.

Then, turning to me, he said, "Ah, Raymonda! What a beautiful liar you are! You promised not to publish . . ."

"Don't forget," I retorted, "we are enemies!"

"I'll never believe you," he said angrily.

"And you?" I flung back bitingly. "Should we believe you?"

Under the circumstances, it was not easy to maintain one's humanity. There were times when it all seemed so hopeless. Here we were, sitting in the comfort of a bourgeois intellectual salon, seeking dialogue, searching for a solution. We complained about the demolition of houses, the torture of prisoners, the arrests and deportations, the collective punishments inflicted on whole communities because of acts of resistance by individuals—and yet, whom were we addressing? Members of the Israeli establishment, people who supported the Alignment, people who enjoyed all the privileges that Israeli society grants to its favored sons! Even Giv'oli, our "liberal-minded" military governor, sometimes attended these discussions—Giv'oli who was in daily charge of carrying out Dayan's repressive policy in our city! What was the point of arguing with such people? Obstinately I clung to the hope that by allowing our adversaries to understand us, by showing our grief and our wounds, we would be able to touch their hearts. There were times when friends of mine lost patience. "What is the use?" they used to ask me. "The Israelis are confiscating land and establishing their settlements all over the West Bank; there are daily instances of brutality, torture, humiliation. What is the use of talking to them?" There were times when I, too, would ask myself, What is the use? Near our home, a three-story house was demolished. There were protests, shops were shut, there was a demonstration—all to no avail. The next day—another house. The family was given half an hour to get out, leaving them with no time to take out their furniture. I rushed to the telephone and called up some diplomatic friends. I got through to Mr. Kay, the British consul in Jerusalem. Hurriedly, I explained the situation and asked him to intervene. Half an hour later, the phone rang; it was Mr. Kay. He told me that he had contacted his ambassador in Tel Aviv, and he would do something, use his influence with the Israeli Foreign Ministry. I let him finish; then, speaking very gently, I said, "Thank you, Mr. Kay. But the house has already been demolished. There is no need to give yourself any more trouble." Two months later, the military court found the young man innocent of possessing explosives. But the verdict came too late: His family's home was a heap of rubble.

Despite all the humanity of my contacts with enlightened Israelis—with Avneri and Mapam and all their like—this, then, was the true image of occupation: that mother, sitting in tears in front of the heap of stones that had once been her home. I have rarely known Da'ud to weep, but this time he cried unashamedly. "I know this man," he explained. "Toukan Hamzi is a client of my bank. He was a refugee from Haifa in 1948. He lost everything, began again from scratch. I saw him pour all his energy, his sweat, into that house. I helped him stand on his own feet. And now—this."

Once again, I told Avneri and the Mapam people; once again they publicized the facts inside Israel. But with few exceptions, the general public response was one of apathy, if not worse. Plenty of Israelis justified such acts, regarding them as "the only method of dealing with terrorists."

As though my own feeling of despondency was not enough, I found myself assailed by a friend, who criticized me for my conversations with Israelis. "You just play with words," he said cuttingly. "It gives you intellectual satisfaction, but it does no good. The repression goes on, occupation remains. What is the use? Only arms and weapons will help us—not words! You are just indulging in intellectualism, you have fallen for the lie that there is an 'Israeli left' that is somehow different. Wishful thinking . . ."

Despite my own doubts and despair, these words stung me into an angry response. "We *must* talk, we *must* explain, we *must* be patient. Maybe our voices *will* be heard. After all, the Algerians made great efforts to convey their cause to French intellectuals, and that helped their struggle, didn't it?" Bitterly, I asked, "Is there no way other than death, violence, torture, destruction? That is what the enemy wants. After all, we have no arms! Is there no way but hate? Is there no way to love, to understand?"

It seemed a forlorn hope, a romantic dream. How could I hope for love and understanding to transcend the enmity between our two peoples when every day fanned the flames of hatred? There was a renewed note of acerbity to the debates in my house. On one of his visits, Eliezer Be'eri spoke of the Israeli occupation as "humane." One of my friends got furious: "Who ever heard of a humane occupation?" he snapped impatiently.

"It could be worse," Be'eri snapped back. "Have you never heard of the Nazi concentration camps? Have you never heard of Auschwitz?"

The debates raged on. Somehow we seemed to have stalled; we were going around in circles, making no progress, each side repeating its own position over and over again.

At the same time, I was under constant pressure because of my contacts with Israelis. Passersby did not know what was going on inside my home. All they knew was that cars with Israeli license plates were always parked outside. There were mutterings of "collaboration," of "espionage." Inside, we were flinging about words like *imperialism, colonialism, repression, denial of national rights.* However, in the comfort of my salon, they were little more than abstractions, theoretical concepts, while for the man who passed by on the street, these terms were a bitter, living reality, connected with the trials and tribulations of his everyday life. It was only natural that I should be regarded with suspicion by many ordinary people in Nablus. Here I was, a woman and a Christian, belonging to a different class, with my foreign-style education, and all these inexplicable dealings with foreigners—particularly Israelis.

At the same time, there were many Palestinians who sincerely doubted whether there was any point in my extensive contacts with groups and individuals belonging to the nation that had for so long been the enemy of my people. To those who genuinely questioned my actions in entering into dialogue with Israelis, I answered frankly. I endeavored to explain that dialogue was vital; it was my contribution to the Palestinian cause. I, too, felt bitter; I, too, sensed a deep internal conflict; I, too, loved my homeland. And I was convinced of the necessity of challenging the Israelis, of confronting them, face to face, with the justice of our case. My explanations rarely produced more than a skeptical raising of the eyebrows. After all, could I point to any real, *meaningful* response from my Israeli collocutors?

One day in 1972, Muhammad Watted brought me a visitor: Guy Penne, an aide to French Socialist leader Mitterand. I invited Mayor Hamdi Kna'an to meet the guest, together with several other Palestinian intellectuals. In the course of the conversation, Kna'an explained our fear of a progressive Israeli takeover of the West Bank with the intention of annexing it permanently.

To clarify his point, he mentioned the case of the village of Akrabeh, whose *mukhtar* (village head) had just informed him of the authorities' pressure on the villagers to force them into selling their land to the Israelis. The villagers refused, saying they would die rather than sell. To step up the pressure, the military authorities then declared a large section of Akrabeh's land a "training area";

the fields were fenced off, and the villagers were forbidden access—"for their own safety." The aim of this measure was to deprive the villagers of their land, since it was hoped that if they were denied the use of their fields, they would be more inclined to sell. But the Israelis did not reckon on the stubbornness of these Palestinian peasants; after a short time, seeing that the land was not, in fact, being used by the army, the villagers broke through the fence and proceeded to plow and sow their fields as they had done since time immemorial. It was a good year, there was plenty of rain, and as the wheat ripened, the farmers hoped for a good harvest.

Their hopes were premature. Enraged at the "presumption" of the villagers in flouting official orders, the Israelis adopted a new tactic. Early on the morning of April 28, 1972, an Israeli plane swooped down over the fields and sprayed them with some mysterious substance. The villagers were mystified and concerned, but they had no idea what was happening. But it did not take them long to find out. Within a short time, the wheat shriveled up uselessly and died. The fields turned black: They had been sprayed with a defoliant of the kind used by the Americans in Vietnam.

Kna'an completed his account; for a moment there was a stunned silence in my salon. Eliezer Be'eri, who was present, refused to believe this story; Kna'an insisted that it was true. There was no way of resolving the argument.

The next day, I drove down to the Jordan Valley with Victor Cygielman, a prominent Israeli left-wing journalist who wrote for the *Nouvel Observateur*. On the way, I mentioned the story of Akrabeh, as Kna'an had related it the previous day. Victor's reaction was similar to that of Eliezer Be'eri. "You exaggerate sometimes, Raymonda," he said reprovingly. His comment vexed me; I had often heard such remarks before, and there was a kind of automatic skepticism about any charges we brought. No one ever wanted to believe us. All too often, we found ourselves the victims of Israeli—and Western—stereotypes of "Orientals with overfertile imaginations."

Stung, I challenged Victor to go and check the story. We drove to Nablus, to see Kna'an. He sent us to Akrabeh, asking us to be discreet in approaching the *mukhtar*. When we arrived in Akrabeh, the *mukhtar* repeated the story I had already heard. Then he took us out to the fields; with our own eyes, we saw the fence, and we saw the wheat fields, blackened and burnt.

We spoke to the villagers. They were broken, dejected, reticent. "How can we feed our little ones?" they asked in despair. In one stroke, their livelihood for a whole year had been destroyed. After the calamity, they wrote letters to the Israeli ministries of defense and agriculture. In response, an official arrived and advised the villagers to keep the affair quiet, promising that if they did so, they would be paid compensation.

Now Victor was convinced. "A true journalist should investigate and see for himself, before casting doubt on what he hears," he told me apologetically. Henceforward, he never again cast doubt on my reliability. Victor promised he would do something about the story. That week, I left for Beirut. On arrival, I bought a newspaper: To my astonishment, I read banner headlines about the incident at Akrabeh. Victor had kept his promise. He had broken the story, and the world press gave it prominent coverage, highlighting the shameful behavior of the Israeli authorities.

The Israeli government was embarrassed and furious. Under pressure from questioners in the Knesset, Defense Minister Moshe Dayan described the use of defoliants on the fields of Akrabeh as "an act of barbarism." Fine words! But they were not followed by action. The spraying had been ordered by a senior Israeli officer, but Dayan did not want to fall out with his generals by punishing the man. Who knows whether, in his heart of hearts, he was not secretly glad that such "barbaric" tactics had been employed; next time, other villagers would sell their land when "requested."

But the Akrabeh incident did not end with Dayan's reply. Perhaps for the first time, the Israeli public really comprehended the true ugliness of occupation and the tribulations imposed upon the population of the West Bank. There were widespread protests, and numerous Israelis—even government supporters—demanded disciplinary action against those responsible. The government did nothing, expecting the whole matter to blow over. This time, however, they were wrong.

Among other Israeli leftist groups, the name Siah (Israel New Left) had been prominent of late. Formed after the 1967 war by groups of dissident intellectuals, students, and kibbutz members, many of them former members of Mapam, Siah had become a small but vocal radical opposition group. Siah proclaimed its support for Palestinian self-determination, calling on the Israeli government to withdraw from the occupied territories and make peace. The Akrabeh incident had especially enraged Siah members; many of them were members of kibbutzim, with a love for the soil and respect for its fruits. They comprehended very well what it meant to a farmer to have his precious crops wantonly destroyed. When they saw that the government did not intend to punish those responsible, members of Siah decided to demonstrate their disgust in a bold and unorthodox manner. Although all political activity was officially forbidden in the occupied territories—for Israelis as well as Palestinians—they decided to hold a demonstration of solidarity with the stricken villagers of Akrabeh.

One day, eighty members of Siah drove down to Akrabeh. They had made no secret of their intentions, and the authorities knew what was afoot. Several miles from the village, the demonstrators were halted at an army roadblock. A large force of green-bereted border guards blocked the way; an officer ordered the demonstrators to turn back. After a short consultation, the Siah people decided to disregard the order. Since their vehicles could not get through, they broke up and made a dash across the fields. Running in small groups and singly, they tried to slip through the military cordon. A manhunt developed, with the soldiers in hot pursuit and the demonstrators making every effort to get through to the village. But the soldiers were too numerous. The demonstrators were rounded up, dragged back to the roadblock, and bundled into their vehicles. Then, under military escort, they were forced to drive to Nablus, where they were detained at the local police station and charged. After some hours in detention, they were released and ordered to leave the occupied territories immediately.

The news of the Siah demonstration caused a sensation all over the West Bank. Time and time again, I had heard people say that "Right and left, Israelis are all the same!" Adherents to this view argued, "They are all Zionists, they all serve in the army—therefore, they cannot be trusted! At most, they might express a few noble sentiments, but they will never show true solidarity with us Palestinians." The Siah demonstration at Akrabeh suddenly opened people's eyes. Here was a group of young Israeli Jews who were prepared to clash with their own army, to risk beatings and imprisonment in order to express anger and disgust with their own government's treatment of a remote Palestinian village.

Several months later, five of the demonstration's organizers were placed on trial before the Nablus military tribunal. I went to hear the case. The proceedings lasted over several sessions. The defendants, appearing without lawyers, confessed to the "crime" of holding a political demonstration in the occupied territories. But instead of arguing about their own guilt or innocence, they endeavored to make the trial into a political case by attacking the moral and legal culpability of those very authorities who had put them on trial. Like all the other spectators, I was astonished as I watched these five proud young men who hurled accusations back at the prosecutor. Yitzchak "Itzik" La'or—later court-martialed and jailed for refusing to do his military service in the occupied territories—addressed the court with impassioned words. The young man, a poet, told the judges that he was ashamed of the actions of the Israeli government. He would refuse to serve in an army that repressed the Palestinian people's struggle for its homeland, he said. "As a Jew, I will defend my homeland; but if you use your arms to deprive a young Palestinian of his land, he will join the Fatah or Black September!"

Yitzchak was followed by Yossi Kotten (he, too, was later court-martialed for refusing to serve in a unit sent to put down Palestinian resistance). Yossi spoke simply and directly; his words had a powerful impact. "The real criminals," he said, "are those who deprive the Palestinians of their lands and their freedom!" The other three accused (Arieh Arnon, Eitan Michaeli, and Yuval Golan) each made a speech replying to the charge of incitement. One of them asked, "Who is responsible for incitement—we or the authorities? Who took away the freedom of these people?"

I could scarcely believe my ears. These five young Israelis represented a new and progressive mentality. By words as well as deeds, they proved that they truly wished for a future in which Israelis and Palestinians could live side by side in dignity and mutual respect.

My admiration for the defendants was not shared by the military prosecutor or the judge. After deliberating, the court issued its verdict. Each of the defendants was sentenced to pay a fine of three thousand Israeli pounds—a large sum at that time. Failure to pay would entail six months' imprisonment.

The courtroom was packed for the reading of the verdict. The military governor was present, as well as other senior Israeli officers. The rest of the spectators' benches were occupied by journalists and citizens of Nablus. After the verdict was read, the court was declared adjourned. The spectators stood up, preparing to file out. Impetuously, I sprang from my seat and rushed forward toward the five defendants. In full view of the whole courtroom, I turned to the Israeli officers, addressing them in Hebrew: *"Hevreh* [fellows]," I said, "this is the path to peace—not with your guns, but following the example of these beautiful young men." Then, stepping up to the defendants, I shook their hands, one by one.

It was a gesture of double defiance on my part. In full view of Israeli military officials who literally held my fate in their hands, I flaunted my appreciation and sympathy for these fine young men, who had just been condemned by Israeli "justice." But my gesture was also directed at members of my own people, at those who said, "Israelis—right or left—they're all the same!" No, I wanted to say, they are not all the same. There are those Israelis who oppress us, and these we must resist; but there are also those Israelis who make personal sacrifices out of sympathy for our cause—and these we must welcome!

After introducing myself to the five Siah members, I invited them for coffee and *knaffeh* (soft Nablus pastry). Taking them home, I phoned Mayor Kna'an to tell him of my guests. His response resembled mine; without any hesitation, he dropped all his work to come directly to my house. On behalf of the people of Nablus and of Akrabeh, he extended his thanks to the five young Israelis. "When a majority of Israelis come around to your point of view, we will make peace based on justice!"

9

Battle on Two Fronts

THE AKRABEH AFFAIR did not end with the Siah demonstration and the court-martial of its five leaders. A further group of Israeli Siah supporters—most of them members of kibbutzim—attempted to get through to Akrabeh to dramatize their protest. They, too, were halted at the entrance to the village and forced to turn back. But this time, they had come prepared for the eventuality; shaking off the military jeeps escorting them, they drove the short distance into Nablus and unfurled banners carrying slogans in Arabic calling for an end to the occupation. The people of Nablus were astonished to see Israelis defying their own government, and risking severe punishment, to express their sympathy with our cause. At the same time, the demonstrators did not forget to stress the national rights of their own people: "Israel for the Israelis, Palestine for the Palestinians!" read one slogan. It was a very important political lesson for our people to see with their own eyes that they had allies among Israeli youth.

When the military governor grasped what was happening, he sent troops to order the demonstrators out of the town. At that moment, I stepped forward. Approaching their truck, I invited the Siah people to come to my home. Since the demonstrators now furled up their slogans, there was nothing the military authorities could do. But as I led the way to my home, we were followed by a heavy military escort. While I invited the demonstrators inside, my house was surrounded by a veritable armored column. Police cars, military trucks, signals vehicles, together with foot patrols—all took up positions as a precaution against the "dangerous conspiracy" being hatched in my home.

Inside my house, we cemented Palestinian-Israeli solidarity with fruit juice and *knaffeh*. I sent the children to offer coffee and *knaffeh* to the soldiers surrounding the house. The offer was refused stiffly. They were "on duty," their officer replied.

Later, at eight o'clock that evening, after the demonstrators left Nablus, I was summoned to police headquarters for a stern warning. "You're to have nothing more to do with these crazy Siah people!" the officer growled at me.

"Crazy?" I repeated in wonder. "You'll never find a better group of youth in Israel!"

He was unimpressed. "These people came here to stir up disorder. If you bring them once more—you'll pay for it!"

The court-martial of the five Siah demonstrators provoked considerable anger in Israel. Jerusalem university students and left-wingers attended a Siah march to protest the sentence. The march ended with a rally outside the Knesset, with the speakers demanding that the sentences be quashed, that the Akrabeh villagers receive compensation for their crops, and that those responsible for the spraying be punished.

My friends from Siah invited me to attend the rally and address it. The invitation caused me some indecision. Despite the fact that these Siah people had demonstrated their goodwill in such an unambiguous fashion, some of our nationalists remained unconvinced.

In addition, I could not overlook the stern warning from the Israeli authorities. They were clearly concerned about the "danger" of Israeli left-wingers making joint cause with the Palestinians. Moshe Dayan described it as a "grave problem" that Israeli kibbutz youth, despite the indoctrination they received, were "working against us."

This was at the time that the United States was forced to end its intervention in Vietnam, largely under the pressure of dissident university and college youth, who displayed their sympathies with the Viet Cong. The Israeli leaders clearly feared the eventuality that one day young Israelis would also chant, "Hell, no, we won't go!" and Israel would be forced to withdraw from the occupied territories in the same way that the Americans were pulling out of Vietnam. Such a prospect was a nightmare for the Israeli establishment, and the government could be expected to act in the most ruthless manner, to nip in the bud any signs of cooperation between Palestinian patriots and Israeli radicals.

Under the circumstances, wouldn't it be foolhardiness on my part to attend the rally, and downright recklessness to stand up and address it? It was not an easy decision to make, but I made it with a clear conscience: I was going.

Victor Cygielman brought me to the rally. The Siah people received me enthusiastically. They were an isolated minority, reviled and denounced by official Israeli propaganda. As many of them told me later, they were desperately in need of a friendly response from Palestinian patriots so as to prove to Israeli public opinion that Israelis and Palestinians could coexist in peace and mutual respect. They knew how difficult and, indeed, dangerous it was for me to attend an opposition rally in Israel, and they showed their appreciation in the warm reception they gave me.

When my turn came to speak, I had a difficult task. In spite of our mutual respect and affection, my views did not coincide with those of numerous Israeli leftists, who retained lingering doubts about recognition of the PLO, which they considered extremist. They criticized the PLO as a "terrorist" organization. At the time, I favored the PLO's current position, which called for a single state for Israelis and Palestinians—a "secular democratic state for Moslems, Christians, and Jews"—while most Israeli leftists preferred the establishment of a Palestinian state *alongside* Israel. I made no attempt to paper over our differences. "Those whom you call 'terrorists' and 'killers' are freedom fighters!" I told them bluntly. "We must find a solution to the conflict between our two peoples. Israel can't make a deal with Jordan. It's the PLO you have to talk to!" Although they may not have liked my views, the people at the rally applauded me enthusiastically.

The Akrabeh episode and its aftermath meant a great deal to me personally. I had played a major role in making world opinion aware of what Israel was doing on the West Bank, vindicating my long and painstaking efforts to foster contacts with the foreign media. The ensuing protests by Israeli liberals and leftists had given me a further opportunity to strengthen links with progressive Israeli circles, justifying my insistence on conducting dialogues with Israelis. And, no less important, the Siah demonstrations encouraged me to confront those Palestinians who doubted whether we could ever find understanding on the part of Israelis.

But while making progress in my public activities, gaining experience and building my self-confidence, I could not afford to neglect my own personal emancipation. Political achievements alone could not satisfy me as long as I remained shackled by the bonds of convention.

Never for one moment could I forget that I was fighting a double battle against repression: I was fighting for the freedom of my people and, simultaneously, for my emancipation as a woman. Together with my almost daily confrontations with the Israeli occupation authorities, I had no few clashes as a result of my insistence on my own personal freedom.

In 1971, at a time when political tension was high and the situation looked particularly bleak, I had an argument with a visiting French journalist. He was openly scornful of Palestinian resistance to Israeli rule, claiming that other oppressed peoples put up a much more vigorous fight. He was particularly critical of Palestinian women, accusing them of being "passive." To drive home his point, he reminded me of what I had told him about the personal restrictions I had to endure as a woman. "Why don't you go away?" he challenged me. "Come to France for a year, study, and equip yourself for your political role!"

I made no reply at the time, but his words planted a seed in my mind. To study in France! That was a magic notion. My parents— my father in particular—had been deeply steeped in French culture, and I had inherited their sympathies. I had always dreamed of studying at the Sorbonne, of living for a time in Paris, the focal point of many romantic fantasies. I imagined myself living the carefree, bohemian life of the Quartier Latin.

Finally, I decided to go ahead with the idea and informed Da'ud that I intended to go to Paris for a year. He was aghast! Over the years, he had grown somewhat accustomed to my nonconformism, but the thought of me going away in this manner left him totally horrified. He expressed his violent opposition and advised me to forget all about it. But I did not give up so easily, and we argued bitterly.

A few days later, we held a reception that was attended by many eminent citizens of Nablus. Hoping that public pressure might have some effect on me, Da'ud lost no time in telling our guests of my latest mad scheme. As he expected, everyone was up in arms against the idea of me leaving my home and family to spend a year alone in Paris, that well-known den of iniquity. Hamdi Kna'an approached me and tried to talk me out of it; when I persisted, he lost his temper, shouting that it would be "criminal" on my part to undertake such a foolhardy venture. "How can you think of abandoning five children?!" he cried in horror.

Emboldened by this support, Da'ud returned to the fray. There and then, in the presence of forty guests, he shouted that he would not permit me to go to Paris. "If you go, I won't allow you to come back! I'll divorce you!" Reminding me of my dependence upon him, he warned me not to expect any money from him. And then he produced his trump card: "And I won't give you permission to apply for a passport!" Under Jordanian law, a married woman requires her husband's written permission before applying for a passport of her own; otherwise, she travels on a joint family passport. In effect, Da'ud was proclaiming that he would use his legal and financial power to keep me a prisoner against my will—but this blatant bullying did not shock any of the assembled guests. On the contrary, they supported Da'ud, raising loud objections to my plan and scolding me for even venturing to propose such a thing.

I was equally indignant. I did not think my actions were anyone else's business, and I was livid with Da'ud for trying to settle private matters by inciting outsiders against me. I, too, lost my temper, and shouted at him in anger and frustration. It was only with the greatest difficulty that they succeeded in calming me down.

Da'ud and all the others pretended to be concerned for the welfare of my children, but I regarded this as no more than a hypocritical pretext. Arab society is obsessed by sex, and these people thought that my main purpose in going to Paris was to live a life of sexual promiscuity. For an Arab man, such a thing is acceptable, but it would be a dangerous precedent if an Arab woman was permitted such freedom. Although no one referred to it openly, it was this "danger" that aroused such violent hostility—and not their pious concern for my children.

Ultimately, I gave in. I abandoned my plan of going to Paris, not because I considered it unreasonable and not because my absence would really harm my children, but because I knew that if I went in defiance of their father's wishes and under the censure of Nablus public opinion, the children would be made to suffer. Having paid part of the price for my own mother's freedom, I was not prepared to subject my children to the same suffering.

I was not permitted to spend a year alone in Paris? Very well, then, I insisted on compensation: I wanted to go to Beirut for a few weeks—on my own! A trip of this sort is unheard of for any Arab woman, married or single. But Da'ud begrudgingly conceded my demand. He was willing to do almost anything as long as I gave up the idea of Paris. Furthermore, he made another far-reaching concession: He gave me written permission to apply for a passport of my own!

And so, on the appointed day, I set off for Amman, armed with Da'ud's written endorsement of my passport application. I was thrilled! For the first time in my married life, I was openly leaving for a trip on my own! How trivial and minor it must sound—and yet, it was a major victory for me. Characteristically, Da'ud still could not come to terms with my freedom: On the first stage of my trip, he insisted that I be "escorted" by his chief cashier, who was charged with helping me to apply for. my passport. Obviously, a weak, helpless woman like me could not be expected to do so alone.

Arriving in Amman in a state of high excitement, I headed for the passport office, accompanied by the cashier. I was dismayed to find an enormous line of applicants. It was after the 1970 Black September massacre of the Palestinians, and the Jordanian authorities made a point of behaving harshly toward Palestinians. A special section of the passport office was set aside for West Bank applicants, who were abused and bullied during their long wait. A Jordanian soldier strutted up and down, "keeping order" by shoving people into line. He was particularly concerned with maintaining a proper segregation of the sexes, repeatedly yelling: "Men over here; over there, the harem!"

The cashier took his place in line. But I was in no mood to tolerate such humiliation, particularly when a clerk warned me that I would probably have to wait a week or more! This was not the way I planned to enjoy my newly won freedom! Leaving the cashier to wait, I headed for the office of the director, knocked at the door, and asked to talk to him. Anyone acquainted with the rigid hierarchy of Jordanian bureaucracy can imagine what audacity this required—particularly on the part of a woman. Perhaps it was this audacity that persuaded the astonished officials to allow me through—and I marched into the director's office. Introducing myself, I reminded the man behind the desk that we had met before: He was none other than Sa'adek al-Shara, the senior Jordanian officer who had plied me with questions when I first arrived from Israel, in 1957. As I have already related, my temerity in speaking with him freely in public sparked off a bitter quarrel with my brother George. Subsequently, al-Shara, together with other progressive officers, planned a coup against the Hashemite regime; the plot was discovered, and al-Shara was sentenced to death. His sentence was commuted; after five years' imprisonment, he was released and given a government appointment.

I found him greatly changed; his imprisonment had aged him. He did not recall our previous encounter, although he made polite efforts to pretend that he remembered. I told him of my surprise at finding him working for the Hashemite regime he had previously opposed. He shrugged resignedly. "A man must strive, do his utmost to seek truth and justice. If he fails, it is God's will. I am here to serve my people."

We now turned to my request. When I explained what I wanted, he gave instructions for my passport to be issued without delay. Gleefully, I returned to the passport office, where I found Da'ud's cashier still waiting patiently in line. Walking up to him, I said, "Go back to Nablus and tell my husband that I arranged my own application—and it took me just one day!"

With that, I promptly set about booking my flight to Beirut. In a defiant mood, I deliberately asked for a night flight. This was yet another outrageous act. If it is out of the ordinary for an Arab woman to travel unescorted, it is unheard of for her to travel at night! This additional act of rebellion only added further savor to my first trip alone. Da'ud's family in Amman made no secret of their displeasure on learning that I was traveling alone. I gave them an additional shock by telling Da'ud's sister that I was contemplating divorce. Horrified, she cried, "We don't do such things in *our* family!" When I insisted that I might do it all the same, she snorted, "Like mother, like daughter!" In a desperate attempt to contain the scandal, she promptly decided to follow me to Beirut, to keep me under supervision!

I had a wonderful time in Beirut. I loved the city—its charm and elegance, its intellectual and cultural life. But above all, I enjoyed the taste of freedom, of being able to go anywhere, at any time, without having to consult anyone else. For the first time in the course of my adult life, I savored the intoxicating flavor of liberty. I went to cafés, visited friends and acquaintances, bought extravagant clothes. My pleasures were innocuous enough; an outsider might have considered them rather exhibitionistic and immature. But it was hardly surprising that my exuberance took this flagrant, adolescent tone. All my life, I had been treated like a child who had to be supervised and disciplined. No wonder that my first bout of freedom led me to behave like a puppy off the leash!

While I enjoyed myself in Beirut, scandalmongers all over the West Bank were hard at work demolishing my reputation. I was staying with the family of Da'ud's brother in Beirut, but rumor had it that, having abandoned my husband and five children, I had eloped to Paris with a lover. To this day, some people in Nablus are convinced that I spent those weeks in Paris, besporting myself with some man.

My abortive bid to spend a year in Paris had a further payoff. In return for giving up the idea, I extorted a concession from Da'ud: If I was to be deprived of a year at the Sorbonne, I insisted on attending the nearest available institute of academic studies, the Hebrew University in Jerusalem. Academic studies for women are still a relative innovation in Arab society; and usually only unmarried girls go to the university. It is almost unheard of for a married woman to study. But I felt the need to broaden my education, and when I made this a condition for giving up my year in Paris, Da'ud was left with no choice but to give his consent.

Accordingly, the beginning of the next academic year found me registered at the Hebrew University in Jerusalem, taking courses in French literature. It is perhaps some indication of the complexity of my feelings toward the Israelis that while immersed in the daily struggle against Israeli occupation, I was attending the well-known Israeli university, listening to lectures from Israeli professors in company with Israeli students. But the paradox is only apparent, not real. For me, the Hebrew University, founded by great thinkers and humanists like the late Dr. Magnes, represented all the great and positive values of Jewish culture and ethics. While I resented the attitude of superiority adopted toward us by Israeli leaders and generals, and the arrogance of their occupation officials and policemen, I fully appreciated that minority of Israeli intellectuals, liberals, and leftists who opposed the militarism of their state. That is one of the fascinating things about Israel—its mixture of modern and progressive elements together with chauvinism and religious fanaticism. I encountered this as a girl, when I learned many of the modern, open ways of thought of my Jewish school friends, and on the other hand, at the convent school in Jerusalem, near the Mea She'arim Orthodox quarter, where I would see fanatical rabbis and religious seminary students who spat at the sight of the crosses we wore.

Although I rationalized my decision to attend the Hebrew University, it was not easy for me to concentrate on my studies there. The university authorities received me warmly, showing no discrimination against me as an Arab, as befits the humanist traditions upon which their institution was founded. And yet I could not help suspecting that there was an element of patronizing benevolence toward me. Or perhaps this was no more than a projection of my own feelings of inferiority and humiliation, coming as I did from Israeli-occupied territory to attend an Israeli institute of higher learning. There were many minor incidents that jarred my sensibility. Not least of these were the cries of wonder when I was introduced as an Arab. *"Non, c'est impossible!"* someone would blurt out, presumably meaning that I did not fit into his stereotyped view of "the primitive backward Arab woman." Doubtless such comments were meant as a personal compliment to me, but I regarded them as a painful affront to my pride as a Palestinian.

Another internal conflict arose from my renewed encounter with French literature. I have always admired the writings of Jean-Paul Sartre and Simone de Beauvoir. More than any of their contemporaries, I saw these two as the foremost representatives of a progressive Western intelligentsia. I was fired by their calls to resist oppression in all its forms; I admired and respected them for their courageous stand against injustice; I knew of their support for liberation struggles throughout the world, particularly their consistent sympathies for the Algerian liberation movement. But my admiration made it all the harder for me to stomach their pro-Israel bias, with scarcely a word about the Palestinians and our sufferings. Several years later, I had an opportunity to confront Sartre personally and tell him of my disappointment in him; but at that time, I could do no more than cry silently: Sartre, de Beauvoir, where are you? What of *my* people? Aren't we oppressed? Don't we deserve freedom like the others? Why do you close your eyes to our agony, why do you shut your ears to our appeals?

It was a stormy period in the West Bank. There were frequent confrontations with the Israeli occupation authorities; there were almost daily strikes, protests, demonstrations; often there were bloody clashes with Israeli occupation troops and police, resulting in arrests and curfews. How, then, could I sit in the comfort and peace of a university auditorium, calmly studying French literature, when Nablus and the rest of the West Bank were in constant turmoil and upheaval? I felt conflicted, but I was keenly aware that studying was an essential part of my personal and political emancipation, and I therefore made every effort to attend regularly.

My efforts were not overly successful. At the beginning of every academic year, I registered at the university and began to attend the lectures while endeavoring not to neglect my political work, my contacts with the foreign media, and my participation in current political campaigns. But I never succeeded in combining it all—and sooner or later, at some point in the academic year, some crisis would erupt, requiring me to devote all my energies and attention to fields very remote from the academic world. After that, I never seemed able to get back to my studies. The final result: In spite of registering annually at the Hebrew University, I have yet to complete a single year's study!

10

The War of Atonement:
October 1973

A FURTHER OUTCOME of the Akrabeh affair was a TV film that Victor Cygielman produced. He asked me to assist him, and I agreed willingly, helping him with contacts and translations. The film contained some moving and revealing sequences. It showed Israeli newcomers benefiting from the confiscated land, while the Akrabeh villagers, its former owners, were forced to seek their livelihood as laborers in Israel. At that time, Israeli official propaganda was continually stressing the "progress" and "civilization" that Israeli occupation was bringing the Palestinians. At one point in the film an old villager was asked whether the Israelis were, indeed, teaching him modern farming techniques. Referring to the confiscation that left him without land to which to apply the "new techniques," the old man asked sarcastically, "Where are they teaching us—on the wall?"

Although I had no doubt of Victor's sympathetic attitude, my work on his film brought me into repeated conflict with his Israeli assistants. When the cameraman tried to take pictures of Arab peasant women, the latter hastily covered their faces with their veils. At that, the cameraman turned to me with a mocking expression on his face: Look how primitive your people are! While we were at work in Akrabeh, one of the villagers—a school teacher—suddenly fell to the ground with an epileptic seizure. It quickly transpired that there was no doctor in the village, and there was a moment of panic until some of the TV crew gave the unfortunate man first aid. After this incident, the cameraman said scornfully, "Look how uncivilized you people are! A village without a doctor or any medical facilities. You should accept Dayan's wishes, agree to be annexed. When you are absorbed into Israel, you will enjoy all the privileges and benefits of a civilized nation."

His arrogance made me furious. "We don't want your help!" I screamed at him. "It's colonialism that has made us retarded! Get out of our land, leave us in peace! We will live, proud and free!"

Such flare-ups were frequent, and Victor was repeatedly obliged to restore calm so that we could go on with our work.

Work on the film began in August 1973, but it was not completed before the 1973 October War. Naturally, all work on the film was halted during the fighting; members of the crew were either mobilized or were serving with news teams at the battle fronts. Then, a few weeks after the war ended, we resumed work once more.

The atmosphere had changed beyond recognition. The war had ended, but the armies were still fully mobilized and in battle positions; on the Golan Heights there were daily bombardments by Syrian and Israeli artillery, with further casualties on both sides. When we met, Peter, the cameraman, just back from Sinai, arrived in uniform. At first, there was no talk, nothing but an exchange of glances; the mood was sad and restrained, our exchanges brief and formal.

I was to be filmed giving my response to the words of Pierre, a newcomer living in one of the settlements established on confiscated Akrabeh land. We began work. The projector whirred, showing a scene in which Pierre recounts the history of the Akrabeh area, pointing to some archaeological relics of ancient Jewish settlements and explaining that even the name Akrabeh is Hebrew; it is a place mentioned in the Bible under the name of Akrab. Accordingly, he concludes, "this land is rightfully Jewish, and we Jews have come back to regain it." When Pierre is asked about Palestinian rights to the land, he retorts that if such a claim is accepted, Israel would have to concede Palestinian rights to Acre and Jaffa too.

Watching the filmed interview and listening to Pierre's arrogant dismissal of my people's rights, I felt the tension rising. Blood rushed to my face.

"Stop the projector!" I shouted. "Stop that crazy fool!" I lost control of myself completely. "What are you talking about? Jaffa and Acre are not ours? I remember Acre, it's my own hometown; it's the place I love most on all the earth! For thousands of years we lived there! Every tree, every stone has a name for us! My family has lived there for five generations, in that Crusader castle—and yet this newcomer comes from his European ghetto, this vagabond speaks of rights?" Quite beside myself, I yelled, "You people need another Yom Kippur! Nazis!"

Pandemonium broke loose.

Everybody in the room was yelling. When I paused for a moment to draw breath, I heard someone shout: "We'll show you! In the Golan, we'll show you! We'll kill the Syrians, every one!" Chaos reigned in the projection room.

I saw Mrs. Cygielman sitting in a corner, crying. Later I comprehended what I had said: Nothing can be more offensive to a Jew than to be called a Nazi, and it was especially painful for Mrs. Cygielman, whose parents had died in a Nazi concentration camp. I felt remorse over offending her; after all, I myself hate the Nazis, and I can never forgive their frightful crimes.

The other Israelis were shouting at me and at one another. Previously, I had had countless rows with Peter, who missed no opportunity to make some hostile remark. Now I was astounded to hear him address the other Israelis, shouting: "Stop it! You don't know what the situation is that we're in! A day may come when those colonists from Akrabeh will have to seek shelter with Raymonda!"

Later, when we had calmed down a little, we resumed filming, but the interview was constantly interrupted by violent rows. I was bitter and vehement. I have Mediterranean blood, and I cannot remain calm in the face of lies and injustice. But I did not want our heated exchanges recorded. Each time, I insisted on stopping the cameras (Victor said afterward, "C'est dommage, it should have been in the movie") while I let myself go, in further heated exchanges. Somehow, we got the debate filmed, and it later became part of the final movie.

After we finished work, I exchanged a few words with Peter. He was not the same man he had been before; his experiences during the war had opened his eyes. "When I was in Sinai," he told me, "I remembered the things you used to say. Once you called me 'Dayan,' and I took that as a compliment. Now I would be offended!" He apologized for his earlier behavior toward me; the war had changed his ideas completely.

My feelings were mixed; I was glad of the change in Peter, but I felt sad at the thought of how much blood and suffering had been necessary to produce this change. With no joy in my heart, I thought: How many young Israelis have had to suffer and die—because of their arrogance?

The October War descended upon us without warning. We had known for a long time that the Israeli occupation of their land was an intolerable affront to the Arab states. We knew that if no political solution was found, they would have to go to war. But the Israelis were so cocksure, so certain of their superiority, so contemptuous of the Arab armies, that at times we began to doubt. Were they, indeed, invincible? Would we live forever with the disgrace of the 1967 debacle? Was it, indeed—as the Israelis contended—tantamount to suicide for the Arab states to take on Israel's mighty military machine?

Before the 1973 war, there was a black cloud of depression over the West Bank. Israeli occupation was entering into a routine "normalcy." Thousands of Palestinians were working in Israel; their work was hard, and they were badly exploited, but they were making relatively good money, even discounting the sharp increase in the cost of living. They did not enjoy the social benefits granted to Israeli workers. One old man explained that, being paid on a daily basis, he did not receive a paid day of rest, nor annual vacations; worse, when he broke his leg, he was left without any means of livelihood. "The Israeli workers have a union to protect them," he said enviously. "We have only God. . . ." His was not the only case of hardship. With repeated devaluations of the Israeli pound, the cost of living was constantly rising. Many people lost their livelihood as a result of land confiscations, which again forced more laborers to seek work in Israel.

At the same time, the cash they earned did create a superficial prosperity, enabling them to buy TV sets and other consumer goods. In addition, merchants who exported to Jordan received bonuses from the military government, bringing more money into the West Bank.

This was all part of Dayan's policy. He believed that if he improved material standards, we Palestinians would resign ourselves to the Israeli occupation, however distasteful we found it. There were some Israelis with a more sober and realistic view who knew we could not be bought. Pinhas Sapir, then Israel's finance minister, said, "Those who believe that raising the standard of living is a compensation for national aspirations have not learned the lesson of history." But most Israelis inclined to Dayan's view; they were sure that if our people were relatively well off, they would tire of their opposition to occupation. Secure in this belief, the Israeli authorities went on with their long-term program to retain control of the occupied territories. Land was confiscated from Palestinian farmers on the flimsiest of formal pretexts—often with no pretext at all—and Israeli settlements were established at key points. Protests were ignored; demonstrations and other forms of resistance were ruthlessly crushed. Under the relentless pressure of Israeli army and police actions, the fedayeen were having considerable difficulty in conducting operations, and hundreds of resistance members were either in jail or forced to flee. We felt powerless, abandoned to our fate. Here and there, a family would sell its belongings and set off to make its home overseas; numerous people went off to the Gulf oil states to make their fortune. At times, it seemed as though we had no future here.

One day, Victor Cygielman visited my home. He was not the only one to come that day; the other guests were a group of friends—Palestinian intellectuals from Jerusalem, Ramallah, and Nablus. As usual in those days of early 1973, the mood was gloomy. The discussion dragged on, covering the same ground that had been covered countless times before, the same attitudes, the same dispirited tone. Even the words were not new: *humiliation, defeat, the powerlessness of the Arab world.* "We live our defeat every day," someone said, "and that means we die every day." In the cynical tone that was becoming so common, talk turned to escape: Europe, the States, the Gulf. To move to a country where one could forget that one is an Arab.

Victor listened to the talk in somber silence. At last he spoke; his tone was earnest, concerned. "I hope," he said, "that the Israeli government will not hear this kind of talk. It will only encourage them to increase the pressure on you, in the hope that you will give up and go away."

There was good reason for our depression. Scarcely a day passed without some new arrogant declaration by Moshe Dayan or Golda Meir, who made it clear they had no intention of withdrawing from the territory they had occupied in 1967. Every day, we saw the Israeli troops—proud, self-confident, fearless, as befits the soldiers of an invincible army. Every day, the Israeli authorities confiscated land, established new settlements, built military camps, fortifications, and roads. Clearly, the Israelis had no intention of giving up their conquests; on the contrary, they were doing everything within their power to tighten their grasp.

How strange it was at that time to listen to the stories of the old people, who reminisced about the days when the Jews were weak and went in fear of the Arabs. Arab demonstrations would strike fear into Jewish hearts: "We used to be able to close down a whole Jewish neighborhood, just by flashing a few pocketknives," they boasted nostalgically. And now the Jews had this powerful state that posed a military threat to the whole Arab world.

At that time, President Sadat of Egypt was making aggressive speeches, warning that unless Israel agreed to a political solution, there would be war. "Our decision is battle!" he declared. "The hour has arrived!" Over and over again, he warned that 1971 was *"sanat al-hassem,"* the Year of Decision, which in both Arabic and Hebrew can be taken to mean "the year of decisive battle." But 1971 drew to a close, and nothing happened. The Israelis made no move toward a political solution, but the Egyptian army, like the armies of the other Arab states, remained in its barracks. After Sadat's aggressive talks, this inaction came as a great disappointment, and there was anger against Sadat and contempt for him. In Egypt, students demonstrated, calling for action. The Israeli papers shrugged off Sadat's threats as "empty Arab bragging," not to be taken seriously—and published highly unflattering cartoons showing him as a pathetic, helpless little man with protruding teeth. We, too, felt humiliated and disappointed. Wry, cynical jokes circulated; people began to refer to the Egyptian president as Anwar Saidat, meaning "womanly Anwar," a cutting remark to make about any man in macho Arab society. But it seemed that in denigrating Sadat, the leader of the largest Arab country, we were showing our contempt for ourselves as Arabs. It seems that every defeated people develops this same kind of self-deprecating humor, to help it to face the fact of its own weakness and helplessness.

On Saturday, October 6, 1973, I phoned Michael Politi, director of the Tel Aviv office of the French news agency Agence France Presse (AFP), to give my usual daily report of events on the West Bank. Suddenly, Michael shouted, "Turn on your radio! There's an attack on the Suez Canal! War!"

Incredulous, I hastened to switch on the radio, but found nothing. All the Arab stations seemed to be broadcasting normally. I thought he might have been mistaken.

At the municipality, Mayor Hamdi Kna'an was meeting with a group of visiting American professors, conducted by Muhammad Watted. I asked Muhammad if he knew anything. "We have just arrived from Tel Aviv," he shrugged. "There is nothing."

We hurried outside into the street. People looked startled, astonished, unbelieving. The taxi drivers had their radios on; they confirmed the report. "On the Canal!" they called in excited voices. "It's war!" They, too, looked as though they could not really believe it. Maybe this was another lie? Another one of Sadat's tricks? But not a war—impossible.

To make sure, I phoned the AFP office in Tel Aviv. Michael Politi answered, and his voice was heavy: *"Oui, ma petite, c'est la guerre."* It was his tone of voice that finally convinced me. Politi is a very proud man, with right-wing, chauvinist views, a strong supporter of the establishment; now he sounded so sad and earnest.

War.

Again.

I was reminded not so much of the 1967 war but of 1956, which occurred when I still lived in Israel. As the tension increased, the school principal decided to send us to our families. We were taken to Haifa, and from there went our separate ways. I remembered the suddenly deserted streets of Haifa. We saw a few men who looked like foreigners—perhaps they were British or French. We waited for the bus to Acre. I looked around, terrified. I saw some Israeli soldiers, looking dirty and unshaven: a sign of mourning, of death. We kept silent, afraid of being noticed; when we spoke, we were careful not to speak Arabic, only French, trying to put on a Parisian accent. In our fear and anxiety, we did not want anyone to notice that we were Arabs. I slipped my cross locket inside my blouse; I noticed that the other girls did the same. We scarcely dared to breathe until we reached Acre.

Now, on October 6, 1973, as the first news of the fighting reached Nablus, the first reaction was also a collective holding-our-breath.

As the reports began to pour in, the mood changed swiftly. It became clear that the Arab attack was heavy and effective, that the Arab armies were on the offensive. Suddenly the people around me lost their frightened expressions; they turned up their radios and walked around with their little pocket transistors, listening to the communiqués, smiling triumphantly, shaking hands and congratulating one another. Then we heard the first official statement by the Egyptian general Shazli, and a wave of happiness swept over us all. There was still a great uncertainty, and everyone endeavored to remain prudent. But the enthusiasm was unmistakable; within a few brief minutes and hours, we were regaining the pride and self-confidence we had lost in the course of six years of defeat and humiliation.

Israeli military vehicles hastened past nervously. The people of Nablus greeted them with fingers outstretched in a victorious V for victory. Some schoolchildren hurled stones at them.

Later, the first newspapers arrived, with the news printed in flaming red headlines. A newly arrived Canadian journalist—an Egyptian Copt by origin—who spoke Arabic but could not read it, asked me for a summary, but I was so excited by the news of the Egyptian army's crossing of the Suez Canal that I could not oblige him.

The Israeli authorities took "security precautions" to maintain their hold on the occupied territories. In Nablus, many young people were placed under preventative arrest. There were tanks and armored cars in the streets and outside the offices of the military governor; the Israelis were putting on a show of force to keep us under control.

Although all attention now focused on events on the battlefronts, some journalists still took an interest in what was happening on the West Bank. The first one to arrive was Jean-Claud Guillebeau of *Le Monde*. He came to see me, and I accompanied him on a tour.

Before the war, thousands of West Bank laborers went to work in Israel every day. But when the fighting broke out, they all stayed at home. The Israeli media made no mention of this fact; when they did, they attributed the workers' behavior to "fear." But when Guillebeau asked some of the laborers why they were not at work, they answered simply and proudly, "Out of solidarity with the Arab armies!" Later, the laborers at Ballatta refugee camp gave the same answer to Uri Avneri. This spontaneous demonstration by thousands of ordinary Palestinians was a striking illustration of the gratitude we all felt toward the armies of Syria and Egypt. Before the war, we went our daily round, helpless, humiliated captives of an all-powerful Israel. Now, as the Arab armies fought valiantly, inflicting heavy punishment upon the Israelis, we rejoiced!

As is always the case in wartime, rumors supplemented the official communiqués. We could see how the Israeli occupation troops were behaving; they were clearly startled and alarmed by this unexpected display of Arab strength and determination. For years, they had been fed on the arrogant propaganda of their leaders, who told them, day in and day out, that they were immeasurably superior to the Arabs, that the Arab peoples were despicable cowards and hopelessly ineffective soldiers. And then suddenly, like a thunderbolt from a clear sky, all their illusions were shattered; their army suffered grave setbacks and paid a heavy price in blood and suffering.

There was no mistaking the shock the Israelis suffered during those fateful days of October 1973. We could see it on their faces, in their behavior, in their voices. Stories began to circulate of Israeli soldiers pulling back from the Jordan Valley, of tanks and trucks heading west, of Israelis proclaiming their reluctance to fight ("Why should we throw our lives away for nothing?"). As these stories came in from various parts of the West Bank, I included them in my daily reports to the Agence France Presse. I did not realize then what a hornet's nest I was stirring up.

The night after I sent in that report, I was summoned to the office of the military governor. A police officer was waiting for me. Without any preliminaries, he challenged me on this report. "You don't know the danger of passing on news like this!" he told me threateningly. "You must issue a denial!" I rejected his demand indignantly; as a journalist, I refused to be dictated to. Our argument was brief but sharp. It ended inconclusively, but that was by no means the end of the episode. The Israeli authorities long harbored resentment against me for sending out this report. The Israeli press also attacked me for it, and it would be a long time before I would hear the end of the incident.

Earlier that year, I appeared on a CBS television program made by Amos Elon. The program was called "The Israelis"—like Elon's widely read book, which was highly critical of the Israeli militarist mentality and of the injustice inflicted upon the Palestinians. I felt uncomfortable at appearing on a program named "The Israelis," but I was reassured by Elon's fair and independent attitude, and I rejoiced at an opportunity to present a Palestinian viewpoint. Later, when I was in the States, I saw the program, which was even better than I had imagined, strengthening me in my belief that I had scored an important success for our cause with my participation. What fortified me even more in my view was the warning I got from the Israeli authorities that I would pay a high price for my sharp tongue.

In answer to the interviewer's questions, I spoke of the chauvinist arrogance of the Israeli occupation army, of their sense of superiority in dealing with us Palestinians. "They need to be hit over the head to awaken them to reality and bring them back to their senses."

Now, a few months later, at the height of the October fighting, I received a phone call from the CBS man who made that program. "Mrs. Tawil," he said, "I would like to remind you that you predicted the war when you spoke on our program." I had issued my warning at a time when most visiting journalists allowed themselves to be dazzled by the forests of TV antennae sprouting above the refugee camps. They seemed to believe that "open bridges" and secondhand washing machines could heal the wounds of our humiliation.

In the year before the war, I attended lectures at Jerusalem's Hebrew University. Driving in to Jerusalem, I had a face-to-face confrontation with the realities of Israeli occupation and expansionism in a most concrete form. The road in from the north passes by the Ramot Eshkol quarter, one of several large-scale housing projects the Israelis have built up around the Arab part of Jerusalem, filling them with Jewish immigrants or young Israeli couples; the aim of this expensive and ambitious plan is to "Judaize" Jerusalem, so as to strengthen the Israeli hold on the city and forestall the "danger" of any future peace conference forcing Israel to relinquish the Arab neighborhoods.

Driving past the huge, ugly apartment blocks of Ramot Eshkol, built on confiscated Arab land, gave us a constant reminder that the Israeli government had no intention of relinquishing its 1967 conquests. Furthermore, these solid-looking buildings were meant to dispel any lingering hope that we would ever be rid of occupation. "Look!" the buildings seemed to say. "Do you really think you can ever move us? You'd better get used to our presence here, accept it, resign yourselves." We often repeated Nasser's slogan, coined after the 1967 defeat: "That which was taken by force, shall be recovered by force!" But these fortresslike blocks of Ramot Eshkol made such talk sound like a "Byzantine" discussion—empty talk, having no impact on realities.

Driving into Jerusalem for the first time after the 1973 war, the buildings of Ramot Eshkol no longer evoked my previous sadness and pessimism. An old man sitting in the car muttered, *"Ustura* [a fable]." Was he expressing his wish and conviction that this apparently solid reality—Ramot Eshkol, the Israeli colonies, the other trappings of Israeli power—would fade away, like a fable or myth? Can power last if it is built on injustice?

Returning to the university after the fighting died down, I did not know what I would find there. Naïvely enough, I had assumed that, with the war drawing to a close, the university would have returned to normal, and I would find it more or less as it had been before. My error was not accidental: I followed the Israeli press and radio, which were making enormous efforts to present the situation in a rosy light and pretend that it was "business as usual" everywhere. There was an interesting reversal of roles: In 1967, it was the Arab media that falsified the news in an attempt to deny the debacle, while the Israeli news reports were usually accurate and reliable. Now, in the 1973 war, it was the Israelis who propagated falsehoods, while the Arab communiqués were precise and correct. At that time, there was a wry joke going around among the Israelis: "We taught the Arabs how to fight, and in exchange *they* have taught *us* how to lie."

What caught my attention at the university was the almost total absence of men—both students and lecturers. Being reservists, they were all away with their units in the Golan or in Sinai. With the exception of a few elderly men lecturers, the university campus was totally dominated by women. Otherwise, everything seemed normal; I attributed the exceptionally quiet and subdued atmosphere to the absence of the men.

I headed for the teachers' lounge of the French Literature Department, where I met with Dr. Zussman to work out my study schedule. I sat down with her at one of the tables, and we were soon immersed in our talk. Out of the corner of my eye, I noticed one or two other lecturers walk in; they looked at me and began whispering among themselves. I paid no attention till one of the younger women lecturers stalked over to our table. "Are you Raymonda Tawil?" she asked me. "From Nablus?" Unsure what she wanted, I answered, "Yes."

Without any warning, the woman suddenly began to shout: "Get out of here! What are you doing here? You are a liar! You published false reports about us, you said our army is fleeing—now get out!"

This onslaught caught me totally unprepared; for a moment, I was so shocked that I remained speechless. But I did not let her rant on for long, and I soon found my tongue again. "This isn't your business!" I told her sharply. "I live under a military government, and if they found anything wrong with my reports, they would have arrested me." But I did not rest content with a formal retort. The events of the past few weeks made me less inclined than ever to accept this kind of arrogance, and when she commented that the Arabs ran away in 1967, I answered, "This time, *we* won the war. Our soldiers took the Bar Lev Line; they didn't flee. This time, it was the Israelis who had to retreat!"

Our heated exchange had attracted several lecturers, and now the grammar teacher took up my remark about living under a military government. "What do you know of occupation?" she shouted. "You live in paradise! Let me tell you what happened to us under the German occupation in Poland! Let me tell you how we lived as children! Let me tell you about the Holocaust!" She looked at me in scorn. "You people don't deserve the humane treatment you're getting!"

Hitherto, Dr. Zussman had not said a word. But now this refined, gentle woman stood up, excused herself, and left the room. As she left, one of the lecturers shouted, pointing at me: "She has been sitting with Dr. Zussman, whose nephew has just been killed by the Arabs!" Until that moment, I had not the slightest inkling that Dr. Zussman's nephew, a young man of twenty-three, had fallen in the Sinai fighting. I was astonished and awed: This woman sat beside me, controlling her grief and overlooking the fact that I was an enemy—and quietly discussed my study schedule, as though nothing had happened.

Dr. Zussman's dignified exit produced a temporary lull in the shouting, and a secretary now succeeded in drawing me away from the group, where the mood was now near hysteria. I was terribly upset by what had just happened with the lecturers, and the secretary tried to calm me down. But our roles were soon reversed; when I regained control of myself, she began to tell me of her own fears and apprehensions. All three of her own sons were in the army, serving in the Golan Heights. At this time, the first reports were circulating about the Iraqis' atrocities against Israeli prisoners, whose bullet-ridden and mutilated bodies had just been discovered by the Israelis. As the secretary talked of this, she broke down and began to weep silently. I put my arm about her, trying to comfort her. "I'm sorry," I said as gently as I could. "I'm sorry for your sons and for all the other young Israelis who are fighting and suffering. We didn't want this war. It is all the fault of your leaders—Moshe Dayan, Golda Meir. They humiliated us, they killed our pride and our spirit, they tried to break our morale. We told you, over and over again, 'We exist! Don't overlook us!' But your leaders continued to underestimate us."

The argument flared up again. One woman shouted, "It's the Americans—they fooled us!" Another cursed Golda Meir. "Go and see the demonstration outside the Knesset! Parents are demanding their sons." The shouts grew louder. At that moment I was summoned to the office of the dean, Dr. Carmel. I walked into his office, my face still wet with tears—the only way I could express all the frustration and anger, the pity and sadness evoked in me by the stormy scene I had just witnessed. I was totally incapable of speaking; it was all I could do to listen to the words of Dr. Carmel, who spoke to me very calmly and sympathetically.

"You showed a lot of courage by coming here in this situation," he told me gently. "Didn't you imagine that emotions would be running very high? Almost everyone has lost some dear one in the war—how do you think they feel toward you? I can't tell you whether or not you should continue to come to the university. You must decide for yourself. But I must tell you that I can't be responsible for your safety if you do come here."

Dr. Carmel added, "I am very sorry for this incident. The lecturers had no right to speak to you in that manner, to humiliate you."

I was still crying, unable to control myself. I got up and left the office. All the way home, I was shaken by the turbulence of my emotions—a medley of fury and overwhelming sorrow. Arriving home, I again burst into tears. I was angry with myself for going to the university and leaving myself vulnerable to such humiliations; I was equally shaken by my compassion for the agony of those Israeli mothers. Safe in my own home, I looked at my children, trying to put myself in the place of those women, trying to imagine what I would feel if my children were in that kind of danger. The thought made my tears flow again, bitter and uncontrollable.

At that moment, a friend walked in—a prominent figure in West Bank political circles. Unable to conceal my agitation, I explained what had happened, attempting to convey my mixed feelings.

My friend rebuked me for being upset. "Don't cry! You should rejoice! The Arabs have gained a victory, and smashed the myth of invincibility that is the foundation of Israel's existence. Forget the human side, forget your pity for the suffering of those Jewish mothers! The fact that the Arabs have gained even one battle will affect the psychology of the whole Middle East. This must have its repercussions—on the Israelis, and on us!"

In time, he himself was to provide a striking illustration of his own words. Deported by the Israelis for "hostile activities," this man reached Beirut, where he was placed on the PLO executive board. In spite of his cavalier treatment at Israeli hands, he played a prominent role in modifying the policies of the PLO toward coexistence with Israel. He personally met radical Arab leaders like Syrian president Assad and Iraqi president Bakker, urging them to support the creation of a Palestinian state alongside Israel. Such a proposal would have been inconceivable without the 1973 war, which restored the Arab sense of pride and dignity and gave us the self-confidence to adopt a more realistic approach.

The Arab victories in the 1973 war did have tremendous psychological repercussions. It was not the war alone: A year later, the United Nations General Assembly arose to give a standing ovation to Yassir Arafat—and in doing so, the international body was acknowledging Arafat, not as an individual but as the spokesman of the Palestinian people. During the same period, the Arab governments also recognized the Palestine Liberation Organization as the legitimate representative of the Palestinian people. For years, the world had ignored us and denied our existence as a people. The very word *Palestine* had been consigned to the history books, as though we were not living people but disembodied ghosts belonging to the distant past. But now, all that had changed.

On the day of Arafat's appearance at the General Assembly, there were strikes and demonstrations all over the occupied territories. The Israelis reacted nervously and violently; the occupation troops put on a brutal show of force in the streets. My daughter Dianna arrived home thoroughly shaken after having been clubbed and dragged by the hair. Other demonstrators, mainly young people, were similarly mistreated, but the Israelis could not prevent our youngsters from parading the streets, bearing the Palestinian flag, chanting slogans, and singing fedayeen songs.

There was something new about these demonstrations. Almost from the very beginning of the Israeli occupation, there had been marches, sit-ins, protests; there had been countless clashes with the Israeli army and police. In the early years of occupation, these demonstrations expressed our protest against the acts of the Israeli administration; arrests, torture, land confiscations, and Israeli colonization. But after the 1973 war—and even more so after the worldwide recognition of the PLO—the protests displayed an element of self-confidence, of a renewed belief in ourselves as Palestinians and Arabs. As Dr. Kamhawi predicted that day, the upheaval produced by the 1973 war had an enormous psychological impact on the Israelis and—no less—on us.

One year before the war—in 1972, after five years of Israeli occupation—the military government announced that municipal elections would be held throughout the West Bank. Israeli propaganda organs trumpeted the decision all over the world, stressing that Israeli rule was "law-abiding" and "democratic," giving the inhabitants of the occupied territories the opportunity to conduct their own affairs as they saw fit.

The aim of the Israeli authorities was clear. They wanted to show the world that the situation in the West Bank was "normal," that their occupation regime was "liberal" enough to permit democratic elections. They were risking little. The elections would be held under Jordanian law, whereby only about one-tenth of the adult population was allowed to vote. Women were barred from taking part in the elections, as were all men who were not property owners. With the suffrage so severely restricted, and with Israeli power at its height, amidst strict repression and with the population largely demoralized and without hope, Israel had little to fear from the outcome of the voting. The Israelis predicted—correctly as it turned out—that the elections would return to power the same traditional, conservative elements who had formerly worked with the Jordanian regime and now largely complied with the wishes of the Israeli occupation authorities.

Under the circumstances, there was little to be done. It was unthinkable to take part in sham elections whose only purpose was to set the seal of legitimacy on Israeli rule. There was some debate—secretly, of course, for such matters could not be discussed in any open forum—that showed clearly that most people were against taking any part in the elections. "Boycott them!" was the slogan. When the candidates' list closed, it became quite evident that no one, outside the traditionalist conservatives, was taking the elections seriously.

The Israeli authorities did their best to destroy any resistance to the elections. At first, they tried propaganda and persuasion. When they saw that their efforts were fruitless, they applied various forms of pressure. The prominent Nablus citizen Hikmat al-Masri was arrested and held in custody for twenty-four hours, while the interrogators accused him of organizing the boycott. Alarmist rumors were spread about; it was whispered that the authorities would stamp the identity cards of those entering the polling stations, and reprisals would be taken against any person entitled to vote whose unstamped card proved that he had refrained from doing so. The Jordanian authorities were similarly eager for a large turnout, hoping that the elections would strengthen their protégés on the West Bank. The Jordanians let it be known they would find ways of punishing persons who refused to vote—and with Jordan our only outlet into the Arab world, this was no trifling threat.

The elections evoked considerable attention in world public

opinion. Israeli propaganda presented them as a triumph for their "liberal" occupation policy, and foreign media representatives hastened to the West Bank to see how Israel was "bringing democracy to the Arabs." At this time, Israeli prestige was at its peak, while anything we said was often treated with skepticism, as in the case of Victor Cygielman, who doubted our accounts of the Akrabeh incident—until he saw the defoliated fields with his own eyes. Foreign journalists were far more inclined to believe Israeli spokesmen, who assured them that the elections would be yet another proof of Israel's "success" in administering the occupied territories.

My own contacts with foreign journalists were growing. Many of them came to see me, for interviews and background information. I spent hours talking, explaining, taking them on tours—even with those who were openly hostile and skeptical. I tried to point out the deceit in so-called free elections held under a reactionary Jordanian law, under the terror and repression of the Israeli occupation authorities. Confidently, I predicted that even among the 10 percent of the population entitled to vote, participation would be minimal. The journalists listened to me, made their notes, took their pictures—and went away. Many of them made no effort to conceal their disbelief.

It was discouraging work—not only because of this lack of faith. There were many prominent Palestinian intellectuals who disapproved of my policy of "open house" toward Western journalists. "What's the point?" they argued. "All the Western media are sympathetic toward the Israelis. They don't believe us anyway. By talking to them, we let them keep up the pretense of being objective and hearing both sides. We should show up their prejudice. We are boycotting the elections—let us boycott the foreign press too!" When I refused to adopt this view, I was subject to widespread censure. But all the same, I did not want to abandon the field to the Israeli propaganda machine. I knew that this sphere was important—no less than the military or political struggle.

Election day came. Of the 10 percent of the adult population entitled to vote, only about one-half cast their votes. Many of those who went to the polling stations did so unwillingly. There were teachers and public officials afraid of losing their jobs if their identity cards remained unstamped; there were businessmen and others with contacts in Jordan who feared reprisals by the Hashemite authorities against those who failed to give their support to the largely pro-Jordanian candidates.

Nevertheless, despite the triumphant trumpeting of Israeli spokesmen, despite the fact that some of the foreign newsmen were deceived into regarding the elections as a proof of "normalization" in the occupied territories, most of the Palestinians who were free to decide for themselves boycotted this sham exhibition of "democracy."

In 1976, the Israeli authorities again announced that, in accordance with Jordanian law—which requires municipal elections to be held every four years—West Bank municipal councils would once more come up for election on April 12. The official announcement immediately provoked heated debates. What was to be done? Some nationalist circles immediately proposed a renewed boycott, precisely as in the previous elections. But although this view had a considerable hold at first, and it did appeal to our instincts, many of us sensed that what had been correct policy in 1972 would be a grave error in 1976. In 1972, when we were in political disarray and psychologically demoralized, we were in no position to contend with the enormous pressures exerted by the Israeli and Jordanian authorities. But so much had changed since then! The intervening period had seen the 1973 October War, Arab and worldwide recognition of the PLO as the legitimate representative of the Palestinian people, Arafat's speech at the United Nations General Assembly. There was a new spirit among us: We were no longer pariahs, ignored outcasts; we had regained our pride and self-confidence. Why, then, should we fear this new test of strength?

The debate was made all the more heated because of some unusual Israeli actions. Since their aim in holding the elections was to show the world how they were "bringing civilization and democracy to the Palestinians," the Israelis were sensitive to criticisms about the undemocratic nature of the existing Jordanian election law, which gave the vote only to male property owners, excluding all women and men of the poorer and middle classes. In consequence, the military government published a decree amending the electoral law in such a way that all households—even those that did not own property—were enfranchised if they paid any kind of municipal tax;

moreover, with each household entitled to as many as four votes, the male head of the family was empowered to grant some of these votes to his female relatives. Although there was still much to criticize in the form of the law and its humiliating aspects—for women especially—its practical effect was a sweeping social revolution: For the first time, the vast majority of the adult population—women as well as men—was entitled to vote! Our feelings were mixed. The Geneva Convention forbids an occupying power to alter the legal structure of the territory it administers. Although this particular modification was beneficial, there was a question of principle involved: If we welcomed the Israeli move in amending one law, would this not serve as a precedent, giving them a pretext for changing our entire legal system? There were those among us who warned of the "Israeli trap," and redoubled their calls for a boycott of the elections—precisely because of the Israeli-initiated reforms!

I could see some justice in this criticism. Nevertheless, I had no difficulty in deciding in favor of the elections. For years, Arab women had dreamed of the right to take part in political activity on an equal basis with our men. Now that we'd gained that precious right—admittedly, from an occupation government—did it make sense to forfeit the opportunity? Certainly not!

The debates raged on for weeks and months, right up to election day. Some circles persisted in their opposition and boycotted the polling stations. But the vast majority of the population went to cast their votes. In almost every West Bank town, there was a radical-national slate of young progressive nationalist candidates, who openly proclaimed their support for, and identification with, the PLO. Despite official Israeli harassment—two leading candidates were deported only a few days before the elections—the nationalist slates won landslide victories. With one or two exceptions, the traditional conservative leaders lost their power in all the towns, and the municipalities were taken over by the pro-PLO groups.

That day, I—along with tens of thousands of other women all over the West Bank—marched proudly and triumphantly to the polling station to cast my vote for the first time.

The victory in the municipal elections carried with it a further success: It was a blow against the "boycott mentality" that has taken root in Arab society. There are plenty of occasions when a boycott is justified; the 1972 elections were a good example. But some of our people see this as a philosophy, not just a tactic. I cannot blame them. We Arabs have good reason to be suspicious of foreigners. They have brought us endless suffering and countless humiliations. There have been many occasions when we were too weak to resist, and we could only take refuge in a proud refusal to have anything to do with these alien powers and their representatives—official and unofficial. But what was correct at times of weakness is not necessarily the right thing to do now that we are strong physically and psychologically. Now that the Arab peoples are a power to be reckoned with, now that the world has had to acknowledge the justice of the Palestinian cause and accord recognition to our representatives, what sense does it make to withdraw inward and evade direct confrontations? In the 1976 elections, we faced a challenge—and we emerged victorious. In the same way, we should welcome every opportunity to meet foreigners, to convey our message to world public opinion, to demonstrate our faith in ourselves and in our rights!

Nevertheless, the "boycott mentality" still persists among many circles. There are some persons quite incapable of changing their ingrained attitudes in keeping with the changed circumstances. They refuse to have anything to do with any Israeli—even genuine opponents of the present regime who have given convincing demonstrations of their support for the Palestinian cause.

On one occasion, I had an opportunity to see how deep-rooted this attitude is, even among my own children. It was after I had been placed under house arrest, when an Israeli friend—Peretz Kidron—came to visit me, accompanied by his son, Yochai. Yochai was wearing civilian clothes, but I knew that he was serving in the Israeli army at the time. Like his father, Yochai is a firm opponent of his government's policy. He is against Israeli occupation, and he sympathizes with the Palestinian cause. Still, as an Israeli citizen, Yochai was bound to do his three years of obligatory military service. Being a soldier, he was not free to express his political opinions. But he had given up one day of his precious leave to show his sympathy for me in my detention, and I appreciated the gesture.

Making my guests welcome, I hurried into the kitchen to prepare coffee. While I was there, my twelve-year-old daughter, Suha, came in, obviously disturbed.

"Mama," she said, "that young man is an Israeli soldier, isn't he?"

"Yes, Suha," I replied.

"Then I don't think we should welcome him in our house!" sne shouted. In recent months, Suha had seen Israeli soldiers break up demonstrations of high school pupils; she had seen Israeli soldiers club and kick her friends; she had seen them shoot and throw tear-gas grenades. Not surprisingly, she felt very hostile toward the young Israelis who had done these things.

I could understand her feelings very well. But I tried to explain my view. We should not boycott the Israeli doves, especially not a young man like Yochai, who would not have anything to do with such brutal behavior, even though he was a soldier under orders. All the more reason to make him welcome! I reminded her that not all the Israeli soldiers behaved the same way, and that some—depending on their background, their upbringing, their parents' views—acted quite differently.

Suha was not convinced. "You told us that you refused to receive the military governor—even though he might be a liberal! When they're in uniform, they can't disobey orders, can they? They are obliged to kill! Who killed Laina Nabulsi, who killed the ten-year-old boy in Ramallah? Yochai is no different from the others."

The other children came into the kitchen and joined in the argument. Gaby said, "In that case, Mummy will have to close the door and refuse to receive *any* Israeli—because all of them, even leftists and doves, are obliged to serve in the army!" He looked at me. "Mummy," he said, "other mothers aren't like you; I can't understand you! Are you convinced of what you are doing? In other countries under occupation, things were different. In occupied France, people who received Germans were regarded as traitors!"

"Our situation is different," I pointed out. "We have to explain our cause to those Israelis who are ready to understand and help. They can be of great assistance in changing Israeli public opinion. Remember the French liberals and leftists! Remember how they campaigned on behalf of the Algerians!" As for Yochai, I reiterated my basic credo: "Behind the soldier's uniform, we must see the man!"

The children rejected my views as naïve. Listening to their vehement words, I, too, felt torn. I recalled how the Israelis had mistreated Dianna; I recalled the soldiers who had wrapped their belts around the necks of demonstrating students, dragging them half-strangled to waiting trucks; I recalled the beatings, the tear gas, the shootings, the funerals of the young victims.

The anger seething within me, I returned to the salon with the tray of coffee. It would have taken little for me to pour out all my anger and frustrations at Yochai. But then, seated there, between sips of coffee, he began to tell me of his experiences as a soldier. He told how his unit was sent to patrol the streets of Bethlehem. The officer who briefed the soldiers ordered them to crush any sign of dissent, giving them a free hand to use force. "I was in charge of a section," said Yochai thoughtfully. "The soldiers knew me, they knew my views. Everyone was watching me, to see how I would behave."

Listening to him, I felt sympathy toward Yochai. I sensed his confusion, his conflict between duty and humanity. Like my own children, like myself. All of us, torn and divided.

I thought of Yochai and my own children. Young Palestinians and young Israelis, trying to find their way in this labyrinth of conflicting pressures and ideals. There was so little one could do to help them. They must make their own decisions about what is right and what is wrong.

11

The United States: "A Democratic, Nondenominational Republic"

AS OUR PLANE FLEW WEST ACROSS THE ATLANTIC, I listened to the conversation of the two men seated in front of us. One, an American engineer, clutched a newspaper; the banner headline was clearly visible: PALESTINIANS MURDER CHILDREN IN KIRYAT SHMONAH. He turned to his neighbor. "Look," he said, "look at what these damned terrorists did! Barbarians!" The other man, a businessman in his fifties, shook his head. "What the hell do these damned Palestinians want? What makes them do a crazy thing like that?"

Sitting behind them, I choked down my urge to answer. Why could these people not understand? How long could the Palestinians live in refugee camps on ten cents' worth of UNRWA assistance a day—and show patience in seeking for truth and justice? Was twenty-five years not long enough? Didn't they know that the attack on Kiryat Shmonah, the previous day, was timed to mark the first anniversary of the Israeli raid on Beirut, where three PLO leaders were murdered in their homes, in front of their wives and children? The fedayeen who attacked Kiryat Shmonah did not intend to kill. They hoped to exchange their hostages for Palestinian freedom fighters languishing in Israeli jails. But the Israeli authorities refused to make a deal, "so as not to create a precedent," as they put it. It was when the Israeli troops stormed the building where the hostages were being held that many of them were killed or wounded.

How could I explain all this to the two men in front of me?

Only the day before, my own children had gone on strike, together with the other pupils of the Al-Aishiya School in Nablus, to protest against conditions in the Israeli jails, where the Palestinian prisoners were on a weeks-long hunger strike. As soon as the students' strike began, Israeli troops surrounded the school, and the military governor tried to browbeat the students into calling off their protest. But the teen-agers defied this show of force; they hoisted the Palestinian flag above the building, chanting nationalist slogans and singing hymns of praise to the PLO, justifying the attack on Kiryat Shmonah. To them—and to me—the fedayeen represent a restoration of our human dignity and self-respect. That is why we love and admire them.

If I tried to explain all this to the men sitting in front of me, would they understand? I doubted it.

Although I did not know it at the time, that conversation I overheard on the plane foreshadowed much of what I was to experience during my tour of the United States.

The well-known French painter and writer Marek Halter and his wife, Clara, were the first to propose that I go to the United States for a speaking tour. Marek, a Jew who survived the Nazi Holocaust, has shown a genuine sympathy with the Arab peoples in general, and with the Palestinians in particular. Clara, editor of the leftist Parisian review *Element,* had extensive links with the Palestinian and Egyptian left. Observing the enthusiasm and devotion with which I endeavored to bring the media around to our cause, the Halters approached various American groups—Jewish and non-Jewish—with the idea of inviting me for a speaking tour.

The proposal appealed to me immediately. It had long been clear that one of the keys to a solution of the Palestinian problem lay in the United States. Much of my work was with American journalists, whom I often found to be sadly ignorant or misinformed on the Middle East. If these newsmen—generally so well-informed—knew so little or were so thoroughly taken in by official Israeli propaganda, I could imagine that the American public at large must be completely in the dark about the Palestinian point of view.

I have always been highly critical of the United States government and official American policies. Even when my column in the *Jerusalem Star* was subject to strict Jordanian government censorship, I once published an article highly critical of U.S. intervention in Vietnam, provoking an angry confrontation with an American consular official. It goes without saying that I was even more critical of American policy in the Middle East, which has given unquestioning political and financial support to Israel and supplied lavish amounts of arms for use against my people. Palestinian refugees in the camps in Lebanon were being killed by American-manufactured bombs dropped on them by Israeli pilots flying American-manufactured Phantoms and Skyhawks. Nevertheless, I had no grudge against the people of the United States; on the contrary, my mother's stories of her childhood in Syracuse had given me a deep affection for her country of birth, and for the American people, whom she always described in the most glowing terms. All the more reason for me to want them to know the truth about our people and their tragedy.

Thus, when that first seed planted by the Halters was followed up by a formal invitation to undertake a speaking tour, I was ready to accept it without any further thoughts. The invitation was transmitted to me by way of the Jerusalem office of the American Friends Service Committee, but it originated from a coalition of American groups and organizations—religious organizations, peace groups, and liberal associations. The initiative came from CONAME (Committee on New Alternatives for the Middle East), a group of prominent American peace activists—many of them Jews—whose object was to seek a peaceful solution to the Middle East conflict.

News of the invitation soon circulated in Nablus; in some quarters, the reaction was highly unfavorable. Not enough that I maintained open contacts with American journalists, diplomats, and politicians—now I was going to venture into the very heartland of American imperialism! All the old suspicions were revived. One friend warned me bluntly, "We will not be ready to defend you from the attacks against you. Who are these people who are inviting you? The Quakers? They're pro-Israel! CONAME? They're Zionists! Look at the names of the committee's members!"

I had no difficulty in refuting these arguments. CONAME had many Jewish members, but these were avowed anti-Zionists like Don Peretz and Noam Chomsky. Chomsky, a famous scholar, was well known for his views on the Israeli-Palestinian conflict and for his advocacy of a binational, socialist state in Palestine.

The other sponsoring groups and individuals were also above any possible suspicion. There were the Quakers, who had done magnificent humanitarian work among our refugees. They could not simply be written off as "Israeli sympathizers"—even though their recently published book on the Middle East, which totally overlooked the Palestinian problem, disgraced their proud record. There was Richard Butler, from the World Council of Christian Churches, whom we had learned to know and trust during his period of service in Jerusalem. In addition, there were other bodies connected with the invitation—the War Resisters League, the Catholic Peace Fellowship, the Fellowship of Reconciliation, the Women's International League for Peace and Freedom. In spite of the various rumors and insinuations that went the rounds in Nablus, there was absolutely no reason to suspect that any of these were acting as agents of the Israeli or American governments.

I got into numerous stormy arguments with people who objected to my tour. They attacked me; I fought back. I do not know if I succeeded in convincing my critics, but I did manage to silence them. But my projected trip to the United States also encountered obstacles of an entirely different nature. Naturally, the invitation had been extended to me personally. But if my American hosts considered it perfectly natural and normal for a woman to travel alone, Nablus society took an entirely different view, as I had learned most strikingly when I dared to consider a year in Paris or when I undertook an innocuous visit to Beirut. If I had gone on a lengthy trip abroad without being "escorted," my reputation would have been left in shreds. And an Arab woman who has lost her reputation is finished!

I was faced with a severe dilemma. Personal freedom is one of my revolutionary ideals. Aside from the political aims of the tour, I looked forward to the idea of traveling freely, alone and unrestricted, outside the narrow confines of Nablus society. On the other hand, if I behaved in a manner my society found "outrageous," the price would be a heavy one. My own mother's sufferings were a vivid example. My problem was not merely personal: In order to serve my people, I had to retain the respect of my social environment. In deciding on which front to fight, I had to give priority to the struggle for national freedom over my struggle for emancipation as a woman. Reluctantly, I gave up my dreams of a short vacation in liberty. Very well, I said, let Da'ud come with me.

With that concession on my part, the way was open for me to go. I cabled my American hosts, notifying them that I was accepting their invitation.

Those weeks in America were an unforgettable experience. I have grown used to living under tension, but the hectic pace and the dynamic tempo of that tour mark it out from any other period of my life. To describe it would almost require a separate book—and even then, I do not know whether it would be possible to convey the special flavor, the delight in discovering a new world, the apprehensions and fears that attended every new encounter, the drama and hostility of some confrontations, the unexpectedly warm welcome and deep comprehension I encountered in others.

Thinking back, my mind turns up a strange kaleidoscope of brightly colored memories: trivial, heart-warming, terrifying. The drive in from Kennedy Airport, with a Jewish taxi driver who warned us repeatedly, "Don't expect much from Kissinger. He'll fail you. Look at Vietnam!" Then, on discovering that we were Palestinians, his tirade against the fedayeen—"gangsters," he called them. But no hostility against us personally . . .

Lee and Tamar Kohns, awaiting us at the hotel; on finding that there was no room reserved for us, they awoke their little son, Daniel, and insisted on giving us their room so that we could rest after the long journey. Tamar and Lee, both Jewish, devoted members of the antiwar movement, who volunteered to welcome and escort us, comforting and reassuring us at some of the most depressing and terrifying moments of our tour . . .

My first encounter with glittering, luxurious New York—a shabby nineteenth-century hotel. My God, I thought, our hotels in Nablus are more presentable . . .

My first American breakfast—the food rich and heavy, with delicious pastries. It was my first encounter with that bizarre American phenomenon: breakfast in a restaurant. It was also my first experi-

ence of another typical American phenomenon: Baffled at my failure—at a moment of some urgency—to gain entrance to the ladies'
room, I appealed to a waiter, who told me to open the door "wid a
dime, lady, wid a dime!" Easier said than done; I did not have my
purse with me. I lost most of my admiration for that wonderful
American pastry as I hurried up and down stairs, seeking salvation
in the form of a humble dime.

My first encounter with the streets of New York. It was a lovely
spring day, and I gazed about me, drinking in the sights and sounds
of this strange and wonderful city. I was overcome with a physical
and mental exhilaration and intoxicating happiness as I enjoyed
every novelty, every new experience. Above all, there was a rare and
unfamiliar sense of freedom. Carried away as I was by my excitement, I could not help thinking back for a moment to my home, to
the curfews and barbed wire, the patrols and the guns and the identification checks that are such an integral part of our daily lives. And
here I was, walking the streets of New York, with no one stopping
me, no sentries, no armed soldiers, no restrictions. I breathed in
deeply; for me, the polluted air of New York carried the unmistakable, delightful flavor of liberty . . .

I was left with little time to enjoy myself: There was a job to be
done. To receive the final details of my speaking schedule, I met
Allan Solomonow, the tour coordinator. Allan, the director of
CONAME, is a Jewish pacifist who spent time in prison for activi-
ties against the Vietnam War. Allan was one of the first members of
the American peace movement to direct his attentions to the Middle
East, and he was the moving spirit in CONAME (later, he directed
Mideast programs for the pacifist Fellowship of Reconciliation,
FOR, and then headed the Middle East Peace Project, MEPP). With
the meager financial and organizational resources at his disposal,
Allan planned a coast-to-coast tour, in which I would address many
different audiences who displayed some interest in the Middle
East—church groups, Jewish organizations, liberal peace associa-
tions, and, needless to say, Arabs residing in the United States.

My relations with Allan were not easy. He was without doubt
sincere in asking me to present a Palestinian viewpoint, and he
worked hard and devotedly to make this possible. But in spite of his

knowledge of the Middle East, in spite of his visits to the region and his direct encounters with the Palestinian people, he still retained a large measure of political naïveté, which produced some painful and almost disastrous blunders. The principal problem lay in the fact that, having previously organized speaking tours for members of the Israeli opposition, who made no secret of their disagreements with their government's policies, he now expected *me,* in my turn, to stand up before American audiences and highlight *my* differences with the PLO! He could not comprehend that there was no comparison between the two cases. Israel is an existing, sovereign, recognized state; it is consequently quite legitimate for Israelis, at home or abroad, to stress their criticism of their national leaders. But the PLO is a struggling, embattled movement, still endeavoring to gain the recognition or just the mere attention of world public opinion. Like the Palestinian people as a whole, the PLO is fighting for its very existence. How, then, could he expect me to stand up before a foreign audience and dissociate myself from the PLO?

At that time, it was still official PLO policy to demand a single state in the whole of Palestine, a "secular, democratic state for Moslems, Christians, and Jews." I was beginning to realize that this aim could not be achieved in the short run. The chief obstacle was the opposition of the Israeli people, who had come to regard Palestinians as inferior or hostile or treacherous. If the Israelis did not now want to live together with us in the same state, such a state would not soon come about. But we could not sit back for further decades, with hundreds of thousands of exiled, homeless Palestinians living out their lives in refugee camps. We had to seek an interim solution. I had gradually grown convinced that we must establish a state of our own, side by side with Israel, as envisaged in the 1947 partition plan. Later, we might be able to join up with the Israelis and form a unified state; but this would take a long time.

This assessment subsequently gained ground and is now shared by many Palestinians, who feel, like Yassir Arafat, that the "secular democratic state" is a long-range dream and not an objective to be attained in the foreseeable future. But whatever my private disagreements with PLO policy at that time, I had no intention of utilizing my speaking tour to voice my criticisms. These were better discussed among ourselves. In addressing my American audiences, I stressed my full support for the PLO and its leadership—and thereby inflicted a grievous disappointment on Allan Solomonow, who dreamed of finding a "Palestinian nonconformist" to counterbalance and match his "Israeli nonconformists." This baseless hope was the source of countless misunderstandings between us. At the time, I was very indignant with Allan, but on looking back, I am convinced that it was an honest error on his part and that his intentions—toward me and toward the Palestinian cause—were sincerely friendly.

Be that as it may, my differences with Allan were only one unsettling feature of an eventful—one could even say frenzied—tour.

Some of my most dramatic and painful, but also at times gratifying, meetings were with Jewish audiences—religious, social, or political groups. These encounters always caused me much apprehension beforehand. I expected to find people who were totally identified with Israel, brainwashed by official Israeli propaganda, and hostile toward me as a Palestinian. Indeed, many of my listeners came clearly prejudiced against me. I tried to address them simply, to explain the Palestinian side of the issue, and to appeal to their sense of justice so as to give them a more balanced view of the situation in the Middle East. Some of these Jews were so fiercely nationalist in their views that my words fell on deaf ears; others listened carefully and seemed to comprehend—in many cases, for the first time—the justice of the Palestinian case.

Following the advice of Rashid Hussein, the exiled Palestinian poet who was living in New York (and recently died tragically in a fire), I endeavored to make my address simple and straightforward, avoiding political theorizing and stressing the aspects of humanity and justice. I would introduce myself as a Christian, and refer to Christian persecution of the Jews. When that happened, I reminded my listeners, the Arab world offered asylum to the Jews. But instead of showing gratitude, the Jews took over that safe haven, making it into their own home at the expense of the Palestinians, who were innocent of any wrongdoing toward the Jews. Any person of conscience—Jew or Christian—should acknowledge this injustice, whereby the persecuted survivors of Nazi concentration camps were given a home by making the Palestinians homeless. "We are like you," I told my Jewish listeners. "We Palestinians are the Jews of the Arab world."

After my address the audience would ask questions. The questioners displayed many different attitudes. Some were sympathetic; others genuinely curious. Many people, obviously long brainwashed by Israeli propaganda, flung rhetorical questions with the aim of tripping me up. I found little difficulty in coping with such questions, but I was often the object of hysterical outbursts by persons who made no attempt to conceal their hatred. For them, all Palestinians were "murderers," "terrorists," "Nazis." Naturally, when such remarks were hurled at me, I did not accept them meekly, and I would reply in kind. The result was often a violent exchange, with no attempt at a reasonable discussion of the issues. These incidents fortified my apprehensions about the hostility of my audiences, and I became more forceful and aggressive in my presentation.

I did not always get a chance to confront an audience, because not all my scheduled meetings came off. For example, I was told I would be speaking at Brandeis University, in a discussion with Sana Hassan. Sana Hassan, an Egyptian woman long resident in the States, was attracting a great deal of attention at that time by virtue of the book she had published with the Israeli writer Amos Elon. The pro-Israeli press praised her as "a reasonable Arab," but her views were not well received in Arab circles. We did not feel that she was presenting our cause in a correct light; she did not stress Palestinian rights, nor was she sufficiently vigorous in denouncing Israeli excesses. Consciously or not, she became an instrument of Israeli propaganda, serving Israeli interests and doing a profound disservice to the Arab cause. I looked forward to challenging her in an open discussion, which would give me the opportunity to show her up. But at the last moment I was notified that the confrontation would not be held on an equal footing. Instead of a discussion in which we would both appear on the platform, I would be permitted to sit among the audience listening to her address and then pose questions. Astounded, I demanded to know the reason for this sudden change; Rabbi Axelrod, the chairman of the meeting, told me that it had been decided to call off my address when it became known that I "supported the Kiryat Shmonah massacre."

We had a long argument over the phone. Rebuking him for his one-sidedness, I made it quite clear that I deplored violence. But I pointed out that the present plight of the Palestinian people made violence inevitable. In the course of our conversation, Axelrod modified his attitude, conceding that there was some justice to my point of view. But he still refused to permit me to address the public meeting. Instead, he invited me to a breakfast where Sana Hassan was meeting a group of Jewish professors. After some indecision, I attended the breakfast, where I engaged Sana Hassan and some of the professors in a fierce argument.

I had a totally different experience in Los Angeles, where I was invited to speak at the synagogue of Rabbi Beerman. When I arrived at the synagogue, he was there to welcome me. My first sight of him gave me a surprise. For me, the title Rabbi conjured up memories of the Orthodox rabbis of the Mea She'arim quarter of Jerusalem, near my convent school. They were fanatically pious men, living in extreme poverty and self-denial, totally absorbed in their study of ancient Hebrew law, their otherworldliness demonstrated by their medieval clothes and long, untrimmed beards.

Rabbi Beerman bore no resemblance whatsoever to such figures. He is a tall, handsome man, elegantly dressed in modern clothes; he is widely educated, a scholar and a lecturer at UCLA. He and a colleague welcomed me most courteously, and their manner somewhat helped me to overcome the inner tension I could sense. The fact was that the tour, the misunderstandings with its sponsors, the ceaseless attacks and confrontations with hostile questioners were all beginning to get on my nerves, and I felt harassed and on edge. As a result, when I addressed Rabbi Beerman, my manner was unmistakably aggressive. "Rabbi," I said firmly, "the sponsors of this tour have presented me in a rather incorrect light. Let me make matters quite clear: I may not be what you expect. I no longer believe in the state of Israel; I am prepared to accept the idea of a spiritual home for the Jews, but not the militarist and expansionist state that exists now. This is my opinion; it is the opinion of the majority of the Arabs. If you don't want to hear that opinion, I'll withdraw, and we'll cancel the lecture. I've encountered enough enmity and hostility, and I don't want to face any more!"

My hosts listened very carefully to what I had to say. Their manner remained polite and unruffled, and I sensed some embarrassment about my needlessly forceful tone. But I was glad that I had spoken my mind and put matters plainly. They, too, seemed glad to discuss matters openly and frankly. Rabbi Beerman's answer was similarly clear and unconditional: "You may say whatever you wish. This is a free country!"

Reassured that there would be no attempt to muzzle me or censor what I had to say, I relaxed, and the atmosphere thawed. In the course of our conversation, I tried to probe my hosts on their views. I wanted a real dialogue.

"Rabbi Beerman," I said abruptly, "tell me, what does the term *Zionism* mean to you?"

He looked at me thoughtfully. "Today, or in the past?" he asked me.

"Today."

"The return to Israel of those Jews who wish to live there," he declared. "In the past, I took it to mean the return to Palestine or Israel of *all* Jews."

"Yes," I agreed with him. "There is a difference."

The time had come to enter the synagogue. As my hosts led the way, I gazed about curiously. It was a most magnificent edifice, modern, elegant, functional. The seats were filling rapidly as the congregants entered for the Sabbath prayers. They were well-dressed, prosperous-looking people, for whom attendance at the synagogue was obviously an important occasion. As Rabbi Beerman showed us to our seats, I caught numerous curious glances flung in my direction. Once again, I sensed an inner tension as I thought of the forthcoming confrontation. But that was not to come immediately; I was scheduled to speak after the service.

I do not go to church often. Even though our Greek Orthodox church was next door to my Nablus home, I rarely went, aside from the festive mass at Easter and Christmas. When I did go, it was more out of respect for family and social convention than through any feeling for the rites, which are half conducted in Greek and which bore me. My visits to synagogues were, of course, even less frequent—with the exception of one or two wedding ceremonies I had witnessed. That Sabbath prayer, then, was something of a novel experience for me, and I followed it attentively.

At first, I was a little reserved. This beautiful synagogue, so airy and luxurious—could it indeed be a house of worship? I gazed at the women in their expensive elegance. Were these like the pious Miriam from the tales of Agnon, "the most blessed among women," she who toiled and scrubbed so that her husband, Raphael the scribe, could do his sacred work in a pure home? And these hand-some, well-groomed men—were they related to Raphael, who carefully selected his quill for the sublime task of penning a Torah scroll in the service of God? What did these people have in common with the secluded society of Orthodox Jews in Jerusalem, living in their enclosed ghettoes, in strict observance of age-old Jewish tradition?

But the service soon brushed away my doubts. Melodious voices soared high, the organ filled the air with its rich tones, the moment of breathtaking mystery as the Sabbath candles were kindled—all this swept me away into a universe of spirituality. "When senseless hatred reigns on earth, and men hide their faces from one another, then heaven is forced to hide its face; but when love comes to rule the earth and men reveal their faces to one another, then the splendor of God will be revealed. In each of us, there is darkness and light. In kindling these Sabbath lights, we turn away from darkness and search for the light; we resist hatred and embrace love."

Listening to these sublime and touching words, I, too, felt myself entering into the same atmosphere of purity and love. I wanted to curse the tragedies and wars stemming from enmity and hatred; let us exchange it all for love and peace. We reject hatred and embrace love! But for God's sake, where is love? In war? In oppression? In bloodshed?

I surveyed the faces about me. These wealthy Los Angeles Jews did not think of emigrating to Israel. They or their parents had fled the persecutions of Europe and made their homes in the United States. They had adjusted to American society, they considered themselves Americans. They had become a social elite, excelling in the liberal professions, in art and music, in education and business and politics. Their success, their new status and respect came as a compensation for past sufferings. But the security they had attained in their new American homeland did not stifle their deep spiritual and emotional attachment to the state of Israel. For them, Israel was not a homeland in a concrete sense; it represented a hope, a dream, a fulfillment of their own dormant nationalism. Could I efface this beautiful, idyllic vision of Israel? Should I even try?

The service drew to an end. It was time for me to arise and address the congregation. As always, I had taken special care in dressing myself for the occasion. I knew that many of these people would be seeing a Palestinian woman for the first time in their lives. Only too well aware of the stereotyped image they carried in their minds—a primitive, backward Bedouin woman—I resolved that my appearance, too, would play its role in conveying my message. I wore a long Palestinian dress, richly embroidered in cross-stitching. This has been our national costume since Crusader times. Even my dress had its political significance, for the Israeli Maskit handicrafts company, headed by Ruth Dayan, bought up hundreds of such dresses and exported them as "Israeli handicrafts." As I thought of the impoverished Palestinian peasant women, spending days and weeks painstakingly producing these beautiful embroideries, stitch by stitch, I was infuriated to think that their efforts were not even acknowledged as Palestinian folk art. This recollection added a further flavor of bitterness to the conflicting emotions I sensed at that moment. Looking at the rows of congregants, I was well aware that they were the enemies of my people. For years they had given their money and their unstinting moral and political support to the state of Israel, directly assisting in Israeli acts of oppression and injustice against the Palestinians. If my people were persecuted and exiled, without a home of our own, these people sitting in front of me had played a direct and active role in causing our plight. With the exception of a few liberal intellectuals, American Jews rarely uttered a word of criticism of Israeli policies; on the contrary, by providing money and political backing, they had given the Israeli leaders carte blanche to act in any way they considered fit.

Yet alongside my enmity and resentment, I also sensed an unexpected warmth toward these people. True, they were strangers; true, I had good reason to harbor resentment and suspicion toward them. But I had just shared in their prayers, I had listened to their voices intoning: "O God, grant us peace!"; I had shared in the sublime atmosphere of their Sabbath service. It was therefore with very conflicting feelings that I prepared to confront them.

Rabbi Beerman said a few words of introduction. Pointing out to his congregation that I was the first Palestinian to address them, he mentioned that I was from Nablus, the Sh'chem of Jewish history, "a place that has significance for all of us." He spoke of the long history of suffering of the Palestinian people, of their links to the land of the Bible. "We should listen, and try to understand," he concluded.

The service had given me a chance to relax and free myself of my tensions; Rabbi Beerman's warm words of introduction also helped to give me confidence, and I began my address in a soft voice, making no attempt to hide my views, but perhaps expressing them in a more relaxed and less aggressive manner than on other occasions. I began by expressing my appreciation for the service I had just witnessed and for the uplifting air of spirituality in which it was conducted. I spoke of my admiration for Judaism, for the great prophets of Israel and their universal message of peace and justice. If only the state of Israel were conducted in the spirit of their teachings, there would be no war or hostility. I told them of my upbringing, my close contacts with Jews, my family's tradition of hospitality toward the Jews. I spoke of the tragedy shared by all of us—Moslems, Jews, and Christians. Whether it was an Arab forced to leave his home and live in exile or a Jew obliged to spend much of his life in military service, we were all victims of this conflict. I told of the conscientious young Israeli left-wingers—Communists, Hashomer Hatzair, Siah, *Ha'Olam Hazeh,* and other groups—who demonstrated against the government's injustices toward the Arabs of Israel and the occupied territories: against military-government regulations, against land confiscations, against all forms of discrimination. To us Palestinians, I said, such Israelis—even though they are a small minority—are a guarantee of future peaceful coexistence.

I told them of the Israeli government's actions in the occupied territories: the expropriation of land, the military repression, the arrests and house demolitions. I depicted the Israelis' arrogance toward the Palestinian people. I showed how this Israeli disregard for our rights and feelings was the direct cause of the October War, with all its pain and suffering for both Jews and Arabs. I pointed out that the American media were one-sided in their reporting: Fedayeen attacks were described in a manner intended to show the Arabs as cruel and barbaric, while Israeli air strikes at Palestinian refugee camps got scant coverage.

This was not a struggle between two rights, I told them. Nor was it a struggle between two religions. The Palestinians, scattered and homeless, await the awakening of the world's conscience. Those who have right without might have lost their rights; those who have might have also taken our rights. Our country, which was the cradle of civilization and justice, deserves better from humanity.

I concluded my address—and to my utter astonishment, the audience broke into loud applause! I felt a warm flow of pleasure and gratification: My message had gotten through.

Now it was the time for questions. I knew that not all of them would be friendly, but I felt confident I would know how to handle them.

"What about the way the Iraqi government treats its Jews?" someone asked. "What about Palestinian terrorist attacks?" someone else added. Some people, obviously well-meaning but not very well informed, asked naïve questions or threw out superficial comments. "You're anti-Semitic!" someone shouted. "Impossible!" I said swiftly, "I'm a Semite myself!"

One woman stood up, making no attempt to hide the hostility in her voice. "You come here," she said venomously, "with your smooth voice and your refined manner, pretending to be humane—but we know who you are! Your people are terrorists, hijackers, killers! I hate you!"

"Did you love us before?" I retorted smartly. Clearly, there was no point in arguing with an irrational outburst like hers.

Some questioners justified their support for Israel, mentioning their feelings of responsibility for the welfare of the Israelis. "Is that why you send them guns—so that they can kill and be killed?" I told them bluntly that their contributions for Israel were an attempt to overcome their feelings of guilt for not emigrating there. "That's why you're prepared to defend the state of Israel, right down to the last Israeli!"

Along with the fanatics, who were hostile and rude toward me, there were those who were genuinely perplexed, torn between their commitment to Israel and sense of Jewish solidarity and their painful awareness of the injustices perpetrated against the Palestinians. Moreover, I continually pointed out that Israel, too, would have to pay the price of those injustices: If Palestinians lived in misery and humiliation, Israelis would never know peace and security.

"All right, then," one man said, "what do you propose? How can the problem be solved without further bloodshed or injustice to one side or the other?"

There was a sudden silence. I could see people leaning forward to hear precisely what I had to say. I sensed that this was the most important issue, and I wanted to give a frank and effective answer. But first, I had to overcome serious internal doubts. By that time I had come to believe that the conflict could only be resolved by the creation of a Palestinian state alongside Israel, rather than the "secular democratic state for Moslems, Christians, and Jews," as advocated by the PLO. But despite my sincere conviction, I felt reluctant to put forward an idea sharply at variance with the PLO program. Was this not an act of disloyalty on my part, at a time when the PLO was fighting for existence and recognition?

Nevertheless, after a brief hesitation, I decided to speak my mind frankly. "For myself," I said, "I would prefer a unified state in the whole of Palestine. I would like a state where we can all live together—Moslems, Christians, and Jews—with equal rights and equal duties, sharing together in building up the country for the benefit of all its inhabitants.

"However," I went on, "I fear that this is not now possible. Therefore, if we cannot live together, let us divide up the country fairly, so that the Jewish and Palestinian peoples each have enough room to build up a state of their own, states that will be viable and self-supporting. To do this, it will be necessary to partition Palestine in the manner that the United Nations envisaged in 1947. Israel will have to give up the territory it occupied in the 1967 war, and also the additional territory it took over in the Palestine war of 1948. That will leave room for a Palestinian state, and we will be able to coexist side by side."

Many people in the audience seemed upset when I spoke of a secular democratic state. They had been taught that this slogan was just a camouflage for plans to liquidate the state of Israel; they were not prepared to accept the idea of Palestine as a democratic, nondenominational republic—even though they themselves were proud and happy to live in the democratic nondenominational United States. Be that as it may, when I spoke of the alternative possibility of a Palestinian Arab state to coexist side by side with Israel, they agreed that this would be a reasonable and just solution. They did not like the idea of Israel returning to the 1947 borders—but then, I did not expect them to agree with my point of view completely.

That meeting in Los Angeles was one of the highlights of my tour. I felt that I had been put to the test—and faced the challenge. Above all, there was the gratification of knowing that I had gained sympathy for our cause among a Jewish audience.

While in California, I was fortunate enough to be invited to the San Jose home of Moshe Menuhin, father of the famous violinist Yehudi Menuhin. This was, indeed, a rare honor. The Menuhins are an aloof family of Russian Jewish aristocrats, who rarely receive guests. During the early years of this century, they lived in Jerusalem, but they later moved to the United States, where Moshe Menuhin attained renown as an active and articulate anti-Zionist.

I was profoundly impressed by this family that has given so much to humanity. My hosts listened most intently to my accounts of the situation in the occupied territories. The conversation touched on the establishment of a Palestinian state alongside Israel. Moshe Menuhin expressed his vigorous opposition to the idea—not because he was against self-determination for the Palestinian Arabs but because he did not want to see a Jewish state perpetuated. He wanted the Jews to have a spiritual home—not a state. "Look," he said, "the Arabs were good to the Jews; they received us in their homes—and we stabbed them in the back! If the two peoples were to live together in harmony and peace, Palestine could once more become a cradle of civilization and culture."

I heard somewhat different views during another highly emotional meeting with an eminent Jew—I. F. Stone, the respected journalist who has achieved such prominence by speaking out fearlessly against oppression and injustice. When I told him of the sufferings of the Palestinians under Israeli occupation, his eyes filled with tears. "I'm a Zionist!" he declared. "I wanted a Jewish state. But I wanted a different kind of Jewish state!" He expressed his concern about the future in store for the Jews in the Middle East if Israel continued its present aggressive policies.

Moshe Menuhin and I. F. Stone differed greatly in their views, but both men showed great sympathy toward me. I was greatly heartened by my meetings with these two distinguished Jews.

My meetings with resident American Arabs were no less emotional. I was not helped by the advance publicity put out—with misguided good intentions—by the sponsors of my tour. By presenting me as a critic of the PLO, they placed me in a false light, and in some places my meetings were boycotted by the local Arab community, who suspected me of disloyalty to the Palestinian cause. But when I succeeded in overcoming this misunderstanding, my meetings with the Arab and Palestinian *ghorba* (diaspora) were exciting and gratifying.

Many of the Arabs in the States are living success stories. Arriving penniless, they succeed, by hard work and by displaying their natural gifts, in establishing a firm position for themselves. They are prosperous businessmen, professionals, scholars, and teachers; they live in comfort, in beautiful homes, enjoying all the material benefits of American society. Many of them are naturalized American citizens; they have adapted to the American life-style. Their American-born children speak English as their mother tongue and mingle freely with their American school friends.

But with all the honor and respect they have attained in their new home, they do not forget their Arab origins. They remain attached to their homeland, their language, their culture. They take a keen interest in happenings in the Arab world; they share the pain of its setbacks and they rejoice in its successes. After 1967, when the Arab armies were defeated, they, too, felt personally humiliated. At the time of my visit, after the 1973 war, when the Arab peoples were regaining their confidence and self-respect, the American Arabs, too, straightened their backs and looked the world in the eye without dismay.

The Palestinian-born Americans live a kind of dual existence. They achieve great personal and material success—and a sizable portion of their money is earmarked to help their relatives in the refugee camps. Outwardly they are completely integrated into American society and culture, yet inwardly they retain their roots and emotional ties with the homeland.

I was given several graphic illustrations of this duality. There was Dr. Ahmed Hindi, a refugee from Jaffa, now a successful engineer with a flourishing business in New York. He used his new wealth to help his relatives in the refugee camps, and he took a deep interest in the Palestinian cause. But when his father—formerly the prosperous owner of orange groves in Jaffa—talked of "returning home," Dr. Hindi was less than enthusiastic. His business was too good to give up, he said. Nowhere else could he dream of achieving what he had achieved in America. Besides, his children had been born and brought up in the United States; this was where they had their friends, their schooling, their roots—they would not want to "return" to a home they had never seen.

Conversely, there was the case of Dr. Mussa Nasser, a successful physician practicing in Los Angeles. His work brought him an annual income in the hundreds of thousands—and yet his dream was to establish a hospital in his native Bir Zeit, even though he knew that he could expect no more than one-tenth of his present salary.

One of my most dramatic encounters with American Arabs was at the Washington conference of the National Association of Arab Americans (NAAA). There were hundreds of participants—elegant, successful people. They congregated in Washington's Hilton Hotel; that opulent environment was a strange setting in which to discuss the plight of the Palestinian people. But if, outwardly, there was a glaring contrast between the comfort and luxury all around and the miserable conditions endured by the masses of the Palestinians, it soon became evident that the Arab Americans, for all their material success and personal comfort, had not forgotten their ties and attachments to their people and culture. On my tour of the States, I took with me Ismail Shamout's film about Palestine. The film included documentary sections and featured Shamout's own paintings dramatizing the tragedy of the Palestinian people. Two of the highlights of the film was the singer Zinab Sha'at singing "The Urgent Call of Palestine," and Mahmoud Darwish's poem "Write Down I Am an Arab."

The film had an enormous impact. Within a few moments, these hundreds of elegant "Americans," sitting in the luxury of Washington's Hilton Hotel, were transported on a flow of overpowering emotion, which conjured up memories of their former homes and brought them face to face with the fate of their less fortunate brethren. The reaction is hard to describe. Well-dressed men and women suddenly buried their heads in their hands, unable to control their emotions. Some left the room weeping. It was a most moving experience, a striking demonstration of the spiritual unity of the Palestinian people, wherever their wanderings may have taken them.

Not all these meetings were characterized by such unity. The painful disagreements that divide the Arab world and the Palestinian people also found their expression in these circles of exiled Palestinians. At a meeting in San Francisco, I witnessed a violent argument between adherents of rival Palestinian groups. The Fatah, the largest constituent of the PLO, enjoyed comparatively weak support among Arab circles in the United States; in contrast, groups and individuals supporting George Habash's Popular Front for the Liberation of Palestine (PFLP) were much more vocal and prominent. At the meeting in San Francisco, PFLP supporters bitterly at-

23

tacked the Fatah leadership, and Yassir Arafat personally, accusing them of "selling out" the Palestinian cause to Israel and the United States. I was most distressed to hear such terms used in relation to Palestinian leaders. True, they had differences of opinion—that is only natural—but it was painful to hear such accusations of "treason" directed against political adversaries who were, nevertheless, brothers-in-arms. In the occupied territories we do everything in our power to maintain unity, whatever our differences; I found it ironic that in the United States political disagreements were conducted in such an unrestrained manner.

I had a similar feeling of irony when I heard the views of these supporters of the PFLP, who totally rejected any idea of a political settlement with the Israelis. Instead, they flung out firebrand slogans of "battle till total victory," speaking heatedly of fighting for the full rights of the Palestinian people, even if it involved a war that would go on "for a hundred years." Listening to these views, I could not help recalling those American Jews who sit in the comfort and safety of their own homes and heatedly support the most extremely nationalist Israeli positions, quite overlooking the fact that the policies they advocate will exact a terrible price from the Israeli people first and foremost. It was an eerie parallel to hear these Arab intellectuals, living in comfort and security, ten thousand miles away from the Middle East, talking unconcernedly of a war that would last for decades. Would they take such a long-term view if they lived under Israeli occupation or in a refugee camp?

Not that it was easy for me to clarify my own thoughts and feelings. Emotionally, I feel a deep attachment to the whole of Palestine. Shortly before leaving for the States, I again drove to my childhood home in Acre, and I seethed with anger at the thought that I could do no more than pay a fleeting visit there. According to Israeli law, I would have to apply for military-government permission if I wanted to spend a night in the town where I was born. What a searing injustice, what a painful humiliation! How could I consent to the partitioning of my homeland?

But this belonged to the realm of feeling; this was homeland as a state of mind, as a myth. In my rational mind, I knew that I had to view my homeland as a reality, as a feasible social and political entity where I and my fellow Palestinians would be masters of our own fate. However painful the wrench, however outrageous the idea of shelving our claim to the whole of Palestine, the real interests of my people required me to accept a realistic solution capable of solving the painful and immediate problems.

I endeavored to explain these views to the Palestinians I met in the States. I was surprised and gratified to find that even though my opinions were not always accepted, they were heard earnestly and with respect. Accordingly, when I joined in these arguments, pointing out that, under present circumstances, a secular democratic state in the whole of Palestine was not an immediately feasible political objective and that we should instead work for the establishment of a Palestinian Arab state alongside Israel, according to the 1947 partition plan, I noticed that the idea was not rejected, nor were there any attacks on me for uttering it.

A salient feature of these meetings with Arab Americans was the strict security: Visitors were carefully scanned, and all bags searched. At this time, the extremist Jewish Defense League was behaving most aggressively, directing terrorist activities against "hostile" meetings. There were numerous cases of physical assaults against prominent Arab activists, and even diplomats representing Arab countries were harassed and threatened by these Jewish fanatics. This campaign created such an atmosphere of fear and insecurity that, as I told the NAAA meeting in Washington, I sometimes felt more vulnerable in the United States than in Nablus under Israeli military occupation. But what I experienced there and at other meetings was nothing compared with what awaited me when I arrived in Philadelphia.

On our way to the train in Washington, the taxi driver turned on his radio for the news. The first item made us catch our breath: Palestinian fedayeen had taken over a school in Ma'alot, in northern Israel, and were holding the pupils hostage, demanding the liberation of imprisoned Palestinians! After that, we waited anxiously for further reports. By the time our train reached Philadelphia, the drama had reached its bloody and horrifying conclusion: Israeli commandos stormed the school, and dozens of pupils were killed or wounded, along with the fedayeen. The news descended upon us like a thunderbolt; the attack was launched while negotiations were in progress between the fedayeen and the Israelis. I had hoped that the episode would be settled without bloodshed. And then, the horrifying reports poured in. The television stations carried direct transmissions, sent by satellite, showing Israeli soldiers carrying out the mangled bodies of the children, with the screams of the wounded clearly audible. It was an awful sight; I shall never forget it the rest of my life. As the camera focused on the bloodstained face of a sixteen-year-old girl I could not help thinking how she resembled my own daughter. It was atrocious. What made it worse was the bias of the reporters, who put all the blame on the Palestinians, making no mention of the responsibility of the Israeli authorities. If I were not a Palestinian myself, the reporters' words, combined with the bloodcurdling sights shown by the cameras, would have made me hate all Palestinians.

I was shocked and upset; the bloodbath at Ma'alot affected me very deeply. I could sense the tension on the faces of those around me. Tamar Kohns, who came to meet me at the station, tried to calm me down, but I was terribly agitated. We spent the evening with Arab friends, and our political discussion turned into a loud and angry argument. Once again, I felt tense and aggressive.

The following morning, the storm broke. Da'ud and I were having breakfast when Tamar came in and spoke to him in a low voice. I demanded to know what was happening, and reluctantly she told me: Since early morning, there had been eight telephone calls to the Jewish community center threatening that the building would be blown up if I were permitted to speak there. The calls came from the Philadelphia branch of the Jewish Defense League, which threatened to kill me "in reprisal for Ma'alot." The threat was not to be taken lightly. The JDL's record of violence showed that they would stop at nothing in their extremism. The realization hit me—if the meeting went ahead, I faced death!

The director of the Jewish community building decided to take no risks. He announced that the scheduled meeting could not take place. On hearing this, my feelings were mixed: I could not help being relieved, but at the same time, I was angry that the Jewish leaders had given way to the JDL terrorists. I was prepared to risk my life; why were they not prepared to defy the threat?

Then another call came. The meeting was going ahead as planned, but it would be held at the Philadelphia headquarters of the American Friends Service Committee. In the afternoon I spoke before a smaller group of committee members, most of whom were prominent Philadelphia Jews. This session was a sorry affair. In the atmosphere of crisis and tension following the Ma'alot incident, and the air of terror created by the JDL's bomb threats, everyone's nerves were very much on edge. I tried to speak as normally as possible, but I was upset and unsettled. My audience did not have the patience to hear me out, and I faced a lot of heckling. When the time came for questions and comments from the audience, matters soon deteriorated into a shouting match, with everyone yelling and no one listening to anyone else. The previous day's events affected everyone. People in the audience shouted at me, calling the Palestinians "murderers," "terrorists," "maniacs." I did not take this onslaught lightly, and I, too, replied sharply, reminding my listeners of what my people had suffered at the hands of the Israelis. The whole hall seemed to be swept by a blind, irrational anger. One woman burst into tears and hurried out. Da'ud followed her and tried to comfort her. But it was no longer possible to keep matters under control.

The session seemed on the verge of total chaos, when there was a dramatic interruption. Father Lewis entered the hall, his face grave and pale. Raising his arms, he managed to restore quiet for a moment, to make an announcement.

"We have just had a call from the police," he said grimly. "They have received warning that if Raymonda appears at the public meeting scheduled for tonight, she will be executed!"

Father Lewis's words had an astounding effect, like a sudden shower of cold water. There was a moment's shocked silence; and then the whole atmosphere changed completely. Only a few moments before, people had been screaming insults at me. Now they suddenly seemed to realize what lay at stake. However heated, our argument had been abstract, theoretical, not touching them personally. Now they comprehended that this could literally be a matter of life or death for me. Suddenly, I found myself surrounded by concerned, sympathetic faces. People put out their hands to touch me, to reassure me.

What was to be done? In view of the police warning, the Quakers felt that they could not be responsible for my safety if the meeting took place. They looked at me, waiting to see what I would propose. They obviously hoped I would refuse to attend the meeting. I was frightened, and probably showed it. At the same time, I had no intention of letting the threat deter me. Perhaps I would be risking death, but I recalled that there were plenty of Palestinians prepared to stake their lives for our cause. If I was fated to pay the price, very well then, so be it!

Da'ud must have realized what was in my mind. He knew me well enough to understand that I wouldn't be influenced by anything he could say. Whether out of despair or as an indirect way of trying to make me change my mind, he addressed me brutally and forcefully. "I know you're stubborn," he said. "Do whatever you want. Don't worry—I'll see that you get a decent burial."

I could scarcely think clearly; I needed the advice of someone I could trust. I picked up a phone and called Sa'adat Hassan, the senior PLO representative in the United States. I told him of the scheduled meeting, of the JDL threat against my life, and of the reluctance of the Philadelphia people to take responsibility for my safety. Hassan listened carefully to what I had to report; mine was not the only problem of its kind he had to deal with that day. He told me that Dr. Mahdi, a prominent Palestinian, had been stabbed in a clash with a JDL demonstrator. After Ma'alot, everything was possible—though he told me that he himself had addressed a meeting the previous evening and it had gone off without incident. "But please be careful," he begged me. All the same, he advised me not to call off the meeting. "If you do, people will say you were scared!" he predicted. "If the organizers can't guarantee your safety, let them call off the meeting." I took his advice and informed the organizers of the meeting that I was prepared to go ahead—if they were. With that, I threw the ball back at them; living up to Hassan's prediction, they informed me that the meeting was off.

The meeting's cancellation did not yet mean that I was out of danger. I was not permitted to return to our hotel for fear that I would be ambushed. While I waited at the home of friends, Da'ud and Tamar went back to pick up our belongings. Then a group of friends closed in around us like a living shield. They escorted us to the railway station, not leaving our sides until the train left.

Politically and intellectually, my trip to the United States had presented me with some very difficult challenges, forcing me to defend my point of view before audiences ranging from fanatical Zionists to Palestinian diehards. In doing so, I had been reviled and abused—and equally, encountered the most heartwarming responses—from both Jews and Arabs, as well as from "plain Americans" without any "Semitic commitment." I had lived through moments and hours of personal confrontation and terrifying drama. One thing is clear—it was not a pleasure trip. Unlike other tourists who are free to savor the many delights and attractions that America has to offer, I felt that I had a mission, and every free moment was devoted to the task I had taken upon myself—speaking, explaining, arguing, propagandizing the Palestinian point of view.

If I concluded my trip to the States with a sense of personal frustration, it was not because I failed to see Las Vegas or Disneyland. Amidst the haste and flurry of my lightning tour, I had some opportunity to observe the American life-style, with its great stress on personal freedom and the rights of the individual to live his or her life. Of course, American society has its constraints and restrictions too—but it differed completely from the Arab society I knew, hidebound and immobilized by a great weight of outworn tradition. I was particularly envious of the American women I met, who were free to participate in social activities, free to come and go, free to live their lives as they found fit—without having to contend with the stifling conventions that reduce the Arab woman to the level of a sex object and a household slave.

As I have related, I wanted to undertake the American tour on my own. It was only with great reluctance that I heeded the warnings of my Nablus friends who, fearing for my "reputation," insisted that Da'ud accompany me. At the time, I swallowed this surrender to tradition, but it saddened me to forfeit an opportunity to savor the adventure of traveling unaccompanied. My smouldering resentment at being thus "chaperoned" burst into flame when I saw American women who did not have to submit to the restrictions of a conservative, male-dominated society. Here I was, a grown woman, a mother, a political figure who could command the respect and attention of large audiences, and yet I was treated like an irresponsible child who cannot be permitted to go about unaccompanied!

Da'ud took his role of chaperone very seriously. Wherever I went in the course of the tour, he went with me. He watched my every move, listened to my every word, supervised every meeting and conversation. Whenever he found my behavior "unbecoming," he did not hesitate to rebuke me.

During the NAAA conference in Washington, there was a reception at the Hilton. It was a pleasant event, one of the few evenings when I could meet friends, relax, and enjoy myself. There was music and dancing, and the atmosphere was very lively. I sat with a group of friends, Palestinian writers and intellectuals, such as Fawaz Turki. There was plenty of arrack; we talked and sang and recited poetry into the early morning hours. At three o'clock in the morning, the reception ended, but our group was in no mood to go home. Unanimously, we decided to go on to another hotel and continue the festivities.

Throughout the evening, Da'ud sat nearby, taking little part in the proceedings. He found little in common with my companions; they were of a different generation, a different mentality, a different intellectual background. He was completely out of his depth. Now when we decided that we were not going home, he got furious. He took me over to one side, berating me for my conduct. He did not like such open, friendly relationships between men and women; he objected to my "intimacy" with these strange men. "Look!" he shouted, "you're the only woman here!"—echoing the reproaches I heard from my brother George at that party in Amman seventeen years earlier. Da'ud told me my behavior was unladylike, that my constant quest for freedom was harming his reputation. Finally, he insisted that we return to our hotel forthwith.

I argued back with equal vehemence. I rejected all his reproaches and refused point blank to go home. I was highly enraged at being treated in this fashion. Our argument was fierce and violent; finally, with great reluctance, I gave in.

This incident marred my enjoyment of a splendid evening, leaving me frustrated and angry. Thousands of miles from home, I had been given a sharp reminder of the shackles and fetters that bind Arab women. Once again exposed to male tyranny, I sensed myself at an impasse, trapped like a homeless child. Admittedly, my plight could have been worse, like that of the women in the refugee camps or the imprisoned women resistance fighters. But this thought was no consolation.

I felt rebellious and angry, and this anger finally made me face an underlying discontent that had long been bothering me. I had never been truly satisfied with my married status. Right from the very start, as a young bride in Irbid and Nablus, I had resented and resisted the curbs that Arab society places on its women. Time and time again, in my social and political activities, I had clashed with convention and behaved in a manner criticized as "unbecoming" and "outrageous." Now I faced the underlying truth squarely: The fact was that married life, as lived in our strictly patriarchal society, was an intolerable burden upon me. Da'ud's chaperoning on the trip had finally brought home to me that I was a captive; society had placed me in a prison called marriage, where my jailer, warden, and custodian was my husband.

My resentment was not only directed at Da'ud. In my eyes, he represented every man in our Oriental society; and consequently, it was not him alone I had to fight. My anger was against the laws and traditions imposed on Arab women. What was the point of striving for freedom for my people if our struggle did not bring freedom to women—indeed, to every individual?

The truth is that I had often thought of my plight before. But what could I do? Could I dare to rebel, to fly in the face of social conventions and leave Da'ud? It did not require much imagination to foresee the outcome. Only too vividly before my eyes I had the example of my own mother, who had been forced to pay a bitter price for daring to seize her freedom. The men who dominate Arab society have framed laws that punish such a woman with the worst penalty imaginable: She is automatically deprived of her children. Could I willingly run the risk of such retribution? Moreover, I would not be the only one to pay the price. Remembering my own sufferings when I was forcibly parted from my mother, I shuddered to think that my own children might undergo a similar fate.

In the past, whenever my thoughts reached this point and I contemplated the probable outcome of any attempt on my part to strike out for freedom, I experienced a deep sense of helplessness and futility. On one occasion, feeling particularly irked by the restrictions I suffer as a married woman, I went to pour out my heart to Sister Marie Louise, a nun who was once a teacher of mine. I told her frankly and honestly of my suffering and my doubts, my anger at my repression, and my fear of the price I would have to pay for my freedom.

She heard me out, listening patiently to everything I had to say. Then, when I had finished and sat there expectantly awaiting her advice, she spoke to me with compassion, but with the calm, inexorable logic of her vocation. She knew of everything that had happened to me in my childhood when my parents divorced and there was no need for her to remind me of that somber period in my life. But she did refer to it indirectly as she urged me most strongly not to take any rash step. Without mentioning Mother by name, she said decisively, "However much you suffer, it is better that you suffer alone, rather than bring suffering upon others." Her meaning was plain: Those "others" were my children.

No, I could not pay that terrible price; I could not subject my children to such suffering. Sadly and reluctantly, I had to concede that she was right; there was no way out. I must submit to the bonds of marriage—though without resigning myself to its restrictions— and strive for the maximum degree of freedom. As far as was humanly possible, I should try to "build a heaven in hell's despair."

It had always been thus in the past. But now my American trip brought me to the end of my tether. Everything erupted: my resentments and frustrations, my sense of humiliation and imprisonment. I made no attempt to control my feelings. I just knew I would not go back to what I had endured for so long.

I told Da'ud of my decision. "I am going to Beirut!" I said. "You can come with me, or return to Nablus!" It was an ultimatum, and Da'ud recognized it as such. In the face of my determination, he gave in, and agreed to move the family to Beirut.

My decision stemmed from various motives, but all were linked with my yearning for freedom. It was not only my own personal predicament as a woman. Like many other Palestinians from the occupied territories, I was often tempted by the thought of going to live elsewhere, to someplace where I would be free of the endless tension that was our daily lot. It was a choice between staying and fighting for our national independence or of flinging it all behind me and going away to enjoy life.

My reluctance to go back also had its practical side. During my tour of the States, I had expressed my opinions most freely; furthermore, I made no secret of my contacts with leading Palestinian exiles, including officials of the PLO. I certainly never doubted that there had been a close watch kept on my activities in the States, with a detailed report going to the Israeli authorities. The military government was most ruthless in dealing with "offenses" such as mine, even when they were "perpetrated" far from Israeli jurisdiction.

Returning to Nablus now, I might incur the vengeance of the Israeli authorities; I could suffer imprisonment or summary deportation, as had so many of my fellow Palestinians. Perhaps it would therefore be more prudent to stay in Beirut—for the time being at least.

I was attracted to Beirut because of its atmosphere of freedom—political, personal, and intellectual. I knew the city well from previous visits. There I would not be under the constant pressure of a foreign occupation army; I would be living in the Arab country with the highest level of political democracy and freedom of expression, whose climate of tolerance offered me a far higher degree of personal freedom and independence than I could hope for in Nablus in the foreseeable future.

Da'ud had long been dissatisfied with his life of enforced idleness in Nablus, where he drew a salary while his bank remained closed ever since 1967. Accordingly, he bowed to my insistence. From the States, we flew to Beirut, where I stayed while Da'ud headed for Nablus to bring the children.

12

Children of Palestine

AT THAT TIME, in the early summer of 1974, a year before the civil war that was to bring such suffering and destruction, Lebanon was a fascinating country. Rudyard Kipling wrote, "East is East and West is West and never the twain shall meet," but if there was one place where "the twain" did meet, it was Lebanon. Beirut was certainly a Middle Eastern city, but its chic and elegance could compete with anything offered by the capitals of the West. Its boulevards and avenues featured luxurious boutiques, charming cafés and restaurants, lively discotheques and nightclubs.

It was not just material luxury I enjoyed in Beirut. Lebanon, with its democratic and liberal society, long served as a refuge and place of asylum for political exiles from other Arab countries. Here, they were granted a relative freedom of speech and political and intellectual activity. They helped to further fertilize the cross-pollination of Arab and Western culture, with the result that Lebanon witnessed an unprecedented outpouring of new Arab creative thought. Eagerly, I flung myself at these cultural treasures, many of them banned by the Israeli occupation authorities. Here, I was free to explore the poetry and novels of exiled Palestinian writers. I read Arabic journals and political magazines that we were never permitted to see on the West Bank. I devoured the writings of Clovis Maqsud, Fa'iz al-Sa'iq, and other Lebanese writers and journalists. I read Sadek Jalal al-Adem's penetrating *Self-Criticism,* with its incisive, clear-sighted view of Arab defects.

Many of these writers, influenced by their own experiences as well as by modern intellectual trends, wove progressive socialist ideas into their works, thus helping to educate their readers and bring them into the mainstream of up-to-date thinking. I was captivated by the depth of their ideas and thrilled by the frank and open manner in which they expressed their criticisms of the Arab world, attacking it for its ignorance and dependence, its passivity and irresponsibility. They castigated the adulation of leaders that characterizes the Arab world—the idolization of kings, sheikhs, and other rulers. Not even Abdul Nasser was spared their criticism, because of the cult of blind worship that became attached to his name.

They did not need to look very far in seeking targets for their criticism. For all its attractive aspects, Lebanon itself had its share of outmoded political structures, of social and economic inequality, of corruption and indifference for the lot of the less fortunate. While chic Beirut lived its life of affluence and comfort, Palestinian refugee camps all over Lebanon were in a state of misery and subjected to recurrent raids by Israeli planes, who sowed death and destruction among their defenseless population. The Lebanese government and army did nothing to prevent these attacks, nor to defend the Lebanese villagers in the south from raids, shellings, and incursions by Israeli forces. Little concern was shown for the victims of these acts. At most, when sitting in some exclusive café in Beirut, one might be accosted by some elegantly dressed ladies from the Lebanese Red Cross, asking for contributions to help alleviate the sufferings of bomb victims.

Not all Lebanese were so detached. The left and the liberals were deeply concerned over what was happening in their country. The students of the American University of Beirut were also in constant turmoil. But other Lebanese shrugged off what was happening in the south. Regarding themselves as Westerners, they were sure they could count on the support of the American Sixth Fleet in case of any threat to themselves. As for the Palestine problem, the Lebanese paid lip service to our cause, but little more. For me, the Lebanese, by their apathy, symbolized the indifference with which the Arab world as a whole regards our plight. It is this shoulder-shrugging attitude that has imbued us Palestinians with a deep mistrust of the Arab world, forcing us to develop our own nationalism and to rely on ourselves for our own salvation.

After spending three weeks in Beirut on my own, I was joined by Da'ud, who brought the children. How wonderful to be reunited with them! It was now nearly three months since I had seen them last, before setting out for the States. Now we could settle down in Beirut and build a new and more pleasant way of life for all of us, far from the pressures and restraints of occupied Nablus. While waiting for their arrival, I had already begun to look for an apartment, and I now redoubled my efforts.

But it was not long before I learned that I was alone in my enthusiasm for Beirut. Without exception, the children were all opposed to staying in Lebanon permanently. They enjoyed the sights; they were impressed by some things and pleased by others. But they regarded themselves as tourists, not as permanent residents. As far as they were concerned, their only home was Nablus, Palestine, and they could not wait to get back.

When Da'ud arrived, he showed me a poem written by Leila, then twelve years old, on the road from Nablus to Kalkilya, as they were driving to Lod Airport.

HOMELAND

They want me to leave you
They want me to emigrate
They asked me to depart to a new home—
I refused.

O my Homeland, I refused to leave
Your sacred olives and soil.
My Homeland, I will not emigrate
To live in a new home.
Why have they decided thus to leave, Homeland?
For what?

I don't want to leave you and don't want to emigrate.
I want to plant a tree in my land, as did my ancestors;
They remained steadfast and immovable and strong
Till the olive tree grew
They remained steadfast.

My Homeland, to remain within you—that's what I want;
I want to die within your bounds
I want, my Homeland, to live from thy sacred soil and sacred olives.
I will not emigrate, not forsake you, my beloved Homeland.

Leila's poem touched me deeply, particularly since I knew she
was expressing not only her own feelings but those of the other children too. The arguments went on, back and forth: Beirut, Palestine,
homeland, freedom. I tried to convince them, but the children remained immovable.

I remained with my doubts. What about the Israeli authorities?
Would I not be jeopardizing myself by returning to their control,
after my outspoken American tour?

But Da'ud reassured me. At his request, Nablus mayor Haj
Ma'azuz al-Masri had approached Amnon Cohen, adviser to the
military governor of the West Bank. Cohen is not one of the hard-
faced Shin Bet officers, with their narrow-minded intolerance of
"dangerous thoughts"; as an intellectual Hebrew University lecturer, he took a more tolerant view, assuring al-Masri that I could
return without fear of retribution. (Eliezer Be'eri of Mapam also denied the idea of me being punished for my views. "Since the 1973
war," he said, "young Israelis have been saying things that are far
'worse' than anything Raymonda has ever said.")

I remained undecided for some time, but the outcome was predictable. Faced by the united opposition of my children, I was
forced to give in.

After two months in Beirut, we packed our possessions and
headed for home.

My short-lived rebellion at an end, I returned to Palestine. The
children were overjoyed and relieved at being back.

We sold our home in Nablus and moved to Ramallah.

With renewed vigor, and with the added assurance and self-confidence I had gained on my American tour, I flung myself once more
into my political activities.

It was 1974—a year after the October War, seven years after the Israeli occupation. Opposition to Israeli rule was growing more active and aggressive. More and more, Palestinian protests were spearheaded by our youth, particularly by that fine generation of young boys and girls, the students of our high schools, who had grown up under occupation and could scarcely remember a time when we hadn't lived under Israeli military domination. Perhaps that was the precise reason why they found occupation all the more intolerable, giving them an increasingly prominent role in all forms of opposition and resistance.

Almost daily, at some place in the West Bank, Palestinian school students clashed with the Israeli occupation forces. There were strikes and sit-ins, demonstrations and processions—most of which ended with violent clashes as Israeli troops and police moved in. But despite the beatings and gassings they suffered, despite the arrests and the brutal interrogations, the heavy fines and terms of imprisonment imposed on them, these young "offenders" continued to defy the occupation authorities.

By now, three of my own children were in their teens, and all attended schools which were the scenes of repeated upheavals. My children took an active part in all these events. During the demonstrations launched to coincide with Arafat's address to the United Nations Assembly, Dianna was beaten and clubbed. At Gaby's school, demonstrations followed a regular pattern: The boys would march out of their classrooms and head for the neighboring girls' school, pelting it with a veritable barrage of stones to "persuade" its teachers into allowing the girls out to join them.

My feelings were mixed. I was proud of our youngsters, of the courage with which they faced armed soldiers, of their persistence and fortitude in reforming whenever their marches were broken up. With tears streaming from their tear-gassed eyes, often bruised and bleeding, they refused to disperse; instead, they picked up their banners, formed up into a line, and, chanting their songs and slogans, marched forward again, to meet the next onslaught.

Although I was proud, I was also anxious. Boys and girls no older than my children were being beaten and imprisoned. Some were so brutally handled they had to be hospitalized. On all too many occasions, Israeli troops used their firearms against the unarmed demonstrators, and their "warning shots in the air" resulted in numerous cases of death and injury. As a mother, knowing the risks and dangers awaiting her children, how could I help feeling afraid?

Of course, I never tried to dissuade my children from doing their duty. It would not have done any good to try. As I followed the dictates of my conscience, they too acted as they considered just and correct. Could I blame them?

On one occasion, a messenger came to summon me to Dianna's school. Hurrying there, I found a scene I had often witnessed before. The girls had marched out of their classrooms, with the aim of going into the streets to demonstrate. The school principal and the other teachers—terrified of being held responsible by the Israeli authorities—endeavored to forestall any "disturbances" by locking the school gate, to prevent the girls from getting out. When I arrived, the situation was at stalemate: The girls could not get out of the courtyard, but they refused to return to their classrooms. They stood inside the locked gate, chanting their slogans and demanding to be permitted out.

The principal, an Italian priest, had called for me, hoping I would exercise my influence on Dianna and the other girls to persuade them to "restore order." If matters had not been so earnest, it could have been a comical scene—the Italian priest turning appealing eyes toward me to rescue him from his predicament, while his pupils, locked in the courtyard, gave vent to their frustrations by chanting slogans against "Italian imperialism."

That particular representative of "Italian imperialism" was in for an unpleasant surprise. Instead of coming to his assistance, as he had hoped, I proceeded to "betray" him by telling him—in a loud voice, so that the girls could hear—that he ought to open the gate and let the girls conduct their demonstration. "It's their right!" I told him loudly, and I was rewarded with a hearty cheer from his pupils.

There were less lighthearted incidents. A man named Muhammad Kawaja, arrested on suspicion of belonging to the resistance, committed suicide in prison. His funeral was to be a mass demonstration of protest. Never having believed in shielding my children from the realities of life, I decided to take my two youngest daughters, Suha and Hala.

It may have been a serious miscalculation on my part. The funeral was a shocking event. Our villagers are primitive, emotional people, not in the habit of containing their feelings. They are uninhibited in their celebrations; equally, their calamities evoke unrestrained displays of grief of a character and intensity quite unknown to Western peoples and, indeed, far more extreme than the behavior of mourners in urban Arab society.

On this occasion, the mourners were even more outspoken in their grief. The man was a political victim, a martyr who had met his death at the hands of the foreign occupying power. As a result, the funeral procession turned into an emotional outburst the like of which I have rarely seen. Men shouted and wailed, women wept and screamed, tearing at their hair and their clothes. When the body was brought out, the scene turned into one of mass hysteria, as the women ululated the traditional mourning cries, while angry shouts arose from all sides. As the procession made its way toward the grave, passions rose to ever higher and more intolerable peaks. People flung themselves on the coffin, weeping uncontrollably. Men and women fainted from emotion. When they were helped back onto their feet, they renewed their semidistracted cries.

It was a moving, overwhelming experience, almost too much for the nerves of an adult, much more so for the sensitivities of a child. Scarcely into their teens, my daughters were totally unused to anything of the sort. Quite unprepared for this nerve-shattering display, they were shocked and horrified, clinging to me fearfully as they gazed about them with pale, astonished faces.

It was a real ordeal for them, far too much for them to take. That night, they could not close their eyes; sleeplessly, they lay in bed, upset and crying, calling to me to come and sit with them. As I sat at their bedsides, trying to calm and reassure them, I asked myself whether I had done right in taking them to the funeral. Perhaps not; but then I reminded myself that there was no point in hiding the truth from them. They were growing up in a land under foreign occupation and repression, and sooner or later they would have to learn precisely what that meant.

As the mother of teen-agers growing up at a time of increasing opposition to occupation, there was a further problem that troubled me. At regular intervals, the Israeli authorities arrested groups of Palestinians, whom they charged with forming underground cells of the Palestinian resistance organizations. Some were accused of carrying out armed attacks; other cells were said to have been uncovered during the early stages of their formation. On most occasions, the authorities claimed to have discovered hidden caches of arms and explosives. Many of those arrested were youngsters, with high school students prominent among them. Some were no older than my own children. Clearly, at least some of our young people, despairing of the political struggle against occupation, had decided that armed resistance was the only solution. But the Israeli security services are highly efficient, with numerous agents and the most sophisticated—and brutal—methods of finding out what was happening in the territory they administered. Most of the groups were caught before they could get properly organized; the young conspirators, lacking experience, were no match for the Israeli Shin Bet. In some cases, one member of a group was caught and then interrogated so brutally that he broke down and revealed the names of his companions. Armed with the lists of names, the Israeli police swooped, netting dozens of young Palestinians.

Without any reservations, my sympathies lay with these young people, ready to risk life and liberty, to face suffering and torture for the liberation of their people. And yet, when I saw the terrible price they paid, their own agony and the distress of their parents and families, I could not help feeling terrible misgivings. As the Israeli security services cracked down again and again, overwhelming and surprising the clandestine groups, these attempts at armed resistance sometimes appeared quite futile. The price these young people paid seemed much too high for the unappreciable extent to which they caused any harm to the Israelis.

What, then, if my own children decided to join such a group? It would be a perfectly understandable act, under the circumstances. I would never dream of reproaching them if they did so; on the contrary, I would not try to conceal my pride. And yet, when I thought of the fearful dangers involved, I could not help shuddering at the prospect. The risks of discovery and arrest, the physical and mental agony to which these young people are subjected, the terrible retribution of the occupation authorities—the idea that one of my own children might face all this was and remains a recurrent nightmare. Such is the lot of a mother in an occupied land.

Still, all these fears notwithstanding, I drew much encouragement from my children's commitment to the burning issues engaging our people. And more and more, their home was becoming a center of political discussion and thought. In many cases, people of opposing views chanced to visit me simultaneously, and the ensuing political discussions often erupted into loud and angry confrontations.

One such confrontation occurred in December 1971, when Herbert Marcuse and his wife came to my house, in the course of their well-publicized visit to the Middle East to study the Arab-Israeli conflict at first hand. They came accompanied by a large group of Israeli intellectuals—professors and lecturers from the Hebrew University and the Van Leer Institute, as well as Eliezer Be'eri and Muhammad Watted from Mapam. To meet them, I had invited a group of prominent Nablus intellectuals and political figures, headed by Mayor Hamdi Kna'an.

Marcuse had refused to make any comment about the conflict before hearing Palestinian viewpoints. His wife opened the discussion by presenting a series of questions about the nature of Israeli occupation. She asked about demolitions, deportations, about land confiscations and torture in prison. In each case, she asked for facts and figures, commenting gently that it was important to be precise and to avoid exaggerations.

"Yes, this we know," replied one of the Palestinians. "Since the Israeli occupation, there are many things we have learned. We have to abandon our old ways of thinking, because our enemies profited from our exaggerations."

Another man—a doctor—attacked Israeli expansionist policies. "They want to hold on to everything, not to give up any territory. They want us to submit! What about Jerusalem, what about the Golan?"

Be'eri butted in, "The Israeli settlements below the Golan were constantly attacked and shelled before 1967. Now we have to hold the Golan, to protect them!"

All this time, Marcuse himself had been sitting silently, listening very intently to the exchange. Now he commented, "But there would be no danger if the Golan were restored and demilitarized. You Israelis are losing an opportunity for peace. It will be a big mistake if you don't take the initiative now and accept the Egyptian peace proposals. You must prepare your people for a mood of understanding and trust, in preparation for an end to the conflict."

Now came the turn of one of the Hebrew University lecturers— Menahem Milson (he later became a prominent official in the military government). Milson alleged that Arabs remain logical until they touch on the Arab-Israeli conflict, and then "they cease to think clearly." He complained that Arab leftists see Israel as nothing more than a tool of imperialism.

Marcuse again made a comment. "There are Arab states that also serve imperialist aims," he pointed out.

One of the Palestinians retorted, "We are not the tools of others. Israel is always the first to threaten those Arab states that are anti-imperialist. *Israel* is a tool—more so than any Arab state!"

The argument raged back and forth. At its conclusion, Marcuse promised to send us a copy of the statement he would make at the end of his stay. A few days later, before leaving Israel, he handed out a carefully worded condensation of his views about the conflict, entrusting it exclusively to those journalists who undertook to publish it in entirety without any editing or omissions. In his statement, Marcuse mentioned that he had always felt sympathy toward Jews suffering persecution, but he could find no sympathy for Jews who persecute others. Marcuse's statement was attacked in the Israeli press, because of its fairness toward the Arab case—side by side with considerable understanding for Israel and its problems.

While Marcuse and the other distinguished guests were debating, my children sat nearby, listening carefully to every word. Naturally, they took no active part in the argument, but there was no mistaking their interest. As a result of these informal "political seminars" they attended at home, on top of their active involvement in the political ferment constantly sweeping the West Bank, my children were quick to reach a high level of political sophistication and independence at an unusually early age.

On one occasion, the whole family was crossing the bridge from Jordan. Da'ud and the children had completed their examination, but, as usual, I was involved in an argument with the officer in charge. Seeing Da'ud and the children sitting there waiting, one of the officers sauntered over to them and said in Arabic: "Don't worry, your mother will soon come!"

Hala—about ten at the time—responded. "You speak Arabic! Are you an Arab?"

"I am from Iraq," replied the officer.

Hala was shocked. "Aren't you ashamed, as an Iraqi, to be serving in the Israeli army?"

The officer smiled. "But I'm a Jew!" he exclaimed.

"A Jew or a Zionist?" Hala asked.

Again the man laughed. "What's the difference?" he asked her teasingly.

"I know," asserted Hala confidently, "but I don't want to tell you."

At this point, Da'ud came over to see what they were talking about. The officer explained that he wanted Hala to tell him the difference between a Zionist and a Jew. Da'ud turned to Hala and said encouragingly: "Go on, tell him."

Hala looked at the officer. "A Jew is a religious person. But a Zionist wears a uniform and carries a gun; he kicks Arabs from their homes and kills them!"

The officer stood there in astonishment. Then, turning on his heel, he went into the office where I was meanwhile having my argument with the officer in charge of the bridge. Flinging open the door, the Iraqi officer shouted: "Leave the mother. Come outside and talk to her daughter!"

13

"Press Officer for the West Bank"

MANY IMPORTANT NEWSPAPERS, radio, and TV networks have reporters in Israel. The area they cover includes the occupied territories. Unfortunately, many of these foreign newsmen come with preconceived ideas and prejudices against the Palestinian people; not only do they oppose our political aims, they bear ingrained notions about "Arab unreliability," believing that we give our imaginations free rein and that therefore anything we say is not to be credited. As though that were not bad enough, since the reporters are being posted to Tel Aviv or Jerusalem, many of them do not trouble to come to the occupied territories to see for themselves. They prefer to sit in comfort in Israeli government press offices, where Israeli public relations experts feed them part truths and distortions. When they do come to the occupied territories, they are often taken on "conducted tours" by Israeli liaison officers, who show them whatever they want them to see, gently shepherding them away from places where they might find out "awkward" truths about the policy of the occupation authorities. On top of all this, the Israeli government keeps a close watch on what foreign journalists send off under the pretext of "military" censorship, and troublesome journalists who ask the wrong questions or insist on seeing for themselves suffer various forms of subtle harassment.

As a result of all this, the world's media were long inundated with Israeli-inspired reports, while little or nothing was heard of our point of view. This one-sided picture was particularly blatant during the early years of Israeli occupation, immediately after 1967. So prejudiced were many of the Western news media that many Palestinians became totally hostile toward foreign journalists, refusing to have anything to do with them. "Whatever we say, they'll misrepresent us!"

I did not give up. On the contrary, I set myself the large task of competing with the Israeli information services, which are lavish with daily news bulletins and handouts. Perhaps without fully realizing what I was taking upon myself, I set out to supply news to those Western journalists who seemed genuinely interested in hearing our point of view. It was hard work, acting as "unofficial press officer for the West Bank." Every morning, I would phone the municipalities of the various West Bank towns, trying to find out what was happening. There was rarely a shortage of events—land confiscations, house demolitions, protests, demonstrations, sit-ins, arrests, interrogations, curfews. Many of these incidents were not reported anywhere. The Arabic newspapers, under strict Israeli censorship, dared not publish "unauthorized" news. Israeli papers, all under some form of established control, naturally cooperated in suppressing "unfavorable" items.

As for the foreign media, they simply did not know. I made it my business that they did find out.

Sometimes, they came to me. Reporters, TV teams, visiting journalists on a tour of the Middle East—all these made it a habit to come to my house and ask me for information on the latest developments. But when there was some event of particular importance, I did not wait to be asked; I would pick up the phone and contact the offices of leading newsmen in Jerusalem. Once the news got out to one or two of them, I could usually rely on the story being picked up by news agencies or other papers.

It was an uphill struggle. At first, I lacked experience. I did not know how to choose the most important stories; I did not know how to present them. It took some time before I found which journalists could be trusted. Conversely, it took time for some of them to learn to trust my reports and not brush them off as the products of my feverish "Oriental imagination." In time, their confidence in me grew, and I had the satisfaction of seeing the world press publicizing incidents that would never have appeared without my efforts to get the news to their representatives.

Israeli journalists posed a particular problem. While the Israeli media generally follow their government's line, and display bitter hostility toward us, there is a minority of honest Israeli journals and journalists who are genuinely concerned for our cause and have proved themselves to be true friends of the Palestinian people. In addition to Uri Avneri's *Ha'Olam Hazeh* and the Israeli Communist party's Hebrew and Arabic papers, which have consistently defended the Palestinian people, there are individual journalists who have had the courage to defy official disapproval in publicizing atrocities and injustices inflicted by the occupation authorities. As a result of their insistence, their reports, highly critical of the Israeli military administration, have appeared in Israeli dailies like *Ha'aretz* and even in papers closely connected with the Israeli establishment, such as *Al-Hamishmar* and *Davar*.

I have always placed considerable stress on fostering close contacts with Israeli opposition journals and even with journalists who, without any clear political commitment to our cause, are yet honest enough to publish the facts without trying to suppress or distort them. After all, if our message is to get through to the ordinary Israeli, we must try to present it by way of the media from which he draws his information. But this view was not always self-evident to people in the West Bank, especially at times of stress and tension. When Israeli security forces clash daily with demonstrators, using the most brutal methods to put down any form of protest or dissension, their victims may be forgiven for harboring resentment against all Israelis, including representatives of the Israeli media. This is well known to Israeli journalists themselves. Recently, employees of Israeli TV refused to undertake assignments in the occupied territories until their employers agreed to take out personal insurance for a quarter of a million Israeli pounds for every TV reporter.

At times, my efforts to assist friendly Israeli journalists have placed me—and them—in situations that were delicate if not downright dangerous. On one occasion, a young man was killed in a demonstration in Nablus. Marcel Zohar of *Ha'Olam Hazeh* arrived, intending to report on the funeral; he asked me to accompany him to the house of the bereaved family. I looked at him in astonishment. Could he, an Israeli journalist, want to visit the family of a boy who had just been killed by Israeli soldiers? And, moreover, could he expect me to accompany him? Didn't he know what a hornet's nest he would stir up? I must confess that I trembled at the thought of the danger to both of us. I told Marcel that if he wanted to, he could go alone with the photographer; I would not go with them.

"If you don't come," said Marcel, "I won't go alone, because I don't speak Arabic and I need an interpreter." Still I hesitated, but Marcel insisted. "It's your duty. If you don't come, you'll be helping the Israeli establishment to hide the truth!" Left with no choice, I consented.

This argument took place in the municipality. The mayor sent a messenger with us, and we made our way to the house. On the way, we encountered an angry mob, who realized that Marcel and the photographer were Israelis. Men shouted, "All Israelis are criminals, murderers!" and they surged around us. The atmosphere was highly charged. The general anger of the population against Israelis was heightened by the preparations for the funeral, with black banners and other marks of mourning. I explained that these men had been sent by Uri Avneri, that they were our friends. The name Avneri had its effect. Some of the more intelligent people in the crowd managed to calm the hotheads, and we were able to go on.

We entered the house. It was a very humble, impoverished family. The unfortunate woman was sitting on the carpet, weeping bitterly. I walked up to her, kissed her, and expressed my condolences. I introduced myself as a Palestinian journalist and asked her some questions. She explained that her son had just left the house for half an hour, to buy a loaf of bread, and while he was outside, Israeli soldiers breaking up a demonstration shot him. Silently, I listened to her sad account, making mental notes of the details for Marcel.

When I sensed that we had stayed long enough, I beckoned to Marcel to come outside. As we were going out, a young man hurled himself at Marcel; later it transpired that he was the dead boy's brother. The young man screamed, "I'll kill you! I'll kill every Israeli!"

People tried to hold the young man back, but he got his hands around Marcel's throat and tried to throttle him. No one could make him loosen his grip; there were shouts and screams from every side. Hurling myself at the young man with tears in my eyes, I screamed at him, "In the name of the Palestinian revolution! In the name of the martyr Samir! Please leave them alone, they are friends!" Where the efforts of the others had failed, my tears and my frenzied screams had their effect. The young man released his hold, and Marcel was free to go. It was a long time before I could overcome my trembling.

Despite such painful incidents, my work with foreign journalists has gained growing appreciation in most Palestinian political circles. But my success in getting our viewpoint across was very irritating for the Israeli authorities. Despite their protestations that theirs is a "liberal" occupation and their claims that we are free to express our opinions, in practice the Israeli authorities are considerably less liberal. Because of their dependence upon foreign—above all, American—support, they are extremely sensitive about their image in the world media, and they become highly irritated when foreign journalists present unfavorable reports. The more effective I became in revealing the truth about Israeli occupation, the more they displayed their displeasure. There was nothing underhanded in what I did. I did not conceal my contacts with foreign pressmen; they were usually conducted over the phone, which is easily tapped. The Israeli authorities had no difficulty in finding who was supplying "undesirable" news items to the press, nor was it difficult to discover who guided foreign journalists to locations skillfully skirted by Israeli liaison officers.

The military government lost no time in showing that it considered my activities hostile. After that first big sit-in in the Nablus municipality—when I brought Uri Avneri and his journalists to witness our protest—I was called in by the military governor of Nablus, who warned me to have no further contacts with Israeli opposition journalists. Later, during the 1973 war, when rumors circulated around the West Bank about Israeli soldiers abandoning front-line positions near the Jordan and generally expressing their reluctance to risk their lives in the fighting, I passed these reports to foreign pressmen, who published them. The Israeli response was not slow in coming: I was again called to the military governor for a severe warning against disseminating "false news," while the Israeli press published vicious attacks on me—one outcome being the hysterical onslaught to which I was subjected by the lecturers of the Hebrew University.

Whenever I met Israeli military officials, I sensed their growing irritation at my activities. In keeping with their "liberal" image, they denied attempting to suppress the truth. On the contrary, their principal complaint against me was the inaccuracy of my reports. Their allegations became more and more absurd. As I have already related, during the demonstrations that coincided with Arafat's address to the United Nations General Assembly, the military governor reprimanded me for reporting that the town was on strike. "But the town is on strike!" I replied, astonished. "Yes, but you sent off the report even before the shopkeepers closed down!" was his furious reaction. Smiling, I pointed out that every journalist tries to get the news as it is "breaking." But he remained unimpressed by my journalistic successes. Somehow, he seemed to suspect that my report to *The New York Times,* ten thousand miles away, had actually caused the strike to break out in Ramallah.

But for all these patent absurdities, I knew that the Israeli authorities were not concerned with logic, freedom of information, or journalistic veracity. Their objective had little to do with such lofty motives. They simply wished to reduce to a minimum any contacts between Palestinians and the foreign media, in the hope of preventing the latter from presenting our viewpoint. In pursuing that aim, they were repeatedly foiled by my increasingly effective and close contacts with Western journalists. In consequence, official warnings grew more and more pointed and direct; if I did not refrain from issuing my "false reports," I was told, I faced "the gravest consequences." There was no need for them to elaborate what these "consequences" could be. Military-government regulations, in force in the occupied territories, gave the Israelis a free hand to apply severe penalties for vaguely defined "offenses." Palestinians accused of "hostile actions," of whatever nature, found themselves under administrative arrest, which sometimes meant spending months or years in prison without ever being brought to trial. There was another form of retribution favored by the Israeli authorities, again without any judicial hearing—deportation. The "offender" would be arrested late at night, held incommunicado till the early morning, and then, without any possibility of legal redress or even of communicating with his family, be driven across the Jordanian or Lebanese border. Once expelled, it was very rare for the authorities to permit a deportee to return to his home.

I had no illusions about the "grave consequences" I faced. Whether arrest or deportation, I knew that I would not be the only one to suffer. My children were young, and I could imagine what a terrible shock it would be for them if they were thus brutally separated from me. The Israeli officials were not above reminding me of the fact. "Don't forget," they would "tactfully" say, "you're a mother." The implied threat was obvious and unsubtle.

Nevertheless, I refused to be deterred. I had undertaken a certain task, and I would not be gagged; nor would I voluntarily accept any restraints.

It was not the military government alone that frowned on my activities. My behavior and life-style were now very unlike those expected of Arab women. I no longer made any pretense of playing the retiring Arab housewife who sits obediently in the corner, serving coffee to her guests and making small talk with the ladies. Instead, I flung myself into the frequent political discussions at our house in a most "unbecoming" manner, freely exchanging opinions with the visiting dignitaries—men for the most part.

This was not my only departure from tradition. Not content with conducting myself in an "unladylike" manner at home, I showed no hesitation about touring the West Bank with strange men— foreigners to boot—and moreover, doing so unchaperoned!

My husband, Da'ud, has moved a long way from the conservative views he held when we first married. All the same, he makes no attempt to conceal his belief that a woman's foremost responsibility is toward her husband and children; she should look after her home and not concern herself with such "masculine" pursuits as politics. Aside from his own views, he undoubtedly felt that my activities reflected unfavorably on his social standing. Since I was increasingly in the limelight, he found himself more and more overshadowed by his own wife—a most unusual situation in male-dominated Arab society. He was sensitive to remarks by his traditionalist friends;

holding him "responsible" for me, they asked him why he tolerated my behavior, hinting that he should impose his masculine authority and bring me into line.

Da'ud made no secret of his discontent. He is a quiet man, who dislikes turmoil and upheaval; the constant coming and going in our house was not at all to his liking. He complained bitterly that my constant preoccupation with politics was taking up my time, to the detriment of the children. "You should be helping them with their French lessons instead of talking to journalists!" With considerable justice, he pointed out that my political involvement was costing him large sums of money: My daily phone calls all over the West Bank and to foreign journalists in Jerusalem and Tel Aviv had sent our phone bill up to astronomical heights, thousands of Israeli pounds every month. Above all, he repeatedly warned me that the Israeli authorities would wreak retribution on the whole family.

But all these complaints and warnings—however well founded factually—were no more than a mask for Da'ud's basic discontent. His wishes were simple and uncomplicated: He wanted me to abandon politics and behave like a traditional Arab housewife and mother.

I found myself facing a strange coalition. Israeli military officials made common cause with my own husband in presenting identical demands. The pressures were very different, the arguments employed bore little resemblance, but the objective was the same: Both Da'ud and the Israelis wanted me to give up my political activity and revert to the traditional role of the housebound Arab wife.

But I was obstinate. By now I was fully launched into political and journalistic activity, and I had not the faintest intention of giving it up. Ignoring Israeli threats and Da'ud's blandishments, I forged ahead. If anyone wanted to limit my freedom, he should not expect my consent! If I was to be restricted to a cage, it would have to be done by force.

At long last, the Israelis got the message. On August 12, 1976, Colonel Ya'akov Katz, military governor of Ramallah, informed me that from that moment on I was under house arrest for an unlimited period of time.

14

Imprisonment
Is a State of Mind

HOUSE ARREST. I am strictly forbidden to leave the house at any time of the day or night.

Every few hours, a patrol passes the house, and the officer inquires about "the lady." Most of the time, the policeman on guard has nothing to do. We take a chair outside and put it in the doorway; every now and then, the children take out a cup of coffee for him. It is painful to see him suffer. It must be especially hard during the night; the nights are cold in Ramallah, and a chilly breeze comes up from the coast.

After a few days, we go a little further in our care for the policeman—in the evenings, when there are no visitors to challenge, we invite him inside to watch television.

One day, an officer passes by and discovers the policeman inside the house. He is furious. After that, the policemen on duty are given strict orders to remain outside the house.

Overnight, I am subjected to forced inactivity. I, who have always been so active, who could never stay at home, perpetually finding something to do, am now confined within four walls. Just like a conventional housewife. I think of my friends and acquaintances, women who follow the traditional role of the Arab mother and housewife, presiding over her narrow little kingdom, rarely venturing outside except for the most immediate needs. Their way of life has always frightened me. Tied to the boredom and pettiness of domesticity, gradually sinking into inertia, with their horizons becoming progressively narrower. It is an awful fate, a vegetative existence without meaning or value.

Is my detention aimed at getting me accustomed to this way of life? Never!

Not content with confining me to my home, the military authorities have disconnected my phone. The legal basis for this act is in the Defense Regulations, which the British mandatory government issued in 1945 as part of its attempts to repress the Jews. And now the Jews are using the same law against us! The bitter irony of history. By disconnecting my phone, the authorities have shown the real motive for my detention. While their spokesmen leak stories accusing me of organizing strikes or demonstrations or civil disobedience—there is a different "explanation" each time—their real aim is to cut my links with the foreign press. Without a phone, and confined to my house, I cannot communicate with my contacts throughout the West Bank. I am unable to collect the news, nor can I pass on reports to the foreign journalists in Jerusalem or Tel Aviv nor continue my work for the San Francisco radio station that has been broadcasting my commentaries.

It is very simple: They want to gag me.

There is a foreign news agency I used to work for on a voluntary basis; I supplied them with regular reports on events in the West Bank. Now my place has been taken by an Israeli Arab, a man whose reports are full of factual distortions and misrepresentations. Many of these are obviously aimed at stirring up trouble and dissension within the Palestinian people. The fact that these reports come by way of an "objective" foreign agency gives them greater credibility; on several occasions, these pieces of "misinformation" have succeeded in sowing grave dissension among our people. He invents stories of clashes between Christians and Moslems. He makes up accounts of "friction" between rival families in an attempt to stir up divisions. When the Israeli authorities order Ramallah schools to expel pupils who took part in protest demonstrations, he lays the blame for the dismissals at the door of Ramallah's popular nationalist mayor, Karim Khalef, trying to smear him as a "collaborator" with the occupation authorities. Yet if ever a man proved himself a Palestinian patriot, it is Karim: This man combines an uncompromising, outspoken opposition to the Israeli occupation with a realistic, moderate policy of future coexistence with the state of Israel.

This "journalist" causes endless mischief; clearly, he is working for the Israeli authorities, but with me under detention, there seems to be no one capable of countering his lies. Israeli friends urge me to take action against this subtle form of psychological warfare, but what can I do, confined as I am?

Within a few days of the arrest order, it becomes clear that the authorities have made one serious miscalculation. They hoped that I would be cut off from the outside world, but they didn't reckon on the loyalty of my friends. As the news of my house arrest gets around, people pour into the house. The visitors come from Ramallah and Nablus, and other parts of the West Bank. Not all my acquaintances show up. Some are frightened away by the knowledge that their visit would be reported to the occupation authorities. Some people—particularly several Nablus notables—are explicitly warned not to visit me. But these measures are only partially effective. Despite the warnings, despite the policeman who notes down their names and addresses, friends come to visit me, to encourage me, to demonstrate their solidarity.

Expressions of solidarity are not confined to residents of the occupied territory. Dozens of Israelis also come to see me, Jews as well as Arabs, old friends and political comrades-in-arms. Uri Avneri comes, accompanied by his friend, the well-known lawyer Amnon Zichroni, a conscientious objector in his youth and a prominent figure in civil rights cases ever since. Amnon undertakes my legal defense before the Israeli authorities, although the arbitrary nature of military-government regulations makes it most unlikely that anything will be gained by approaching the courts. Avneri's visit reassures me: I know from past experience that whenever he tackles a problem, he goes about it in a thorough manner.

There are other eminent Israeli visitors. Dr. Yisrael Shahak of Israel's League of Human Rights comes to encourage me to stand firm. Several members of the Knesset, the Israeli legislature, also pay me visits: Avraham Levenbraun, of the Communist party (Rakah), comes with his wife; they are followed by Marcia Friedman, of the Independent Socialists, and by one of the most prominent Israeli doves, Aryeh (Lova) Eliav. Eliezer Ronen, of Mapam, a member of the government's Knesset coalition, comes to talk to me and subsequently approaches Defense Minister Shim'on Peres, demanding my release.

Another sign of solidarity: telegrams from numerous Israeli lawyers, Jews and Arabs, offering to undertake my defense.

Another miscalculation of the Israeli authorities: They thought that by detaining me at home and depriving me of my phone, they would sever my contacts with the foreign press. But they are wrong. My friends among the Western journalists do not forget me. Whenever they tour the West Bank, they drop in to see me. As before, they ask me for news of what is happening in the area, and I endeavor to supply them with whatever I know. Often, they have the opportunity of meeting other Palestinians, of posing questions and hearing the views of prominent West Bankers. Even more than ever before, my home is a "political salon" and a place for informal meetings and discussions, where foreign journalists and visiting politicians can meet Palestinians.

Furthermore, the foreign pressmen publicize my detention. The world press carries articles written in a sympathetic vein: William Farell publishes two pieces in *The New York Times;* Mike Cubric inserts an article into *Newsweek.* Amnon Kapeliuk and Victor Cygielman of the *Nouvel Observateur* and Greenway of the *Washington Post* also report on my arrest.

Denied entry into my home, an Italian TV team slips around to the back of the house. They "interview" me from a distance of several dozen yards, while I stand at the window and shout my replies.

The Israeli authorities receive the daily list of visitors; they must be extremely frustrated when they see the names of those coming here. And they can surely guess what goes on in the house. Have they installed bugging devices to overhear our conversations? Perhaps. I hope they enjoy what they hear.

Foreign newspapers print the news of my detention. Charles Weiss, Ann Lash, and Jim Fine of the American Friends Service Committee report to their parent organization after visiting me. Israeli friends contact my acquaintances abroad. The news reaches the groups I addressed during my American tour. Church leaders, prominent members of the peace movement, liberal Jews, several well-known rabbis—all contact local Israeli missions and register their protests at my detention. The Israeli consuls and diplomats, embarrassed by the queries, take refuge in downright lies, such as accusing me of "incitement to acts of violence that caused damage to property and loss of life," or carefully phrased evasions.

The Arabs in the States also come to my assistance. The AAUG demands my release. Abdeen Jabana, the famous lawyer, offers to take over my defense.

My detention is the occasion for a rare display of Arab-Jewish press collaboration: Uri Avneri's *Ha'Olam Hazeh* publishes a long article about my detention, bitterly criticizing the occupation authorities for the way they treat me. The article is illustrated with pictures of me, including one taken through the fence, to show me "behind bars." The article is translated into Arabic and republished in the newspapers in Kuwait and other Arab countries. Other Israeli journalists publish sympathetic articles—Gabriel Stern of *Al-Hamishmar,* Kazma of the Arabic *Al-Anba,* as well as Yehuda Litani. Noami Gal interviews me for *Ha'aretz.*

Despite this wave of encouragement and solidarity, I sense the pressures. Being confined within the house is nerve-wracking; on the other hand, the constant flow of visitors, however welcome, also has its drawbacks. Every morning I have to dress hurriedly, make myself presentable, and prepare the house for guests. Some overzealous American reporters are quite capable of turning up at eight o'clock, and I must be ready to receive them. At almost any hour of the day the doorbell can ring; unable to phone me, the visitors must perforce come unannounced. There are days when I do not have a moment's rest from morning to night. Guests, talk, coffee, refreshments, journalists. It is wonderful to know that I am not forgotten, but how long can I stand up under the strain?

One day, the assistant military governor comes on a visit of inspection! I notice that he is observing me closely. Clearly he wants to see if I am showing signs of stress. Even more than usual, I endeavor to look and sound cheerful and unconcerned. I will not let him see my suffering—on the contrary. Let him report to his superiors that Raymonda Tawil is flourishing!

On one single occasion since it was disconnected the telephone rings. For one joyful moment, I think it has been reconnected—but my jubilation is short-lived. It's Captain Duddy, at the military governor's office. His tone is friendly, but his questions are probing and pointed. He asks if there is anything I need.

"Nothing," I reply politely.

"Don't you get bored?" he asks, with something of a superior tone of voice. "Do you have a TV set?"

I endeavor to make my own tone even more superior. "Oh, yes!" I explain triumphantly, "I have a TV!"

There is much to contend with as I try to keep up my morale. As the weeks go by, I try my hardest to appear cheerful and undismayed when entertaining visitors. Running the household is difficult, since I cannot even go outside to do the shopping. The young girl who used to help me with the housework is not allowed to remain. Concerned about the detrimental effects of my "permissive" household and about her friendly talks with the policemen, her family takes her away. It is hard to cope with everything.

But aside from day-to-day concerns, there are also more long-term worries. Will the Israeli authorities rest content with house arrest? Every now and then, there are rumors and hints that they intend to impose stricter restrictions and more severe punishment. What does this mean? Will they close the house to visitors? Or do they intend, if there is no other way of silencing me, to send me to prison? Above all, there is the ever-present fear of deportation.

Now that I am confined to the house, Da'ud has to take responsibility for anything that needs to be done outside, whether it is shopping or looking after the children's education and meeting their teachers. Da'ud is of course highly indignant over my punishment. He never ceases to remind me that I was always the one who risked flouting West Bank public opinion by welcoming Israeli visitors to my house and maintaining an open dialogue with them—"and now see how the Israelis repay you!" He is also deeply concerned over the future and worries about what might yet be in store for me. I sense that he is not entirely displeased by what has happened. Perhaps he hopes that this will be a lesson to me, reducing my commitment to my "unfeminine" political activity. Or perhaps, after failing to persuade me to spend my time at home, he is gratified at seeing me forced into "domestication" whether I want it or not.

We make jokes about it—especially about the phone. Since it has been disconnected, he is saving a great deal of money on phone bills. One day, some guests asked playfully, "Was it Da'ud who made a deal with the military governor to have the phone disconnected, so as to make you into a housewife?"

"They can't make me into a housewife," I snap, "because being a housewife is a state of mind!"

But although this is said in a lighthearted manner, it does not really conceal my resentment. I cannot help noticing that men are in collusion against me—Arabs and Jews alike. The military governor—a man—has forbidden me to leave the house; the policeman—another man—is on guard outside, to make sure I obey; Arab society—dominated by men—is ruled by laws that fetter and humiliate me as a woman. Men—all men, friend and foe alike—personify and represent all these forms of oppression together.

On one of their visits, I tell Uri Avneri's wife, Rachel, "I have two guards—one outside the door, and the other inside." She glances at Da'ud and then back at me, nodding her head in understanding.

Even now, when I am under house arrest, there are some circles that disapprove of me and my actions. "Why are you only under house arrest?" someone asks me venomously. "Why aren't you in jail? You must be a very special case for the Israelis to display such favoritism." I seethe with anger at the insinuation that I enjoy some kind of privileged status with the Israelis.

One day, I am seeing some visitors off; as they leave the house, I walk out with them to the front gate. At that precise moment, Major Maurice of the Ramallah military government happens to drive past. When he sees me outside, he becomes furious. Turning to the policeman, he shouts, "She is not allowed out of the house! I don't want her to see the sun!"

I am not even allowed out to smell the flowers in the back garden. The flowers are in bloom, and the garden is very lovely. But it seems that if I go out there, I endanger the security of the state of Israel.

I am overwhelmed by a profound feeling of bitterness. By what right does this man forbid me to see the sun? Does the sun, too, belong to the Israelis alone? But I remain clearheaded, not letting my anger overwhelm me: My bitterness is directed against the Israeli army, against Israeli occupation, against men like Major Maurice. But I have no hostility against ordinary Israelis.

The Israeli authorities are trying to break me, adopting a whip-and-carrot policy. The whip is my detention, the disconnected phone, the ban on showing my face outside, the recurrent rumors of worse penalties in store. But there is also the carrot. My visitors include many Israelis—liberals and leftists, for the most part. They all endeavor to help; they offer aid and advice. But the advice varies, depending on the individual and his ideas. Even members of the same party hold utterly conflicting views. For example, there is Eliezer Be'eri from Mapam, one of the party's "Arab experts." We are old acquaintances—and adversaries: We have met on various occasions, mostly for debates and arguments, in which we clashed sharply. Following my detention, Eliezer comes to see me several times. On one occasion, he comes up with an idea for procuring my release. He advises me to write an official letter to the Israeli authorities proclaiming my innocence of any action harmful to the state of Israel and undertaking not to behave differently in the future. Such a letter, he assures me, will persuade the authorities to release me.

"What?" I shout indignantly. "Apologize? Beg for mercy? Humiliate myself? Never!"

We are soon arguing vehemently; he accuses me of extremism. Before leaving, he warns me again that unless I write the letter, I shall remain in detention for a long time.

That is the carrot.

The Israeli authorities need the letter to discredit me, to humiliate me. By displaying my capitulation, they will eliminate me as a political opponent whose views carry any weight.

Shortly afterward, another visit from members of Mapam Mordechai Bentov and Latif Dori. I tell them of Be'eri's proposal. Latif does not hesitate for a moment. "Don't write any such letter!" he entreats me. "Whatever happens, don't write them a letter. It's a trap!"

Bentov's response is different. He is furious when he hears me declare that I would die rather than write a letter asking for mercy. But I retort, "I am a Palestinian! I am entitled to resist occupation!"

Be'eri, Bentov, and Dori—all three members of Mapam.

Avneri and Zichroni hear of the proposed letter of mercy. Both men pointedly refrain from persuading me to write it.

Dr. Yisrael Shahak, the Israeli human rights champion whose activities and statements have made him very unpopular among his own countrymen, comes to visit me. He, too, advises me against writing any letter to the Israeli authorities. "They want to silence all the Palestinians. In Beirut, the Palestinians are being subjected to physical annihilation. In your case, they are practicing psychological annihilation. Keep your self-respect—don't appeal for clemency!"

I cannot go outside, but the outside can come in. My prison—my home—is invaded by news from the outside world: In Lebanon, the civil war rages on. Hundreds of Palestinians—men, women, and children—are killed by Falangist attacks. I watch the television reports, listen to the radio. Yet again, Palestinian blood is spilled, and the world stands by, unmoved and apathetic.

Western newsmen, recently arrived from Lebanon, explain, in cool, dispassionate voices, that the Lebanese fighting has eliminated the PLO as an independent political and military force. Their words are painful to me; but although they call up "objective" facts, I do not permit myself to become depressed. I have faith in the Palestinian cause.

I believe in the PLO fedayeen. There can be no doubt about it: It is due to them that the world is taking an interest in my people. When Palestinians scarcely kept body and soul together with skimpy UNRWA rations, the world never showed any concern for us. When we were the dust of the earth, despised and humiliated by all—Arab states as well as foreign countries—no one showed any pity for us. The world only began to take us into consideration when young Palestinians hijacked planes and threatened important interests. Then they sat up and took notice of us. I love the "terrorists," because the "terrorists" have made the world recognize us as a people!

These young Palestinians called infiltrators and terrorists—they were simply rebelling against humiliation. They wished to be treated as human beings, to be recognized as a people. They left their university studies and joined the resistance. "What is the use of having a degree?" one of them asked his Israeli judges. "What good is a degree when I don't have a homeland? When I am not allowed to rejoin my people, while a Russian Jew is permitted to come and live in a country he never knew?"

There is one thing that puzzles my visitors, especially those who still swallow Israeli propaganda about their "liberal" occupation. "But tell me," someone invariably asks me, "why are you being detained?"

"I don't know," I reply patiently.

"What d'you mean you 'don't know'? They have to give some reason!"

"They don't have to give any reason. I am detained by an arbitrary order of the military authorities. There were no legal proceedings, I have never been told what my 'crime' is, and I don't know how long I am to remain under detention."

Late in October, after over two months under house arrest, I am summoned to the offices of the military governor. There I again encounter the same burly Shin Bet (Israeli intelligence) officer who warned me earlier about passing on "false information." Possibly with the aim of frightening me, he conducts our interview in the basement, evoking thoughts of interrogations and torture chambers.

This time, there is no pretense of courtesy in his manner. "It seems your house arrest isn't enough for you!" he bellows. "You are still opening your mouth too much!"

"My God, aren't I allowed even to speak?" I cry in amazement. "I don't use explosives, there is a policeman standing outside the door twenty-four hours a day, my phone is disconnected. What harm can I do?"

My words infuriate him even further. He slams his fist down on the table. "We know how to shut you up! I warn you—if you're not careful, you'll suffer far more severe punishment!"

I am horrified. What further cruelty do they have in mind? But I do not knuckle under to his bullying. "You'd better listen to me and people like me!" I shout. "If not, you'll have another October War! Your son could be killed in it! And then, when it's too late, you'll remember me and my warnings!"

He does not tell me what I am accused of doing, nor does he give me any idea of the punishment they have in store for me. He goes away, leaving me shaking with anger. Above all, there is a profound sense of foreboding. What else do they intend to do to me?

A few days later, the blow falls. One evening, a police officer calls with new instructions. Henceforward, I am to be permitted no visitors. The policeman is to deny entry to everyone except members of the household.

This new restriction causes consternation. Dianna is about to go to the Arab countries, to register for the university. Da'ud is to accompany her. The other children are at school. I will be left alone in the house, with my police guard, and with no way of communicating with the outside.

The children begin to cry, "How can you stay at home alone? What if you need something? We won't leave you!"

One of my daughters bursts out, "God damn them! I'll join the fedayeen. That'll show them!"

A soldier comes in and orders the neighbors to leave the house. There is an armored troop carrier outside. What is happening? I think in panic.

Da'ud goes to the neighbors and phones Amnon Zichroni. Later, we learn that Amnon called Avneri and Bentov, who in turn called Peres at home in the middle of the night.

All that night, we remain awake, unable to close our eyes.

Early the next morning, the order is rescinded. The protests were effective.

My house arrest was ordered by the military government. Under military law, there is no legal way of appeal or redress against such a decision. The governor's word is final. But Amnon Zichroni, my indefatigable attorney, tries the only legal path open to him—he asks for my case to be brought before a review board. The board has no authority; it can hear cases of administrative detention, such as mine, and then make recommendations. These recommendations are not binding. The last word rests with the military government.

Although it does not seem promising, Amnon urges me to present my case to the board. It is a form of pressure, and it might do some good. I give my consent, and he presents the application.

The hearing is set for early November.

On the appointed day, Amnon and I enter the military-government building for the hearing. We are ushered into the courtroom. The proceedings commence.

According to the military-government representative, I am guilty of the following "crimes":

Between the years 1969 and 1974, Raymonda Tawil engaged in organizing protests by the Nablus women's organization, an association that is a subversive body and that has, since June 1967, mounted extreme protest actions: incitement and sit-in strikes.

In April 1969, Raymonda Tawil, together with other women, organized a sit-in strike.

In June 1969, she transmitted information about events in the law courts to the Popular Front for the Liberation of Palestine.

In August 1969, she organized a women's meeting, inciting them to demonstrate in protest against torture in prisons.

In December 1969, she issued a statement about the mistreatment and torture of detainees.

In March 1970, she incited pupils to demonstrate in protest against the killing of a young man.

In April 1970, she organized a sit-in of women at the Nablus municipality.

In October 1971, she organized a sit-in and hunger strike in protest against the torture of prisoners at Ashkelon Jail.

In January 1973, she took an active part in a women's demonstration in Nablus in protest against the authorities' treatment of detainees.

In March–April 1973, she demonstrated, together with members of Siah, at Akrabeh. Some of the Siah members were arrested and indicted.

In April 1973, she warned residents of Nablus to refrain from celebrations during the days of mourning that followed the Israeli army raid on Beirut.

In May 1973, she engaged in collecting contributions for the families of terrorists killed in battle with the Lebanese army.

That same month, she was detained for a number of hours, after an attempt to resist the demolition of a house in Nablus.

In June 1973, on the anniversary of the Six-Day War, she engaged in organizing a women's demonstration and asked schoolteachers to explain the significance of the date to their students.

In October 1973, she took part in a sit-in strike by women in Nablus and invited foreign consuls to be present.

In December 1973, together with Israeli leftists, she demonstrated against deportations, near the Nablus municipality.

In December 1974, she was arrested by the military government for agitation.

After moving to Ramallah, she kept up her subversive activities. In November 1975, she incited demonstrations in Nablus, like those being held in Ramallah.

During the past year, in her contacts with foreign journalists, she presented herself as the PLO spokesman for the Judaea and Samaria area.

Early in May 1976, she was connected with the persons planning a march in protest against the march of Gush Emunim [Israeli religious nationalists].

Early in June 1976, she attended the funeral of Muhammad Kawaja, a member of a terrorist organization who committed suicide in prison; she came accompanied by foreign journalists.

In June 1976, she urged members of Ramallah's municipal council to organize a strike in protest against arrests at the Bir Zeit college.

On July 21, 1976, she was summoned to the Ramallah military government and requested to desist from her subversive activities. In spite of this, it became known to the security services that, early in August 1976, she incited shopkeepers in Ramallah to close down their businesses in protest against the imposition of Valued Added Tax.

On October 27, 1976, she was again summoned to the military-government offices for a warning and appeared at the meeting wearing a PLO badge on her lapel.

As I sit listening to the indictment, I sense a kind of detachment, a slight sense of wonder. What a list! Does that all refer to *me?* To the little girl who was torn away from her mother? To the teen-ager whose heart was broken as she sought her brothers beyond the Mandelbaum Gate? To the young woman so cruelly separated from parents and dear ones?

Are they talking about the "imperialist missionary"? About the woman reviled for trespassing on masculine preserves, condemned for her "unladylike" contacts with foreigners?

Does this woman now represent such a threat to the mighty state of Israel?

Do they really mean me?

It is cold in Ramallah's military courtroom. Entering the building, I see the women squatting in line outside; they are wearing long black Palestinian dresses, their faces are wrinkled, their hands toil-worn. They sit there patiently, as they have been taught, ready to defer to anyone in authority. How astounding! Many of these women are the mothers of fedayeen—the bold, fearless young men and women who have restored our pride and self-respect. But they—the mothers—remain humble, submissive, resigned.

I do not resemble those women. I am wearing my chic blonde wig; I am dressed in European clothing. I talk to foreigners; I can even address the Israelis in their own language. To the Israeli soldiers who crowd into the courtroom, I must represent a new and unfamiliar type of Palestinian woman. They stare at me inquisitively; boldly, I return their stares, enjoying their embarrassment as their eyes meet mine.

Alien faces. The judge, the prosecutor, the soldiers. I remember Father's words: "Strangers in my homeland. *La maison me regarde plus.*" I feel sad, despondent. Father was referring to Acre, after the Israeli conquest—but he might just as well have been speaking about Ramallah, now also under alien occupation.

And here, in the Palestinian town of Ramallah, I must now face an alien court, in a bid to regain my freedom.

I am not permitted to speak; Amnon conducts the case for me. Being an Israeli, he can present my case with a vehemence and a power that an Arab lawyer would find hard to equal. He tears the "indictment" to shreds, attacking the authorities for giving me no indication of what I am permitted and what I am forbidden to write in the foreign press. He castigates the military government for its "arbitrary acts" in depriving me of my "elementary human rights."

The hearing lasts for four hours. Amnon does wonders, despite the absence of proper legal procedure. He challenges every charge the "prosecutor" presents.

At one point, the chairman of the review board asks in amazement, "If she is guilty of all these offenses, why has she not been placed on trial?"

Embarrassed, the prosecutor mumbles something about "security" and "secret sources of information."

Later, Amnon brings out a clipping from *The New York Times,* which writes most favorably about me and criticizes the Israeli authorities for detaining me. "Raymonda's arrest is harmful to the interests of the state of Israel," Amnon points out.

The "prosecutor" loses his temper. "We don't care what *The New York Times* writes!" he shouts.

The "prosecutor" is wrong. Clearly, there are influential persons in Israel who *do* care what *The New York Times* writes. Israeli friends who have been working for my release tell me that they have promises from "the highest quarters" that I will soon be released. It seems that Shim'on Peres, the Israeli Defense Minister, is soon to visit the United States and he does not want to face an unfavorable press on account of my detention.

But while the political leaders are obviously concerned over the constant stream of protests from within Israel and, even more, the continual pressure on Israeli representatives abroad, the military authorities are determined to keep me confined and gagged.

A special messenger from the military government arrives at Amnon Zichroni's office, bearing the recommendations of the review board. The application for my release has been rejected. Unofficially, we learn that the review board even recommended that my detention be made more stringent.

On December 10, 1976, at eight o'clock in the morning, I was summoned to the Ramallah military governor. In great wonder and apprehension, I entered his office. What did they want of me now?

The governor received me courteously; smiling, he invited me to be seated. "You know the review board rejected your application. The military governor of the West Bank has confirmed the findings of the board."—

Was this what he called me in for?

—"Nevertheless, because Ramallah has been quiet and peaceful"—I stared at him in astonishment: This was after two days of protests and demonstrations had created turmoil in the center of town—"I have decided to employ my own discretion. I have decided to release you from your detention."

He decided? What kind of yarn is he trying to sell me? He got orders from his superiors—probably from the very top.

"You are free." He smiled at me again.

Only then did I begin to think. To let the news sink in. To feel.

The sense of relief, the feeling that the nightmare was at an end. I was too shaken to say anything.

His manner remained friendly. "What will you do now?" he asked. "Are you going back to the university?"

I muttered something indistinct.

Then I went home.

I was released from house arrest.

Was I then free?

Of course not.

How could I be free?

I am a Palestinian living under occupation.

I am a woman living in a male-dominated reactionary society.

I am a wife in a society that has made men into gods and women into submissive dolls.

My house arrest has ended. My enslavement persists.

My battle for emancipation has only begun.

Postscript
by Peretz Kidron

AT ONE O'CLOCK on the morning of March 23, 1978, eight Israeli police—some uniformed, others plain-clothed, including one woman soldier—forced their way into Raymonda Tawil's home. Three of the agents arrested Ms. Tawil, driving her away in a police car escorted by five additional military and police vehicles. The remaining agents conducted a thorough search of the house, confiscating books, cassette recordings, a Palestinian flag, photographs (even leafing through wedding albums), as well as albums of clippings from the world press about Ms. Tawil.

While Ms. Tawil was detained at police headquarters in Jerusalem, the authorities tried to justify her arrest by leaking reports to the Israeli press, accusing her variously of "incitement to riots," "taking photographs of Israeli troops mistreating demonstrators," "contacts with PLO leaders in Beirut," and "contacts with terrorist cells in the West Bank." The charge entered on her detention order was "terrorist activity"; this was subsequently erased and replaced by "causing public disturbances."

During the first two weeks of her detention, Ms. Tawil was interrogated daily, at times from eight in the morning till eleven at night. The matters on which she was questioned had nothing to do with the official "charges"; her interrogators dealt exclusively with her contacts with the media, with public personalities, and with organizations in the United States and Europe. She was also asked about her contacts with the Soviet bloc. She was repeatedly questioned on alleged links with PLO leader Abu Jihad in Beirut. She was accused of contacts with the PLO radio, by way of her broadcasts for a San Francisco radio station.

During this period of her detention, she was kept in solitary confinement. She was not permitted visits from her lawyer or her family, nor was she allowed to receive books or clothes. She was subjected to combined physical and psychological pressure—kept at times in an unlit cell, blindfolded during interrogation, subjected to threats. During the interrogations no actual physical violence was employed.

On April 4, while in her cell, Ms. Tawil was subjected to a beating by wardens and police officers. This was followed by a visit from the Red Cross and—at her demand—by Ramallah's military governor (she was not permitted to see her lawyer till a week later). After this, there were no further cases of brutality, and the interrogations were called off.

On April 5, a police interrogator came to the prison and formally charged Ms. Tawil with having assaulted an Israeli officer during a demonstration at Ahaliya College on March 16.

On April 10, after eighteen days of detention—the maximum period a person may be legally detained without a judge's remand— Ms. Tawil was placed under "administrative detention" for a thirty-day period, by an order signed by the West Bank's military governor, General Hagael.

During the period of administrative detention, Ms. Tawil was not subjected to any interrogations until the Israeli weekly *Ha'Olam Hazeh* published a report of the April 4 beating. Following the publication, Ms. Tawil was questioned several times, with the interrogators threatening her with dire consequences.

During the period of Ms. Tawil's detention, there was worldwide interest in her case. Dr. Nahum Goldman, Jean-Paul Sartre, I. F. Stone, and Noam Chomsky published protests or intervened with the Israeli authorities on her behalf; leading newspapers in the West highlighted her detention in a sharply critical light; a number of Israeli journalists also published articles condemning her detention. Prominent Israeli liberals and political figures made vigorous approaches for her release.

On May 7, with the expiration of the thirty-day detention order and after over six weeks' imprisonment, Raymonda Tawil was released.

Epilogue

THIS BOOK WAS COMPLETED early in 1978. Since then, Egypt and Israel have concluded a peace treaty. This treaty rests upon the Camp David agreements, which were to provide a framework for a peaceful solution to the Mideast conflict. Among other provisions, the agreements proposed to "solve" the Palestinian problem by granting a form of "administrative autonomy" to the West Bank and Gaza Strip. The innocent-sounding term *autonomy* has taken in many well-intentioned people, who honestly believe that this "autonomy" will permit the Palestinians to enjoy the national independence that is the fundamental and inalienable right of every people.

But the facts are otherwise. "Autonomy" is a sham.

What kind of freedom will the West Bank and the Gaza Strip enjoy under the "autonomy" plan? Israeli troops will remain in occupation; Israel will retain control of internal security as well as supervising the coming and going of our people across the Jordan bridges; Israeli settlements set up since 1967 will remain, and new ones will be added. Is that "Palestinian independence"? What rights will we enjoy? The right to collect municipal taxes and supervise our own sewage works?

As this book explains, we have nothing against the secure existence of the state of Israel—within its own recognized borders. But we Palestinians want a state of our own, with our own flag and our own anthem. We want our own national identity. We want to safeguard the interests of our exiled brethren of the Palestinian diaspora. We want to protect Arab rights in Jerusalem.

This so-called autonomy will give us none of these rights. On the contrary, the plan is an attempt to bury the Palestinian cause forever, to relieve the conscience of the world by creating the impression that the Palestinian issue has been "resolved"—while we remain under Israel's yoke.

That is why I reject the "autonomy" that is to be imposed upon us. I reject "autonomy" because it is a gigantic hoax designed to mislead Palestinians, Israelis, and world public opinion. I reject it because it is a lie.

That does not mean that I am a "rejectionist," in spite of what has been said and written about me. I champion the national rights of my own people—without questioning the national rights of the Israelis. I believe in the rights of *both* peoples; that belief is illustrated in this book—and, indeed, in the very manner in which it was written.

While working on the manuscript, I was under continual pressure from the Israeli occupation authorities. My house arrest, my subsequent month-long imprisonment, and other harassments were all attempts to gag me as an advocate of the Palestinian cause.

But that was not the only difficulty I had to contend with. This narrative was put together with the assistance of Peretz Kidron, who is an Israeli; and for that reason, I was subjected to very heavy pressure from fellow Palestinians. Some friends and political associates did everything they could to dissuade me from working with a citizen of the very state whose army is repressing my people. I was warned that if I went ahead with the project in conjunction with Peretz Kidron, I would ruin my personal standing—socially and politically. Prominent Palestinian moderates—such as PLO officials Said Hamami and Iz-al-Din Kallek—were assassinated for advocating views similar to mine; in view of their fate, I could not take such warnings lightly. Nor could I overlook the protests of my own family, who feared that they would be made to share in my "disgrace." The pressures were enormous; only those acquainted with the conformist norms of Arab society can imagine what I had to withstand. There were times when the atmosphere of near-hysteria almost induced me to give up.

All the same, my convictions compelled me to go ahead, for the sake of the Palestinian cause and of my own emancipation as a woman. That is how this narrative came to be completed.

Let the reader judge whether it lives up to expectations.

RAYMONDA HAWA TAWIL

Ramallah
April 1979